MENU DESIGNS

HANSPETER SCHMIDT

MENU DESIGNS

RIZZOLI
NEW YORK

Menu Designs
© 1981 by Office du Livre, Fribourg
First published in the United States of
America in 1981 by:
Rizzoli International Publications, Inc.
712 Fifth Avenue/New York 10019

Library of Congress Catalog Card Number:
81-51380
ISBN: 0-8478-0395-3

Printed in Switzerland

Table des matières   Inhaltsverzeichnis   Table of Contents

Préface de Wolfram Siebeck	7	
Introduction	9	
Check-list pour graphistes et réalisateurs	12	
Cartes de restaurants	16	
Cartes de grill-rooms et rôtisseries	70	
Cartes de bars	82	
Les petites cartes	90	
Cartes spéciales	118	
Cartes de compagnies d'aviation	130	
Cartes de compagnies maritimes	150	
Index	160	

Vorwort von Wolfram Siebeck	7	
Einführung	9	
Checkliste für Gestalter und Hersteller	12	
Speisekarten für Restaurants	16	
Speisekarten für Grill-Room und Rôtisserie	70	
Karten für die Bar	82	
Die «kleine Karte»	90	
Spezialkarten	118	
Luftfahrtgesellschaften	130	
Schiffahrtslinien	150	
Register	160	

Foreword by Wolfram Siebeck	7	
Introduction	9	
Some hints for the designers and producers of menus	12	
Restaurant menus	16	
Grill-room and rôtisserie menus	70	
Bar menus	82	
'Small menus'	90	
Special menus	118	
Airlines	130	
Shipping lines	150	
Index	160	

Promesses sur papier à la cuve

Madame Giusti, de «La Merenda», dépose sur notre table une grande ardoise; Monsieur Schmitt jr, des «Schweizer Stuben», présente avec élégance et discrétion ses cartes de menu sur papier à la cuve: deux façons dissemblables de nous faire découvrir leur «liste des mets». Sur l'ardoise, inscrits bien sûr à la craie, figurent d'excellents plats, mais en nombre réduit, qui toujours nous inciteront à revenir dans le petit bistrot du Marché aux fleurs niçois: moules marinière, tripes niçoise, pâté au pistou, mesclun huile d'olive, daube provençale, mousse au chocolat... un grand interligne: le très apprécié boudin aux pommes ou les sardines farcies ont été effacés par la main de Madame Giusti; une manière pratique de retirer de la carte ce qui fait défaut en cuisine!
Si l'on sait que la fine et très noble gastronomie des «Schweizer Stuben» de Munich les a aussi fait connaître internationalement, peut-on en déduire qu'il n'y aurait, entre l'ardoise du bistrot et la carte du restaurant trois étoiles, d'autres différences que la matière dont elles sont faites et le prix de «l'impression»? Oui et non.
En fait, nous l'avons vu, l'une et l'autre jouent le même rôle; la carte est au client de restaurant ce que la table des matières est au lecteur de livres: énumération des titres de récits et indication des pages. Mais nulle évocation de leur forme ou de leur fond; seul le nom de l'auteur peut donner une idée du style.
Quels renseignements supplémentaires la carte de menu donne-t-elle? Les plus prometteuses désignations, le papier le plus précieux et autres illustrations alléchantes ne précisent pas si la crème de truffes est fade ou relevée et la selle de chevreuil juteuse ou sèche. En revanche, nous découvrirons si le chef a de l'imagination, du goût pour la présentation graphique... ou le contraire; nous apprendrons aussi le prix du repas; nulle carte, la plus remarquable soit-elle, ne nous dira non plus si les mets proposés valent le prix demandé.

Hoffnung auf handgeschöpftem Bütten

Wenn Madame Giusti im «La Merenda» die große Schiefertafel auf unserem Tisch abstellt, dann unterscheidet sich das nur unwesentlich von der diskreten Eleganz, mit der Herr Schmitt jr. in den «Schweizer Stuben» die Speisekarten verteilt: wir lesen ein Inhaltsverzeichnis. Da stehen, mit Kreide geschrieben, die wenigen, aber vorzüglichen Dinge, deretwegen wir immer wieder das kleine Bistro am Blumenmarkt in Nizza besuchen – die moules marinières, die tripes niçoises, die pâté au pistou, der mesclun huile d'olive, die daube provençale, die mousse au chocolat ... Ein großer Zwischenraum zwischen zwei Zeilen deutet darauf hin, daß die beliebten boudin au pommes oder die delikaten sardines farcies bereits ausgegangen sind, weggewischt von der Hand der Madame Giusti: zweckmäßiger geht es nicht. Besteht also der Unterschied zu den Speisekarten in der besternten Edelgastronomie nur in der Qualität des bedruckten Büttens, im aufwendigen Farbdruck? Ja und nein.
Für den Gast, der sich in einem Restaurant zu Tisch setzt, ist die Speisekarte genau das, was das Inhaltsverzeichnis eines Buches dem Leser bedeutet: wieviele Erzählungen das Buch enthält, welche Titel sie haben und auf welcher Seite der Leser sie finden kann. Über den Inhalt einer Erzählung, ihre Form und ihre Qualität sagt das Inhaltsverzeichnis nichts aus; allenfalls garantiert der Name des Autors einen bestimmten Stil. Nicht anders ist es mit der Speisekarte. Die vielversprechendsten Bezeichnungen «à la», das edelste Papier, die schönsten Illustrationen geben nicht den geringsten Hinweis darauf, ob die Trüffelsuppe aromatisch oder fade, der Rehrücken saftig oder trocken ist. Sehr oft erfahren wir zwar viel über die Selbsteinschätzung des Kochs, über seine Vorstellung von grafischer Dekoration; wir sehen mit einem Blick, ob wir ein preiswertes oder ein teures Essen vor uns haben – aber die eine, einzig wichtige Information, ob das Essen seinen Preis denn auch wert sein werde, diese In-

The hope that springs from a sheet of handmade paper

When Madame Giusti, who runs the little bistro 'La Merenda' on the flower market in Nice, places a large slate board in front of her guests, what happens is not markedly different from what diners experience in the discreet and elegant 'Schweizer Stuben' where the menu cards are handed around by Herr Schmitt jr.: in each case the client is confronted with a list of the dishes that await him. Chalked on Madame Giusti's slate are the few delicious specialities she is so famous for: *moules marinière, tripes à la niçoise, pâté au pistou, mesclun huile d'olive, daube provençale, mousse au chocolat*. If a big space is left between two lines, this means that the popular *boudin aux pommes* or *sardines farcies* have been sold out, and so Madame has neatly wiped these dishes off the board. Can one therefore say that the sole purpose of a menu in a high-class gastronomic restaurant is to impress diners with the costly hand-made paper on which it is printed? Yes and no.
A restaurant menu is to the client what a table of contents is to someone reading a book of stories. In the latter case he or she learns how many tales the book contains, what their titles are, and which page each of them begins on. But nothing is revealed about the content, form or quality of any of the stories; one can only go by the author's name, in the hope that this will guarantee a certain style. It is much the same with a menu. The promising phrase 'à la', the finest paper and superb illustrations do not tell us whether the truffle soup has a subtle flavour or not, or whether the venison is gravy-rich or dry. But we do very often discover what the chef thinks of himself or what kind of ideas he has about graphic art; we see at a glance whether we are going to get an expensive meal or a cheap one. But the one thing we really want to know – whether the price will correspond to the quality of the food – cannot be found out from even the most splendid menu. So can we conclude that Madame Giusti's slate board is good enough?

Doit-on en conclure que l'ardoise de Madame Giusti suffit? Ce serait méconnaître ce que peut «transmettre» une carte, hormis le nombre, description et prix des mets disponibles. J'apprécie les cartes de petits restaurants, chaque jour réécrites et attestant d'une «cuisine de marché»; de même l'adjonction, sur les cartes des grands établissements, de la «spécialité du jour».

Elle est également instructive la comparaison entre le nombre de mets proposés et l'importance de la brigade de cuisine!

Examinons maintenant les viandes: nous offre-t-on l'éternelle variation sur les steaks de bœuf, ou un cuisinier se serait-il plu à mijoter des abats ou du lapin? Un filet de poisson suggéré avec le pauvre choix de deux sauces m'informe du... jeune âge du chef de cuisine; un unique accompagnement (pommes frites, tomate grillée, salade mêlée) pour tous les principaux plats me décourage. La suspicion me gagne lorsque, sur une même carte, un cocktail de crabe côtoie un saumon sauvage mariné, tant ces deux entrées sont représentatives de styles culinaires différents. Certains chefs usent également de l'intimidation: cartes aux dimensions exagérées, citations de Brillat-Savarin et autres aux seules fins d'en imposer; et souvent le service sera à l'avenant, malheureusement.

S'il est utopique d'espérer des cartes définissant le degré d'excellence d'une cuisine, il faut en revanche bien admettre que certaines mettent ses faiblesses en évidence, parfois même de manière éloquente... et bien avant que soit dégusté le premier plat. Raison supplémentaire de les bien étudier. Un bon nombre d'entre elles, d'ailleurs, présentent des qualités de pièces de collection!

En définitive, qu'elles aient l'ardoise ou le papier à la cuve pour support, toutes les cartes ont un point commun: elles sont porteuses d'une promesse. Promesse d'un véritable plaisir de la table! Elles suggèrent aussi la confiance en un art culinaire et en l'heureuse issue de cette aventure toujours renouvelée qui débute par ces mots: «Sortons manger...!»

Wolfram Siebeck

formation vermittelt auch die aufwendigste Speisekarte nicht. Also genügt die Schiefertafel der Madame Giusti?

Wohl doch nicht. Denn eine Speisekarte verrät mehr als die Anzahl, Bezeichnungen und Preise der vorrätigen Speisen. In kleinen Lokalen freue ich mich, wenn sie täglich neu geschrieben wird: das signalisiert eine «Küche des Marktes». In großen, eleganten Häusern weiß ich aus dem gleichen Grund einen angehefteten Hinweis auf eine Tagesspezialität zu schätzen. Die Zahl der angebotenen Gerichte mit der mutmaßlichen Größe der Küchenbrigade zu vergleichen, ist nicht weniger aufschlußreich, als zu lesen, wie es mit dem Fleisch bestellt ist: Überwiegt das traditionelle Rind mit seinen ewig gleichen Steakvariationen, oder wagt sich hier ein Koch an Innereien und Kaninchen? Die angekündigten zwei Saucen zu einem Fischfilet enthüllen mir das Alter des Küchenchefs (noch sehr jung), die Drohung, daß alle Hauptgerichte von Pommes frites, Grilltomate und gemischtem Salat begleitet werden, macht mich mutlos. Einen Krabbencocktail und marinierten Wildlachs auf ein und derselben Karte zu finden, scheint mir fast unmöglich, so verschieden sind die Stile, die jede dieser Vorspeisen verkörpert.

Eine Speisekarte kann einschüchternd wirken, sei es durch ihre übertriebene Größe, sei es durch Imponierzitate von Brillat-Savarin und Konsorten, und es ist dann sehr wahrscheinlich, daß auch der Service mit einschüchternden Ritualen arbeitet. Wenn Speisekarten auch nie verraten, wie gut eine Küche wirklich ist, so können sie doch deren Schwächen auf geradezu geschwätzige Art schon preisgeben, bevor der Gast den ersten Bissen überhaupt probiert hat. Auch deshalb lohnt es sich, sie gründlich zu studieren. Ihre Beliebtheit aber, die sie sogar zu Sammelobjekten hat werden lassen, verdanken Speisekarten letzten Endes jedoch der einen wichtigen Eigenschaft, die ihnen allen, der Schiefertafel des Bistros wie dem handgeschöpften Bütten im 3-Sterne-Restaurant, gemeinsam ist: sie verkörpern das Prinzip Hoffnung. Die Hoffnung auf die Freuden des Essens; der Glaube an die Kochkunst, an den glücklichen Ausgang des immer wieder unternommenen Abenteuers, das da heißt: Laß uns essen gehen...!

Wolfram Siebeck

No, we cannot. A menu does tell us a bit more than just the number of dishes, their names and prices. In a small unpretentious restaurant I am always glad to find a menu that is written out anew each day, for this suggests that the food will also come fresh from market. Similarly, in an elegant establishment I like to know what the speciality of the day is by consulting a separate piece of paper tacked on to the menu card. One has a chance to compare the number of dishes on offer with the size of the kitchen staff, or to see whether the chef knows what to do with meat: does he just chop up beef into the usual types of steak, or does he dare to experiment with offal or rabbit? If I see two sauces accompanying a fillet of fish, I can tell how old the chef is: still quite a young man! And if all the main courses are served with French fries, grilled tomatoes and mixed salad, I lose heart straightaway. One would scarcely find crab cocktail and marinated salmon on the same list of hors d'œuvres, for the simple reason that each goes with a very different sense of style. A menu can put one off if it is unduly large or bristles with impressive quotations from Brillat-Savarin or his confrères; in that case one can expect the service to be equally distinguished by intimidating rituals. Although a menu can never tell one how good the cooking really is, the chef's weaknesses are revealed at once, before the diner has even taken his first mouthful. That is why it is worth while studying the menu. The popularity of menu cards, which even become collectors' objects, is due to something that all of them have in common, from the slate board in a bistro to the fine handmade paper ones in a three-star restaurant. This common quality is that they embody the idea of hope: hope of a satisfying meal and faith in the chef's culinary skill. After all, eating out is always something of an adventure!

Wolfram Siebeck

Introduction

La carte de restaurant, qu'elle soit «de menus», «des mets» ou «des boissons», est en fait une énumération de ce que propose l'établissement; à cela s'ajoutent souvent les compositions de plats et leur préparation et, bien entendu, les prix. Exception faite de la simple liste manuscrite ou dactylographiée, la carte est le moyen de présenter au client, de la façon la plus efficace et convaincante, une offre bien précise; conçue avec goût, elle constitue davantage qu'une présentation des mets et boissons: elle transmet l'image de marque de l'établissement, jouant le rôle d'une carte de visite dont la conception et la réalisation doivent répondre aux impératifs de la publicité.

Les techniques classiques ou modernes d'impression et de reproduction, de reliure aussi, les matières, souvent fort belles, rendent possibles une infinité de variations. On pourrait en déduire que l'imagination et l'esprit créatif ont libre cours pour leur réalisation, mais ils sont en fait limités par quelques facteurs importants: la situation, le style de l'établissement, l'étendue de l'offre et la clientèle spécifique, entre autres.

Le présent ouvrage propose une sélection de cartes classiques, d'autres particulièrement originales, exemples d'une harmonie réussie entre les divers éléments de réalisation: format, matière, caractères d'écriture, couleurs, illustrations, rédaction.

En quel endroit la carte sera-t-elle utilisée? Il est évidemment important d'en tenir compte. Le genre et le style de l'établissement, nous l'avons déjà dit, doivent être considérés, mais également ceux du local même où a lieu le service. Toute disharmonie dans ce domaine risque de créer une sensation de malaise chez le client.

Ainsi, un grand établissement disposant de plusieurs salles ou locaux de styles différents prévoira avantageusement une carte spécifique pour chacun d'eux, les mets et boissons qui y sont servis étant également variables. A défaut, une carte fonctionnelle

Einführung

Menukarten-, Speise- und Getränkekarten sind eigentlich nichts anderes als eine Aufzählung von Speisen und Getränken, von Zusammenstellungen und Zubereitungsarten der Gerichte mit den dazugehörigen Verkaufspreisen. Sieht man einmal von den einfachen hand- oder maschinengeschriebenen Listen ab, so dienen die meisten dieser Karten dazu, ein ganz bestimmtes Angebot dem Gast so wirkungsvoll und überzeugend wie möglich vorzulegen. Eine gut gestaltete Karte will daher mehr als nur Speisen und Getränke anbieten; sie trägt auf besondere Weise zum Gesamteindruck eines Gastbetriebes bei und ist gleichsam die Visitenkarte des Hauses. Sie steht damit im Dienste der Werbung und muß folglich unter der Berücksichtigung werbewirksamer Gesichtspunkte konzipiert, gestaltet und hergestellt werden.

Menukarten erlauben es dem Gestalter und Hersteller, seinem schöpferischen Gestaltungsdrang fast uneingeschränkt freien Lauf zu lassen. Eingeschränkt wird seine gestalterische Freiheit von einigen wichtigen Faktoren wie der Lage und dem Stil des Hauses, dem Umfang des Angebots, welches zu berücksichtigen ist, oder einer speziellen Gästegruppe. Die modernen Gestaltungsmittel in Verbindung mit Reproduktions- und Drucktechniken, die unterschiedlichen Papiere und die buchbinderische Verarbeitung bieten zahllose Variationsmöglichkeiten. Das vorliegende Buch vereint eine Auswahl klassischer wie besonders origineller Beispiele, die die ganze Breite realisierbarer Lösungen anschaulich belegen. Jedes einzelne gestalterische Element, Format, Papier, Schrift, Farbe, Bild, Text usw. bestimmen den Gesamteindruck der Karte mit.

Wichtigstes gestalterisches Prinzip einer Menukarte ist die Berücksichtigung des Ortes, an dem sie Verwendung finden wird. Die Karte muß dem Stil des Hauses oder dem individuellen Stil eines Raumes entsprechen, wenn sie nicht störend wirken soll. Dieses Prinzip bestimmt und leitet die

Introduction

Bills of fare, menus and wine lists are essentially an enumeration of dishes and drinks – a compilation and description of items giving their prices. Most owners of restaurants aim at a convincing and effective presentation of what they have to offer, unless they are satisfied merely with handwritten or typed lists. A well laid-out menu is, however, much more than just a list of things to eat and drink. It makes a major contribution to the general impression of the establishment, and is, so to speak, its visiting card. Thus it counts as advertising and must be conceived, designed and produced with this aspect in mind.

Menus give designers and producers an extensive opportunity for free expression, limited by such important factors as the establishment's location and style, the size of its business and whether or not special groups of clients are to be catered for. Modern type-setting, reproduction and printing techniques, paper and binding offer endless variations. This book combines a choice of classic and original examples, showing the whole range of solutions that can be achieved. A menu is a combination of many artistic elements: format, paper, type, colour, design, text, etc.

The most important feature to be borne in mind when designing a menu is the place where it will be used. If it is not to produce a jarring effect, the menu must be in keeping with the style of the establishment or of the room where it is used. This principle determines and guides the choice and use of the various design elements. The menu must be functional and match the given locality. It may therefore be advisable for a large restaurant to have a special menu for each of its rooms, listing the different dishes and wines that are served there. The variety of items offered influences the design of the menu and may require several separate cards. A badly arranged, overloaded card is useless. In order to offer new dishes, cards

et polyvalente remplira parfaitement son rôle si elle est représentative de l'établissement considéré dans son ensemble.

La richesse et l'étendue de l'offre peuvent également imposer le fractionnement en une série de petites cartes distinctes et clairement conçues, valant mieux qu'une seule surchargée et finalement illisible.

Diverses propositions gastronomiques sont aussi faites au gré des heures, des jours ou des saisons. La lecture de cartes s'y rattachant directement est plus agréable à la clientèle, dont les habitudes conditionnent à leur tour le choix des aspects pratiques. Cette clientèle varie en effet d'un jour à l'autre, elle est cosmopolite ou au contraire uniforme dans ses habitudes et ses goûts. Il est donc évident que, dans un cas, le multilinguisme de l'information sera préférable et que, dans l'autre, un langage et une présentation d'un seul style seront choisis. La clientèle étrangère apprécie également les annotations et traductions d'expressions locales ou nationales.

A circonstance exceptionnelle, carte exceptionnelle: un jubilé, un événement justifient aussi l'édition d'une carte de circonstance si les propositions de menus s'en inspirent.

Toutes différentes sont les cartes présentées à bord d'aéronefs et de bateaux; leur conception s'inspire soit du pays d'origine de la compagnie, soit des lieux géographiques desservis.

Techniquement, il est possible de distinguer deux genres fondamentaux de cartes:
- celle faite d'une pièce, pliée une ou plusieurs fois et exécutée en une seule matière;
- celle composée d'une couverture, parfois luxueuse, et d'une partie à insérer exécutée en matière différente. Cette seconde catégorie impose le respect d'un certain nombre de points essentiels évoqués dans la check-list qui suit.

Le budget à disposition conditionne principalement la conception graphique et la

Wahl und den Einsatz der einzelnen Gestaltungselemente. Die Karte muß funktionell und den örtlichen Gegebenheiten angepaßt sein, wobei für jeden Raum andere Voraussetzungen gelten können. So mag es empfehlenswert sein, daß ein großer Gastbetrieb für jeden seiner Räume eine besondere Karte, vielleicht mit einem jeweils anderen Speise- und Getränkeangebot, vorsieht.

Auch die Reichhaltigkeit des Angebots beeinflußt die Gestaltung der Karte entscheidend und kann die Aufteilung in mehrere getrennte Karten erforderlich machen. Eine unübersichtliche, überfüllte Speisekarte ist unbrauchbar. Nicht selten werden im Verlauf eines Tages oder im Wechsel der Jahreszeiten verschiedene Karten aufgelegt, um jeweils neue Speisen anbieten zu können.

Die Menukarte wendet sich an eine ständig wechselnde Kundschaft und wird täglich von Menschen unterschiedlicher Herkunft gelesen. Trotzdem muß versucht werden, mit gestalterischen Mitteln auf jeden einzelnen Gast einzugehen. Wird ein Gastbetrieb bevorzugt von ganz bestimmten Gruppen aufgesucht, so ist auch dem bei der Gestaltung der Karte Rechnung zu tragen. Bei internationalem Publikum sollte das Angebot mehrsprachig abgefaßt sein, und nationale oder lokale Ausdrücke sollten gegebenenfalls erklärt werden. Außergewöhnliche Anlässe, zum Beispiel Jubiläen, stellen besondere Anforderungen, weil dann auf das jeweilige Ereignis eingegangen werden muß. Eine eigene Gruppe bilden die Karten von Luftfahrtsgesellschaften und Schiffahrtslinien, die einen stärkeren geographischen oder nationalen Bezug haben.

Grundsätzlich sind zwei Kartenformen zu unterscheiden:
- Einteilige Karten, ein- oder mehrfach gefalzt, aus einem einzigen Material
- Zweiteilige Karten aus mehreren Materialien mit einem Deckel – meistens in luxuriöser Ausführung – und davon unab-

may have to be changed at the beginning of each season or even during the course of each day.

A menu is aimed at a continually changing clientèle and is read daily by people from different backgrounds; yet it is important that it should appeal to each patron individually. If an establishment is preferred by specific groups of clients, the menu must take this into consideration too. For an international clientèle the text should be set out in various languages. National or local expressions should, if necessary, be explained. Exceptional occasions, for example anniversaries, call for special treatment to reflect the nature of the occasion concerned. Airlines and shipping lines, if they have some regional or national association, form a separate category. We distinguish here between two basic formats:

- Single-sheet menus, with one or more folds, made from a single material;
- two-piece menus, made from assorted materials, with a cover, mostly in luxurious style, and an independent insert. In the latter case specific production factors have to be considered.

The graphic design and manufacture of menus will be determined by the amount of money to be spent on them, which will in turn depend less on the quantity to be produced than upon their quality: whether several colours are used, how they are folded and stamped, etc.

Here the rule holds good that even a few colours and well-chosen stylish illustrations or the print layout can be attractive without having to be expensive. By engaging experts for design and production effective results can often be achieved at no additional cost.

Considering all these points, a menu can be created whose design matches the text

réalisation des cartes; le nombre et la variété de celles-ci aura moins d'incidences financières qu'une luxueuse présentation, la polychromie ou le façonnage et l'estampage compliqués. La règle prévaut dans ce domaine aussi qu'une carte de bon goût se contente souvent d'un nombre de couleurs restreint et d'illustrations bien choisies. Nous avons apprécié plusieurs cartes étonnantes de simplicité parce que de conception originale et de réalisation économique, dues à des professionnels du design et de l'impression.

En résumé, quels que soient la forme, le nombre de pages ou les subdivisions d'une carte de restaurant, l'essentiel est de présenter une réalisation harmonieuse, équilibrée, lisible, adaptée au style de l'établissement ou de ses divers locaux, ainsi qu'à sa clientèle. Le plaisir de la table en dépend aussi.

hängigem Innenteil. Für diese Karten sind spezielle verarbeitungstechnische Gesichtspunkte mitzuberücksichtigen.

Das vorgesehene Budget bestimmt die ganze graphische Gestaltung und den Herstellungsprozeß. Die Anzahl der benötigten Karten wirkt sich auf die Herstellungskosten nicht so entscheidend aus wie eine aufwendige Gestaltung, Verwendung mehrerer Farben und komplizierter Stanz- und Falztechniken. Dabei gilt die Regel, daß sich auch mit wenigen Farben und stilsicher ausgesuchten Illustrations- oder Textelementen erstaunliche Wirkungen erzielen lassen, ohne daß die Karten zu teuer in der Anfertigung kommen. Durch die Mitarbeit von Fachleuten für Design und Herstellung können oft bei gleich hohem Einsatz wirkungsvollere Ergebnisse erzielt werden.

Berücksichtigt man diese Gesichtspunkte, so läßt sich eine Menukarte gestalten, die in Ausstattung und Aussage einheitlich und wie aus einem Guß wirkt, bei der Außen- und Innenteil harmonisch miteinander verbunden sind und die sich unter Berücksichtigung der jeweiligen Kundschaft an Art und Stil des Hauses anpaßt.

perfectly and where cover and insert are in harmony, adapted to the clientèle and the house style.

Check-list pour graphistes et réalisateurs

Checkliste für Gestalter und Hersteller

Some hints for the designers and producers of menus

Destination

1. Où sera présentée la carte? Sur un bateau, à bord d'un avion, dans un wagon-restaurant, à l'hôtel, au bar à café, au café-glacier, dans une brasserie, une cave à vin ou à bière, une pizzeria, un restaurant à spécialités, etc.
2. Que mettre en valeur? Le symbole national ou régional, la marque distinctive de la société ou association, la raison sociale, le sigle, un élément d'ordre géographique, des armoiries, les couleurs nationales, un site particulier, etc. Il s'agira de plus de définir si un de ces éléments (éventuellement plusieurs) sera utilisé comme unique déterminant ou s'il apparaîtra sous forme de rappel dans les différents constituants de la carte.
3. Les symboles peuvent être en relation avec les particularités nationales ou régionales, par exemple culinaires, climatiques, culturelles, folkloriques, etc.

Verwendungszweck

1. Wo soll die Karte verwendet werden? Auf dem Schiff, Flugzeug, im Speisewagen, Hotel, Bar, Café, Eisdiele, Bier- oder Weinkeller, Pizzeria, Spezialitätenrestaurant usw.
2. Nationale Symbole, spezifische Merkmale einer Gesellschaft – Signet, Marken- bzw. Firmenzeichen, geographische Stilelemente, z. B. Wappen, Farben, Trachten, besondere Landschaftsbilder usw. sollen als bestimmende Kennzeichen wirken. Nach Eignung können derartige Merkmale rapportähnlich immer wieder auftauchen, das heißt je nach Verwendunszweck der Karte (Dinerkarte, Frühstückskarte, Getränkekarte usw.) eingesetzt werden.
3. Nationale bzw. regionale Besonderheiten (kulinarische, klimatische, kulturelle, folkloristische usw.) lassen sich mit Symbolcharakter verwenden.

Purpose

1. Where is the card to be used? On a ship or aircraft, in a train restaurant-car, hotel, bar, café, ice-cream parlour, beer or wine cellar, pizzeria, speciality restaurant, etc.?
2. Are national or other symbols to be used, e.g. crests or logos of a specific firm, geographical indicators (scenery, local costume, etc.)? If suitable, such symbols can form points of reference and recur on each of several cards, e.g. dinner and breakfast menus, wine list, etc.
3. National or regional peculiarities (culinary, climatic, cultural etc.) may be indicated by appropriate symbols.

Eléments constitutifs

Doivent être pris en considération:
1. Les couleurs propres à l'établissement ou la société, le caractère d'écriture habituel, le décor, les particularités ornementales, les associations auxquelles l'établissement est lié (chaîne, groupement, etc.) et dont le symbole devra figurer sur toutes les cartes de façon exacte et complète.
2. Les personnalités de haut rang ou faits historiques liés directement à l'établissement ou à la société exploitante, et qui pourraient lui tenir lieu d'image de marque.
3. L'image générale de l'établissement: sobre, cultivée, snob, hautement culturelle, rustique, romantique, décontractée, ultra-moderne, etc. Toutes ces particularités peuvent être traitées graphiquement.
4. La façon dont est présentée la carte est évidemment importante: est-elle en permanence sur la table ou remise à la clientèle par le personnel? L'exécution sera fonction des divers degrés d'usure prévisibles, les-

Gestaltungselemente

1. Bei der Konzeption einer Karte sind eine Reihe von Gesichtspunkten zu berücksichtigen: gesellschaftseigene Farben, Schriftzug, Dekor, Ornamente, Assoziationen zu wesentlichen Tätigkeitsbereichen des Unternehmens usw. Gehört das Lokal (Restaurant usw.) zu einer Kette, dann sollte unbedingt das Symbol (Signet, Schriftzug, Farbe usw.) dieser Organisation auf allen Karten immer wieder auftreten, um die Zugehörigkeit deutlich zu machen.
2. Gibt es Bezüge ganz persönlicher Natur: hervorragende Persönlichkeiten nationalen oder internationalen Ranges, die stellvertretend für das Bild des Unternehmens eingesetzt werden können, sind historische Ereignisse oder Gegebenheiten vorhanden, die mit der Geschichte der Gesellschaft bzw. des Unternehmens in Verbindung zu bringen sind?
3. Wie ist das allgemeine Image der Gesellschaft bzw. des Unternehmens: streng sachlich, kultiviert, snob-appeal, kulturell

Elements in the design

1. When designing a menu attention should be paid to such points as: use of the firm's house colours, lettering, decoration and ornament, indication of the firm's other fields of activity, etc. If the establishment is part of a chain, the latter's logo, lettering, colours and so on should be reproduced on all the menus in order to underline their common association.
2. There may be individual characteristics to be taken account of, e.g. prominent individuals of national or international renown, or historical events or episodes that may be associated with the firm and help to define its image.
3. The character of the firm's image may be severely functional, cultivated, rustic, romantic, olde-worlde, technically advanced, etc. All these characteristics may be rendered visually.
4. The design will depend on whether the menu is to be set out on each table before the meal or whether it is to be handed to the

quels auront une influence sur la durabilité et l'aspect de la carte.

•

anspruchsvoll, rustikal, romantisch, verspielt, technisch-fortschrittlich usw. All diese Eigenschaften lassen sich im Bild bzw. in der grafischen Gestaltung sichtbar machen.

4. Liegt die Karte auf dem Tisch bereit oder wird sie dem Gast vom Personal überreicht? Entsprechend muß auch die Aufmachung sein – der Abnützungsgrad bestimmt in entscheidendem Maß das Aussehen einer Karte.

guests individually by the staff, for a card's appearance will be affected by the amount of use it receives.

Les services offerts

Raison d'être de la carte, leur présentation exige que l'on tienne compte de divers facteurs:

1. La clientèle, exigeante souvent: personnes seules, voyageurs individuels ou en groupes, touristes, randonneurs, voyageurs de commerce, représentants, gastronomes amateurs de viandes ou de poissons, végétariens, consommateurs de vins ou de bières, amateurs de spécialités, etc. Les subdivisions par catégories de mets et de boissons leur faciliteront le choix: viandes, poissons, potages, salades, entrées, desserts, spécialités nationales ou régionales, plats étrangers typiques, vins rouges et blancs, alcools, boissons sans alcool, etc. Un public cosmopolite incitera à ne pas oublier la mise en valeur des spécialités nationales; également à son éventuelle non-consommation de diverses sortes de viandes (le porc, par exemple), ou de boissons alcoolisées.

2. Les mets de saison doivent être immédiatement repérables, donc graphiquement traités différemment.

3. Les taxes sur boissons, de séjour ou autres qui majorent les prix de base, éviteront toute réaction négative si elles sont clairement indiquées; de même, la mention «service compris» ou «non compris» éliminera les éventuels malentendus.

Das Angebot

1. Für wen ist die Karte im Rahmen der Dienstleistungen des Unternehmens beziehungsweise der Gesellschaft bestimmt?: für anspruchsvolle Gäste (Einzelreisende), Gruppenreisende, Touristen, Ausflügler, Geschäftsreisende (Managerservice), Fleisch- bzw. Fischliebhaber, Vegetarier, Wein- oder Biertrinker, Spezialitätenliebhaber usw. Diese Kategorien bestimmen in hohem Maß Stil und Ausführung einer entsprechenden Karte. Ebenso wichtig ist eine sinnvolle Unterteilung der Karte in die einzelnen Speise- beziehungsweise Getränkekategorien: Fleisch- und Fischspeisen, Suppen, Salate, Vorspeisen, Desserts, Spezialitäten nationaler oder internationaler Art, Weiß- und Rotweine, Spirituosen usw. Bei internationalem Publikum ist vor allem auch an nationale Besonderheiten zu denken: Ablehnung verschiedener Fleischsorten (zum Beispiel Schweinefleisch) oder von alkoholischen Getränken usw.

2. Ist das Angebot nach der Saison verschieden, kann und sollte das schon bei der Gestaltung einer Karte zum Ausdruck kommen.

3. Getränkesteuer, Ortstaxen u. ä., die zu den Speisepreisen beziehungsweise Getränkepreisen noch hinzukommen, sollten gesondert und nicht versteckt angegeben werden. Spätere Bekanntgabe verärgert den Kunden, genauso wie auch der fehlende Hinweis, ob der Service inbegriffen ist oder nicht.

Content

1. For what type of customer is the menu designed: individual patrons with discriminating taste, parties, tourist groups, daytrippers, or business people (personalized service)? Is there to be an emphasis upon certain kinds of food and drink, e.g. meat, fish, vegetarian dishes, local specialities, wine or beer? This will affect the style of the menu to a very large degree, for it must be divided into appropriate categories for hors d'œuvres, soups, meat and fish, salads, desserts, national or international specialities, red and white wines, liqueurs, etc. It should not be forgotten that some international clients may have special dietary requirements (e.g. rejection of pork, alcoholic liquor).

2. If the dishes vary according to season, reference should be made to this on the menu.

3. Local taxes, beverage taxes, etc. should be indicated separately from the price of the dishes, but not hidden away. The customer is likely to be irritated if these charges are added to his or her bill later. It should also be stated whether the tip is included or not.

13

L'aspect (forme, typographie)

Le client y est sensible et il émettra diverses remarques, le cas échéant pas nécessairement flatteuses. Facteurs à considérer:

1. Format et épaisseur: ils pourront conférer à la carte un aspect élégant ou plein d'ostentation, noble, sobre, plaisant, trop volumineux, peu pratique, déplacé, simple, bon marché ou coûteux, etc.

2. La typographie peut être simple et objective, moderne ou ancienne, décontractée, romantique, froide, austère, sobre, serrée, aérée. L'essentiel est bien entendu d'harmoniser la typographie avec le format et les différents éléments évoqués plus haut. Le caractère choisi pour le texte n'échappe pas à la règle: la gamme des possibilités s'étend du style classique à l'écriture manuscrite, en passant par le «tendre» Biedermeier et le pop-art; il est toutefois judicieux de tenir compte des difficultés de lecture que présentent certaines écritures.

3. Les papiers: rugueux ou doux au toucher, lisses, grainés, satinés, brillants, etc., ils contribuent à la première impression du client lorsque celui-ci prend la carte en main.

4. La finition: une réalisation typographique imparfaite est parfois sauvée par un pliage solide et impeccablement exécuté, une couverture à l'avenant, agrémentée éventuellement d'un estampage ou d'un gaufrage.

5. Des éléments interchangeables peuvent être fixés de différentes manières à l'intérieur de la carte et porter mention d'un événement ou d'une spécialité du jour. Tout comme les cordelières, rubans armoriés et autres ornements, ils confèrent à la carte une certaine noblesse.

Die Gestalt (Form, Typografie)

1. Format und Umfang. Aus beiden Gegebenheiten resultieren gewisse Empfindungsreaktionen: elegant, protzig, stilvoll, vornehm, ansprechend schlicht, zu umfangreich, unübersichtlich, aufdringlich, schlicht, billig, teuer usw.

2. Typografie: sachlich, modern, antikisierend, großväterlich, romantisch-verspielt, kalt, nüchtern, gedrängt, viel Raum lassend. Sämtliche Stilrichtungen sind möglich, müssen aber unter den vorgenannten Stichpunkten geprüft und ausgewählt werden, damit nicht eine Diskrepanz zwischen Inhalt, Verwendungszweck und Form entsteht. Diese Stilmerkmale drücken sich vor allem in der gewählten Schrift aus, die von klassischer bis zur Schreibschrift, von zartem Biedermeierstil bis zur Pop-Art variieren kann, wobei besonders zu bedenken ist, daß nicht überall alle Schriften gelesen werden können, z. B. Fraktur.

3. Papier: Die Wahl eines richtigen Papiers kann allein schon für den ersten (und weiteren) Eindruck entscheidend sein. Rauhes, samtiges, glattes, genarbtes, satiniertes, glänzendes usw. Papier bestimmt das beim In-die-Hand-Nehmen auftretende Gefühl.

4. Verarbeitung: solide, handwerklich einwandfreie Falzung und entsprechender Umschlag vermögen unter Umständen sogar eine drucktechnisch nicht ganz gelungene Gestaltung wettzumachen. Dabei können Gags durch Stanzung oder Beschneiden mithelfen, die Karte «interessant» zu gestalten.

5. Solche «Gags» können auswechselbar in verschiedene Haltevorrichtungen eingeschoben und somit dem «Tagesereignis» angepaßt werden. Auch Kordeln, Wappenschnüre u. ä. Verzierungen lassen Karten «vornehm» erscheinen.

Design (form, typography)

1. Size and format will determine the client's reaction: whether he or she finds the menu elegant, ostentatious, stylish, agreeably straightforward, too big, fussy, 'hard-sell', simple, etc., and whether the dishes seem cheap or expensive.

2. The typography may be functional, modern, olde-worlde, Victorian, romantic, or merely cold and sober; the lettering may be close together or well spaced-out. Any lettering is acceptable provided that it does not lead to a discrepancy between content and form. Any type-face may be chosen, from classic to typewriting, from Tudor to Pop, but one should bear in mind that some type-faces (e.g. Gothic) may not be readily intelligible to certain clients.

3. The choice of paper may decisively affect the client's reaction: on picking it up, he or she will notice whether it is rough or smooth, soft and velvety or thick and grained, etc.

4. The make-up, if effectively done, with an appropriate cover, may on occasion offset faulty printing. Punching and stamping or cutting off corners may add points of interest.

5. Such 'gags' can be inserted separately to draw attention to special features of the day. Knotted string, seals and other trimmings may be added to enhance the effect.

Devis

1. A l'instar de toutes réalisations graphiques et imprimées, une carte de restau-

Kalkulation

1. Die Kalkulation ist die Grundlage für alle im Vorgenannten zu bedenkenden Bemü-

Cost calculation

1. Cost calculation is the basic step to consider when devising a menu, for the amount

rant dépend, pour son aspect, essentiellement du budget à disposition. Une calculation correcte et complète s'impose donc.
2. La carte est-elle destinée à être offerte au client, ou éventuellement vendue? Certaines compagnies d'aviation et de navigation, ou autres entreprises similaires, offrent généralement leur carte aux passagers; ces souvenirs deviennent ainsi des cadeaux publicitaires durables; les restaurateurs sont peu nombreux à pratiquer de même. Il serait judicieux d'envisager la vente d'une carte particulièrement soignée, laquelle constituerait un message publicitaire d'importance non négligeable.
3. Indépendamment des possibilités évoquées sous le point précédent et qui ont une influence non seulement sur le nombre d'exemplaires du tirage mais également sur le prix unitaire, des économies sont réalisables, par exemple en prévoyant des éléments interchangeables à encarter dans diverses couvertures standard.
4. Autres éléments du devis: les frais de composition, d'impression, de papier, les travaux de reliure, les droits de reproduction, les honoraires pour graphiste et photographe.

hungen bei der Gestaltung einer Karte, denn der zur Verfügung stehende Kapitaleinsatz bestimmt nicht zuletzt Umfang und Aussehen.
2. Zu überlegen ist auch von vornherein, ob besonders gut gestaltete aufwendige Karten von Interessenten gekauft werden können. Im allgemeinen geben jedoch speziell Fluggesellschaften, Schiffahrtslinien und ähnliche Unternehmen ihre Karten kostenlos an jeden Passagier als Erinnerungsstück und damit als beständiges Werbeobjekt, während das bei Restaurants kaum üblich ist. Die «Kaufmöglichkeit» einer Karte sollte aber stets mit in Betracht gezogen werden, denn darin liegt ein beachtlicher Werbewert.
3. Entscheidend für die Höhe der Auflage sind nicht nur die vorerwähnten «werblichen» Überlegungen, sondern auch die rationellen Möglichkeiten bei der Fertigung: standardisierte Teile, die vielfach verwendbar sind, austauschbare Teile usw.
4. Die Kalkulation muß alle Gesichtspunkte für die Gestaltung und die Herstellung der Karte berücksichtigen: Satz-, Druck- und Papierkosten, Bindearbeiten, Reprogebühren, Honorare für Grafiker und Fotografen, unter Umständen Reproduktionsgebühren für verwendete Fremdfotos oder andere Unterlagen sind dabei zu beachten.

of money available will determine its size and appearance.
2. The prior consideration is whether a well-designed luxurious menu can be sold to those interested. In general airlines, shipping lines and similar concerns present menus without charge to their clients as a souvenir and for advertising purposes, whereas restaurants as a rule do not do so. However, one should always bear in mind the possibility of sale, since this provides valuable advertising.
3. The print order will depend not only on considerations to do with advertising, but also on the degree to which production can be rationalized by use of standardized or exchangeable parts.
4. The calculation should take into account all the costs involved: paper, composition and printing, binding, photocopying charges, fees for designers and photographers, as well as costs of reproducing photos and other materials.

Cartes de restaurants

Speisekarten für Restaurants

Restaurant menus

Classés par régions, ces intéressants exemples illustrent la vaste gamme de créations personnalisées et réalisations possibles. L'utilisation des particularités et styles locaux ou nationaux est remarquable, de même que la précision de l'indication d'appartenance à une chaîne de restaurants. Le choix opéré va du restaurant traditionnel à celui offrant des spécialités typiques. Certains grands hôtels accueillent leur clientèle dans des locaux de caractère différent: restaurant français, bar, café-terrasse, etc. Les cartes qui s'y rapportent présentent néanmoins une unité de style propre à l'établissement.

In diesem Teil sind nach regionalen Gesichtspunkten geordnet interessante Menukarten von Restaurants und Hotels aufgenommen. Diese Beispiele zeigen das breite Spektrum individueller Gestaltungsvorschläge, welche zur Anwendung kommen können. Die Anpassung an örtliche, nationale oder stilistische Eigenarten kommt dabei klar zum Ausdruck, auch die Einreihung in ganz bestimmte Schemata (Restaurants von Ketten). Die Auswahl geht vom traditionellen Restaurant bis zum typischen Spezialitätenlokal.
Große Hotels bieten ihren Gästen oft mehrere Restaurants im gleichen Hause an, das «Französische Restaurant», die Bar, das Terrassencafé usw. Diese verschiedenen Karten sollen aber trotzdem einen Hausstil sichtbar machen.

This section contains restaurant and hotel menus arranged according to region. These examples show the wide range of designs that are possible and illustrate the degree to which local, national or stylistic characteristics may be expressed, and the way in which menus may be adapted to a certain scheme (e.g. in a chain restaurant). The selection extends from the traditional restaurant to the establishment serving speciality dishes.
Large hotels often have several restaurants under the same roof – French restaurant, bar, terrace café – each of which has a separate menu that must, however, keep to the basic house style.

1a–b Le Moulin de Mougins, Mougins, France
Carte de menu. Création: Editions 06, Le Cannet. Photo Touillon
224 × 395 mm, ouvert 448 × 395 mm, 4 pages. Chromo double face. Page 1 offset 4 couleurs, pages 2–4 offset noir. Laminé, rainé, plié
Les prix sont reportés à la main. La couverture de la carte de menu est décorée d'objets de l'art culinaire.

1a–b Le Moulin de Mougins, Mougins, Frankreich
Speisekarte. Gestaltung Editions 06, Le Cannet. Foto Touillon
224 × 395 mm, offen 448 × 395 mm, 4seitig. Chromokarton zweiseitig. Seite 1 Offset 4farbig, Seiten 2–4 Offset schwarz. Laminiert, gerillt, gefalzt
Die Preise werden von Hand eingetragen. Der Umschlag der Menukarte zeigt Objekte der «art culinaire», der großen Kochkunst.

1a–b Le Moulin de Mougins, Mougins, France
Menu-card. Designed by Editions 06, Le Cannet. Photograph by Touillon
224 × 395 mm, open 448 × 395 mm, 4 pages. Two-sided cast-coated paper. Page 1: 4-colour offset printing, pages 2–4: offset printing in black. Laminated, scored, folded
Prices are entered by hand. The cover of the menu-card depicts objects of the art culinaire, the grand art of cooking.

LE MOULIN DE MOUGINS

ROGER VERGÉ

Roger Vergé aujourd'hui vous suggère...

LE CONSOMMÉ D'HUITRES AU CITRON VERT

LA SALADE DE TRUFFE DU VAUCLUSE AU VINAIGRE DE JEREZ

LE BOUQUET DE SALADES GOURMANDES
AUX QUEUES D'ÉCREVISSES

LA PETITE SOUPE DE GRENOUILLE AUX FEUILLES DE MENTHE

LE GRATIN D'HUITRES DE BELON AUX ÉPINARDS

LA FRICASSÉE DE St PIERRE DU PAYS AUX PETITS LÉGUMES

LE CIVET DE HOMARD AU VIEUX BOURGOGNE

LA DAURADE ROYALE DU PAYS ROTIE AU LAURIER,
AVEC LA FONDUE D'ORANGE ET DE CITRON

LE BISCUIT DE LOUP AUX ASPERGES SAUVAGES, SAUCE LÉGÈRE

LA COMPOTE DE GIGOT D'AGNEAU A LA SARRIETTE ET
AUX AUBERGINES AVEC LES TARTINES DE PURÉE D'AIL

LE SUPRÊME DE VOLAILLE DE L'ALLIER ÉTUVÉ
AUX HERBES VERTES DU JARDIN

LA TRUFFE DE GRILLON CUITE SOUS LA CROUTE AU SEL

LA FAISSELLE DE FROMAGE BLANC A LA CRÈME

LES FROMAGES DE LA FERME SAVOYARDE, AVEC LE PAIN
DE SEIGLE AUX NOIX ET AUX RAISINS

Menu conseillé

LE FOIE GRAS FRAIS DES LANDES AVEC LE BOUQUET
DE TRUFFES FRAICHES EN SALADE

LE GRATIN DE HOMARD ET D'HUITRES AU BARSAC

LE SUPRÊME DE CANARD DE CHALLANS AUX ÉCHALOTTES,
SAUCE BORDELAISE

LES DESSERTS ET LES GOURMANDISES DU MOULIN

Les prix indiqués sont calculés par personne.
Service 15% en sus.

Vins   : 1/1 à partir de   Frs. - 1/2 à partir de   Frs.
Infusion :   Frs. - Café :   Frs. - Eau Minérale : Frs.

1b

Desserts

LE MOULIN DE MOUGINS

2

---

2   Le Moulin de Mougins, Mougins, France
Carte des desserts. Création: Editions 06, Le Cannet.
Photo Touillon
224 × 395 mm, 2 pages. Chromo double face. Page 1
offset 4 couleurs, page 2 offset noir. Laminé

2   Le Moulin de Mougins, Mougins, Frankreich
Dessertkarte. Gestaltung Editions 06, Le Cannet. Foto
Touillon
224 × 395 mm, 2seitig. Chromokarton zweiseitig. Seite
1 Offset 4farbig, Seite 2 Offset schwarz. Laminiert

2   Le Moulin de Mougins, Mougins, France
Dessert card. Designed by Editions 06, Le Cannet.
Photograph by Touillon
224 × 395 mm, 2 pages. Two-sided cast-coated paper.
Page 1: 4-colour offset printing, page 2: offset printing
in black. Laminated

3 Casino, Grands Hôtels de Divonne,
France
Carte de menu. Création: Van der Wal,
Genève
Couverture: 224×323 mm, ouvert
446×323 mm, 4 pages. Couvrure 20/10
contre-collée. Pages 1 et 4 offset 4 couleurs. Laminé, coins arrondis, pliés,
tranche or. Des onglets collés à l'intérieur permettent l'insertion de la carte
du jour
Des cartes de jeu rappellent le casino.

3 Casino, Grands Hôtels de Divonne,
Divonne, Frankreich
Speisekarte. Gestaltung Van der Wal,
Genf
Umschlag: 224×323 mm, offen
446×323 mm, 4seitig. Pappe 20/10 ka-
schiert. Seiten 1 und 4 Offset 4farbig.
Laminiert, abgerundete Ecken, gefalzt,
Goldschnitt
Auf dem Innenteil aufgeklebte Ecken
ermöglichen das Einstecken der Ta-
geskarten. Spielkartenmotive als Hin-
weis auf das Spielkasino

3 Casino, Grands Hôtels de Divonne,
Divonne, France
Menu-card. Designed by Van der Wal,
Geneva
Cover: 224×323 mm, open
446×323 mm, 4 pages. Mounted card
20/10. Pages 1 and 4: 4-colour offset
printing. Laminated, folded, gilt-edged.
Reinforced corners glued to the inside
pages enable insertion of cards for
'Menu of the Day'. The playing card
motif alludes to the casino.

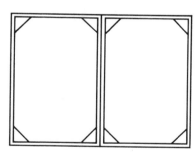

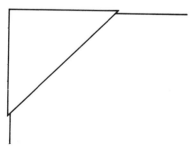

3

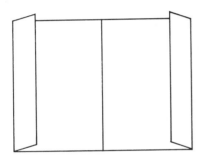

4 Château du Domaine St-Martin,
Vence, France
Carte de menu. Création: Editions 06,
Le Cannet. Photo Appollot
Couverture: 248×370 mm, ouvert
616×370 mm, 4 pages et 2 rabats de
60 mm. Chromo double face. Page 1
offset 4 couleurs. Rainé 3 fois et plié
Les deux rabats maintiennent la carte
de menu de 4 pages.

4 Château du Domaine St-Martin,
Vence, Frankreich
Speisekarte. Gestaltung Editions 06,
Le Cannet. Foto Appollot
Umschlag: 248×370 mm, offen
616×370 mm, 4seitig und zwei 60 mm
breite Klappen. Chromokarton zweisei-
tig. Seite 1 Offset 4farbig. 3mal gerillt,
gefalzt
Die beiden Klappen halten die 4seitige
Menukarte.

4 Château du Domaine St-Martin,
Vence, France
Menu-card. Designed by Editions 06,
Le Cannet. Photograph by Appollot
Cover: 248×370 mm, open
616×370 mm, 4 pages plus two flaps
of 60 mm width. Two-sided cast-coated
paper. Page 1: 4-colour offset printing.
Three times scored, folded
The two flaps hold the 4-page menu-
card in place.

Château
du Domaine
St Martin

4

5

5 Les Frères Troisgros, Roanne, France
Carte de menu. Création: Ateliers I.A.G., Riorges,
d'après un tableau de Gilles Coudour, Roanne. Impression: Presses d'arts graphiques, Riorges
Couverture: 318×250 mm, ouvert 636×250 mm, 4
pages. Chromo mat une face. Page 1 offset 4 couleurs,
page 4 en gris. Rainé, plié
Intérieur: 314×250 mm, ouvert 628×250 mm, 4
pages. Papier offset couleur. Pages 2 et 3 offset noir.
Plié et inséré dans la couverture
Le double portrait de la couverture crée un contact
personnel entre le client et le «Grand Chef».

5 Les Frères Troisgros, Roanne, Frankreich
Speisekarte. Gestaltung Ateliers I.A.G., Riorges, nach
einem Gemälde von Gilles Coudour, Roanne. Druck
Presses d'arts graphiques, Riorges
Umschlag: 318×250 mm, offen 636×250 mm, 4sei-
tig. Mattchromokarton einseitig. Seite 1 Offset 4farbig,
Seite 4 grau. Gerillt, gefalzt
Innenteil: 314×250 mm, offen 628×250 mm, 4seitig,
Offsetpapier farbig. Seiten 2–3 Offset schwarz. Gefalzt
und in den Umschlag eingelegt
Das Doppelporträt auf dem Umschlag schafft eine per-
sönliche Beziehung zwischen Gast und «Grand Chef».

5 Les Frères Troisgros, Roanne, France
Menu-card. Designed by Ateliers I. A. G., Riorges, after
a painting by Gilles Coudour, Roanne. Printed by
Presses d'arts graphiques, Riorges
Cover: 318×250 mm, open 636×250 mm, 4 pages.
One-sided cast-coated card with matt finish. Page 1: 4-
colour offset printing, page 4: grey printing. Scored,
folded
Contents: 314×250 mm, open 628×250 mm, 4 pages.
Coloured offset paper. Pages 2–3: offset printing in
black. Folded and inserted into the cover
The double portrait creates a personal relationship
between the guest and the 'grand chef'.

Nos Menus

Les Hors d'œuvre

Soupe de poisson ....
Potage du jour ....
Consommé chaud ou froid ....
Terrine de lapin à la farigoulette ...
Jambon de Parme ....
Salade d'écrevisses (en saison) ....
Ratatouille froide ....
Salade niçoise ....
Terrine de rougets ....
Foie gras de canard frais ....
Aiguillette de canard séchée Bastide .

Nos Suggestions

Terrine de légumes
Asperges mousseline
Foie gras poêlé au vinaigre
Parfait à l'orange

Terrine de lapin à la
farigoulette
ou
Foie gras de canard frais
–
Mousse de Saint-Pierre
au cerfeuil
ou
Feuilleté de ris de veau
–
Entrecôte au poivre vert
ou
Poularde farcie Bastide
–
Salade de saison
–
Plateau de fromages
–
Pâtisserie du jour

Coulibiac de saumon
–
Selle d'agneau rôtie
Tomates provençale
–
Salade de saison
–
Plateau de fromages
–
Pâtisserie du jour

Les Entrées

Soufflé de rascasse au pistou (20 minutes)
Artichauts barigoule
(en saison) 20 minutes ....
Tourte Bastide (30 minutes) ....
Petits farcis niçoise (15 minutes) ...
Tian de légumes (15 minutes) ...
Truffe en feuilleté (30 minutes) .

Les desserts

Plateau de fromages ....
Coupe Dame Blanche ....
Pâtisserie du jour ....
Glaces et sorbets ....
Crêpes suzette (30 minutes) deux pers.
Corbeille de fruits ....

LA BASTIDE DE TOURTOUR

Les Poissons

Assiette du pêcheur aux légumes ....
Suprême de loup à l'oseille ....
Petits rougets à la graine de fenouil ....
Cassolette de queues d'écrevisses (en saison) ...

SUR COMMANDE :
Loup en croûte (min. deux pers.) par pers.

Les Viandes

Paupiettes de volaille à la vapeur ....
Râble de lapin au basilic ....
Pieds et paquets marseillaise ....
Carré d'agneau provençale (deux pers.) ....
Entrecôte au poivre vert ....
Tournedos sauté aux truffes ....
Côte de bœuf béarnaise ou bordelaise (deux pers.)
Noisettes d'agneau aux herbes ....
Magret de canard aux poireaux ....

PRIX NETS

6

6 La Bastide de Tourtour, Tourtour, France
Carte de menu
243 × 348 mm, ouvert 486 × 696 mm, 4 pages. Chromo une face. Imprimé une face offset brun et noir. Rainé, pli anglais, fentes estampées
Carte du jour : 93 × 183 mm, 2 pages. Chromo une face. Texte dactylographié. Estampé

Carte des spécialités : 80 × 89 mm, 2 pages. Chromo une face. Page 1 offset noir, texte dactylographié. Estampé. Un renforcement du pli médian, dépassant les fentes, évite le glissement latéral des deux cartes qui y sont introduites.

6 La Bastide de Tourtour, Tourtour, Frankreich
Speisekarte
243 × 348 mm, offen 486 × 696 mm, 4seitig. Chromokarton einseitig. Einseitig bedruckt Offset braun und schwarz. Gerillt, Englischer Falz, gestanzte Schlitze
Tageskarte : 93 × 183 mm, 2seitig. Chromokarton einseitig. Text Schreibmaschine. Formgestanzt

Spezialitätenkarte : 80 × 89 mm, 2seitig. Chromokarton einseitig. Seite 1 Offset schwarz und Text Schreibmaschine. Formgestanzt
Tages- und Spezialitätenkarte sind in die Schlitze eingeschoben. Eine hinter dem Mittelfalz angebrachte Verstärkung über die Stanzschlitze hinweg verhindert das seitliche Verschieben.

6 La Bastide de Tourtour, Tourtour, France
Menu-card
243 × 348 mm, open 486 × 696 mm, 4 pages. One-sided cast-coated card. One-sided offset printing in brown and black. Scored, English 8-page fold, die-cut slots
'Menu of the Day' card : 93 × 183 mm, 2 pages. One-sided cast-coated card. Typed text. Die-cut

'Specialities' card : 80 × 89 mm, 2 pages. One-sided cast-coated card. Page 1: offset printing in black. Typed text. Die-cut
The cards for 'Menu of the Day' and 'Specialities' are inserted into the slots. Reinforcement applied behind the centre-fold and continued beyond the die-cut slots prevents a sideways shift.

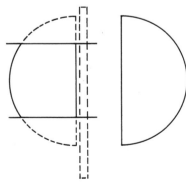

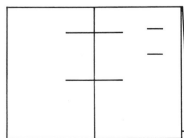

LE BRISTOL

Aujourd'hui nous vous recommandons

Entrées
Rouelle de ris de veau aux queues d'écrevisses 75
Vrai confit d'oie aux haricots blancs 75
Civet de canard au Brouilly 90
Aiguillettes de filet de bœuf au Meursault 80
Selle d'agneau en croûte. Paillasson de légumes 80
Mignon de veau au citron vert 80
Salade de saison • Salade mixte •

Chasse Selon saison
Emincé de perdreau au chou rouge
Grande assiette de gibier: Marcassin - Chevreuil - Lièvre
Le chariot de fromages 25

Desserts
Assiette de sorbets aux fruits frais 30
Œufs montés Vieille Epoque aux trois parfums 25
Mousse de cassis avec son coulis 30
Feuilleté chaud aux mangues et gingembre confit 35
(commander au début du repas)
Symphonie au chocolat 30 Petits fours glacés Elysée 30

• Selon marché   Prix Nets

7a   7b

7a–b   Le Bristol, Paris
Carte de menu. Création et impression: Akila/Pasquet, Pantin
Couverture: 240 × 320 mm, ouvert 480 × 320 mm, 4 pages. Papier à la cuve. Pages 1 et 4 offset brun clair. Page 1 dorure à la feuille et gaufrage. Rainé, plié
Intérieur: 233 × 310 mm, ouvert 466 × 310 mm, 4 pages. Papier à la cuve. Offset brun clair et brun foncé. Plié et inséré dans la couverture. 4 fentes estampées permettent d'insérer la carte du jour
Gaufrage, dorure et harmonie des couleurs sur le papier à la cuve confèrent beaucoup d'élégance à cette carte.

7a–b   Le Bristol, Paris, Frankreich
Speisekarte. Gestaltung und Druck Akila/Pasquet, Pantin
Umschlag: 240 × 320 mm, offen 480 × 320 mm, 4seitig. Büttenpapier. Seiten 1 und 4 Offset hellbraun. Seite 1 Goldfolien- und Blindprägung, gerillt, gefalzt
Innenteil: 233 × 310 mm, offen 466 × 310 mm, 4seitig. Büttenpapier. Offset hell- und dunkelbraun. Gefalzt und in den Umschlag eingelegt. 4 gestanzte Schlitze ermöglichen das Einstecken der Tageskarte
Blindprägung, Goldprägung und geschmackvoll abgestimmte Farben auf Büttenpapier lassen diese Karte besonders elegant erscheinen.

7a–b   Le Bristol, Paris, France
Menu-card. Designed and printed by Akila/Pasquet, Pantin
Cover: 240 × 320 mm, open 480 × 320 mm, 4 pages. Hand-made paper. Pages 1 and 4: offset printing in pale brown. Page 1: gold embossing and blind embossing, scored, folded
Contents: 233 × 310 mm, open 466 × 310 mm, 4 pages. Hand-made paper. Offset printing in pale brown and dark brown. Folded and inserted into the cover. Four die-cut slots enable insertion of the 'Menu of the Day' card
Blind embossing, gold embossing and tastefully harmonized colours on attractive hand-made paper give this card its particularly elegant touch.

8a–b   L'Archestrate, Paris
Carte de menu. Création: Etablissements K.S., Paris
280 × 378 mm, ouvert 560 × 378 mm, 4 pages. Véritable Arches à la cuve. Page 1 offset jaune et brun, pages 2–4 offset brun. Plié. Le bord à la cuve subsiste à droite

Les menus sont rédigés à la main sur des lignes pointillées imprimées. A page 4, reproduction d'un fragment d'un ancien plan de Paris et bref texte sur l'Archestrate de Gela.

8a–b   L'Archestrate, Paris, Frankreich
Speisekarte. Gestaltung Etablissements K.S., Paris
280 × 378 mm, offen 560 × 378 mm, 4seitig. Echt Büttenpapier Arches. Seite 1 Offset gelb und braun, Seiten 2–4 Offset braun. Gefalzt. Der Büttenrand bleibt rechts bestehen

Die Menus werden von Hand auf vorgedruckte Linien geschrieben. Auf Seite 4 Ausschnitt eines alten Stadtplans von Paris und kurzer Text über Archestratos von Gela.

8a–b   L'Archestrate, Paris, France
Menu-card. Designed by Etablissements K.S., Paris
280 × 378 mm, open 560 × 378 mm, 4 pages. Original hand-made Arches paper. Page 1: offset printing in yellow and brown, pages 2–4: offset printing in brown.

Folded. The deckle-edge remains on the right-hand side
The menus are written by hand on to pre-printed lines. On page 4: detail of an old map of Paris and a short text about Archestrate de Gela.

8a

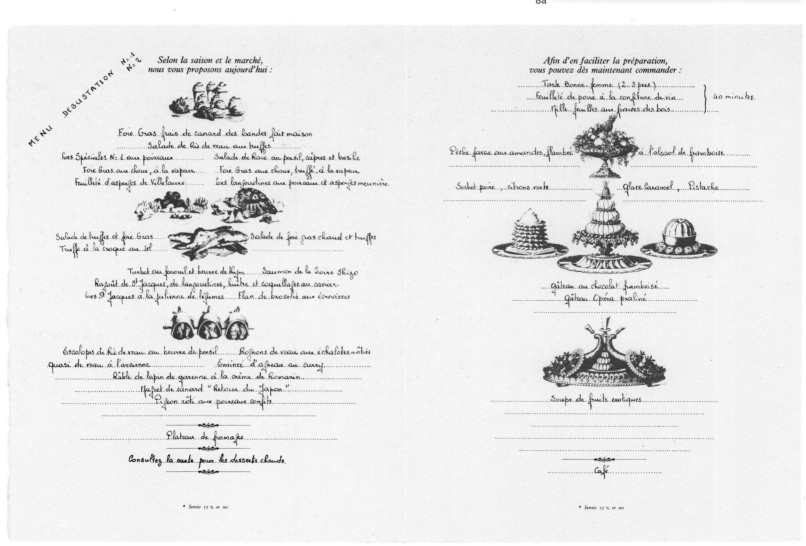

8b

9a–b Alain Chapel, Mionnay, France
Carte de menu. Création: Florent Garnier, Lyon
Couverture: 245 × 330 mm, ouvert 490 × 330 mm, 4 pages. Chromo une face. Pages 1 et 4 impression typo argent et brun-rouge. Rainé, plié
Intérieur: 240 × 320 mm, ouvert 480 × 320 mm, 6 pages. Papier structuré à la cuve. Offset gris et brun-rouge. Pliage 4 pages avec feuillet encarté, le tout inséré dans la couverture
La gravure sur bois du XVIIIᵉ siècle reproduite en réduction dans les pages intérieures constitue l'emblème de l'établissement. Belle typographie classique.

9a–b Alain Chapel, Mionnay, Frankreich
Speisekarte. Gestaltung Florent Garnier, Lyon
Umschlag: 245 × 330 mm, offen 490 × 330 mm, 4seitig. Chromokarton einseitig. Seiten 1 und 4 Buchdruck silber und rotbraun. Gerillt, gefalzt
Innenteil: 240 × 320 mm, offen 480 × 320 mm, 6seitig. Papier mit Büttenstruktur. Offset grau und rotbraun. 4seitig gefalzt und Einzelblatt. Beide Innenteile werden in den Umschlag eingelegt
Der abgebildete Holzschnitt aus dem 18. Jahrhundert ist die Hausmarke und wird verkleinert auch auf dem Innenteil verwendet. Schöne klassische Typographie.

9a–b Alain Chapel, Mionnay, France
Menu-card. Designed by Florent Garnier, Lyons
Cover: 245 × 330 mm, open 490 × 330 mm, 4 pages. One-sided cast-coated card. Pages 1 and 4: letterpress printing in silver and red-brown. Scored, folded
Contents: 240 × 320 mm, open 480 × 320 mm, 6 pages. Paper with texture of hand-made paper. Offset printing in grey and red-brown. Four-page fold and one single sheet. Both inside pages are inserted into the cover
The woodcut from the 18th century is the house logo which is also used on the inside pages, but reduced in size. Attractive classical typography.

9b

9a

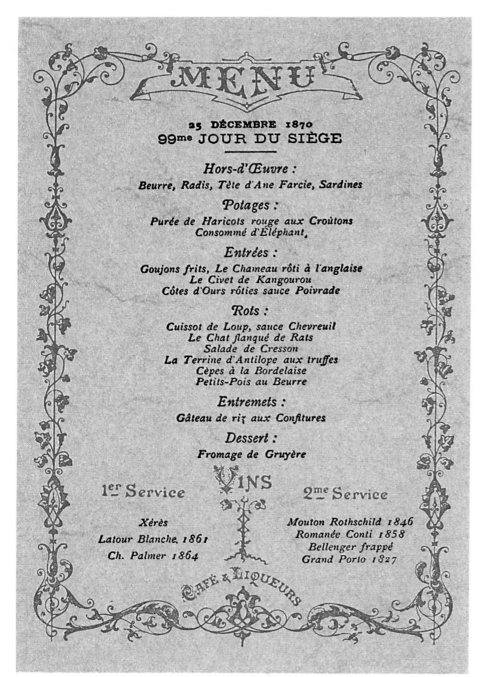

MENU

25 DÉCEMBRE 1870
99me JOUR DU SIÈGE

Hors-d'Œuvre :
Beurre, Radis, Tête d'Ane Farcie, Sardines

Potages :
Purée de Haricots rouge aux Croûtons
Consommé d'Éléphant,

Entrées :
Goujons frits, Le Chameau rôti à l'anglaise
Le Civet de Kangourou
Côtes d'Ours rôties sauce Poivrade

Rôts :
Cuissot de Loup, sauce Chevreuil
Le Chat flanqué de Rats
Salade de Cresson
La Terrine d'Antilope aux truffes
Cèpes à la Bordelaise
Petits-Pois au Beurre

Entremets :
Gâteau de riz aux Confitures

Dessert :
Fromage de Gruyère

1er Service   VINS   2me Service

Xérès
Latour Blanche, 1861
Ch. Palmer 1864

Mouton Rothschild 1846
Romanée Conti 1858
Bellenger frappé
Grand Porto 1827

CAFÉ & LIQUEURS

10

Au gré des temps, au rythme des saisons
nous vous proposerons plats de tradition
et recettes nouvelles.

DES HUITRES CHAUDES

LE TURBOT DUC D'ORLÉANS
beurre blanc, citron vert et cumin

UNE ESCALOPE DE RIS DE VEAU
A LA MODE
écrevisses, rognons et crêtes de coq
purée verte (cresson, épinards, haricots verts)

LA BÉCASSE ALAIN ROUSSEL
et
LA POULARDE RENÉ GOSCINNY
marinée, sautée au vinaigre de champagne
- petits légumes -

UN SOUFFLÉ MAISON BOURGEOISE
au pralin

Cette cuisine demande beaucoup de temps
Faites-nous la faveur d'ordonner par avance

11

10, 11 La Tour d'Argent, Paris
Un petit musée à l'intérieur du restaurant reflète la tradition historique et gastronomique de l'établissement. Les hôtes retenus dans le fichier des clients reçoivent parfois des propositions de menu (ill. 11) avec la reproduction d'une ancienne carte de menu (ill. 10). La carte reproduite est celle du 99ᵉ jour (25 décembre 1870) du Siège de Paris pendant la guerre franco-allemande 1870/1871.
Ill. 10: 120×180 mm, 2 pages. Papier imitation parchemin. Page 1 impression typo noir et brun
Ill. 11: 86×115 mm, 2 pages. Papier offset couleur. Page 1 impression typo brun ou gris

10, 11 La Tour d'Argent, Paris, Frankreich
Ein kleines Museum im Restaurant weist auf die geschichtliche und gastronomische Tradition des Hauses hin. Die in der Kundenkartei aufgenommenen Gäste erhalten von Zeit zu Zeit Menuvorschläge (Abb. 11), dazu die Reproduktion einer alten Menukarte (Abb. 10). Die hier gezeigte Menukarte gilt für den 99. Tag (25. Dezember 1870) der Belagerung von Paris im Deutsch-Französischen Krieg 1870/71.
Abb. 10: 120×180 mm, 2seitig. Papier mit Pergamentimitation. Seite 1 Buchdruck schwarz und braun
Abb. 11: 86×115 mm, 2seitig. Offsetpapier farbig. Seite 1 Buchdruck braun und grau

10–11 La Tour d'Argent, Paris, France
A small museum in the restaurant refers to the historical and gastronomic tradition of the house. From time to time, guests who have been entered on to the files on customers receive menu suggestions (ill. 11), as well as the reproduction of an old menu-card (ill. 10). The menu-card depicted here is for the 99th day (25 December 1870) of the siege of Paris during the Franco-Prussian war of 1870–1.
Ill. 10: 120×180 mm, 2 pages. Paper with vellum imitation. Page 1: letterpress printing in black and brown
Ill. 11: 86×115 mm, 2 pages. Coloured offset paper. Page 1: letterpress printing in brown and grey

Fines de Belon
Salade Notre-Dame
Caviar Blinis
Foie gras
des trois Empereurs
Cocktail de langouste
Serge Burcklé
Saumon fumé

POTAGES

Consommé Isabelle
Consommé Fabiola
Consommé Julienne
Bisque d'écrevisses
Potage Tour d'Argent
Potage glacé à l'indienne
Potage Claudius Burdel

ŒUFS

Œufs Mornay
Œufs en meurette
Œufs La Rochejacquelein
Œufs en brouillade aux truffes
Œufs en cocotte Chanoinesse
Omelette à votre plaisir
Œufs Tom Curtiss

POISSONS

Sole Mingori
Filets de sole Gloria
Filets de sole Cardinal
Filets de sole Concorde
Sole en Belle Meunière
Cari de sole à l'Indienne
Filets de sole grillés Frédéric
Coquille de Lauzun Barbue Botticelli
Homard Lagardère Barbue de Citeaux
Tournedos de saumon Vlasto
Croustade de barbue Lagrené
Langouste à la Mahonnaise
Goujonnettes de Mostelle
Quenelles André Terrail
Sole Daniel Saint
Langouste Winterthur
Turbot Duc d'Orléans

ENTRÉES

Côte de veau en casserole Côte de veau Charlemagne
Carré d'agneau
Côtes d'agneau à la grille Filet Tour d'Argent
Noisettes des Tournelles
Chateaubriand sauce Béarnaise Filet sauté de Lauzières
Rognon grillé Béarnaise Rognons Saint-Louis
Le filet charolais aux quatre poivres
Tournedos Yella Escalope Viennoise

CANETONS

Le caneton Tour d'Argent
Caneton aux quartiers de pêches
Caneton grillé aux pommes de reinette
sur commande
Aiguillettes de caneton à la gelée de porto
Le caneton Marco Polo aux quatre poivres
Caneton aux huîtres à la façon
de M.-A. Carême
Caneton poivré Lavallière
Caneton Daniel Sicklès

Caneton de la cerisaie
Caneton Venaissin aux olives
Caneton en terrine des Yvelines
sur commande
Caneton aux pistaches Claude Foussier
Caneton Bourdaloue à la julienne de citron
Le caneton Mazarine aux oranges
Caneton d'au-delà les mers à l'ananas,
aux pamplemousses
Caneton des vendanges

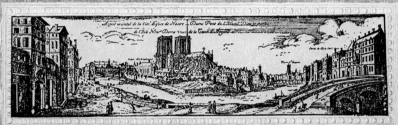

TEMPS ET SAISONS

La grande cuisine exige beaucoup de temps

Marmite d'écrevisses Philippe Peschaud
Caneton aux navets de Croissy
Soufflé aux framboises

A chaque saison ses fruits et ses apprêts

Faites-nous la faveur d'ordonner par avance

RÔTS

Poularde René Goscinny
Poularde Gustave V
sur commande
Poularde à la broche
Chapon en papillote
Poularde Tour d'Argent
sur commande
Poularde grillée Henri III
Poularde Charles Berthiez
Poularde sautée
Princesse Palatine
pour deux personnes
Curry de poulet Max Perez

LÉGUMES

(suivant saison)
Petits pois
Asperges vertes de Lauris
Endives sauce meunière
Fonds d'artichauts soufflés
Champignons à la Bordelaise
Haricots verts Gloire de Deuil
Épinards à la crème double
Pommes Alain Roussel
Pommes soufflées
Salade de l'Orbrerie
Salade Sully
Salade Roger

FROMAGES

Glaces
Sorbets 3 valses
Les mignardises
Flambées de pêches
Soufflé de Garavan
Soufflé aux amandes
Soufflé au Cointreau
Soufflé Sainte-Geneviève
Soufflé Kocisky Soufflé Valtesse

ENTREMETS

Poire en soufflé «Vie parisienne»
Poire Charpini
Fraises Valentinoise-Framboises
Soufflé au Grand Marnier
Pannequets des Tournelles
Profiteroles au chocolat
Crêpes Princesse Anne
Crêpes Suzette
Ananas

CAFÉ en filtre de grès

12

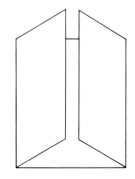

12 La Tour d'Argent, Paris
Carte de menu. Création: Y. de Farcy
254 × 380 mm, ouvert 514 × 380 mm, 6 pages. Carton argenté double face. Impression typo rouge et noir. Gaufrage structure argent. Rainé, pli fenêtre
Le choix des mets est présenté sur une série imprimée de plats en argent. Au dos, texte présentant la Tour d'Argent au fil des siècles et des informations sur quelques clients célèbres.

12 La Tour d'Argent, Paris, Frankreich
Speisekarte. Gestaltung Y. de Farcy
254 × 380 mm, offen 514 × 380 mm, 6seitig. Silberkarton zweiseitig. Buchdruck rot und schwarz. Silberstrukturgeprägt, gerillt, Fensterfalz
Die Auswahl der Menus wird auf Silberplatten präsentiert. Auf der Rückseite Text über die Geschichte des Tour d'Argent im Laufe der Jahrhunderte und Angaben über einige seiner berühmten Gäste.

12 La Tour d'Argent, Paris, France
Menu-card. Designed by Y. de Farcy
254 × 380 mm, open 514 × 380 mm, 6 pages. Two-sided silver card. Letterpress printing in red and black. Silver grained and embossed, scored, gate fold
The choice of menus is presented on silver salvers. On the back page: text gives information about the history of the Tour d'Argent throughout the centuries, as well as about some famous guests.

13a–b Gualtiero Marchesi, Milan, Italie
Carte de menu. Création: Giorgio Lucini, Milan
Couverture: 208 × 295 mm, ouvert 416 × 295 mm, 4
pages. Chromo une face. Pages 1 et 4 offset 4 couleurs
sur fond brun. Laminé, rainé, plié
Intérieur: 205 × 292 mm, ouvert 410 × 292 mm, 4
pages. Papier couché mat. Impression typo gris et
rouge. Plié et inséré dans la couverture

13a–b Gualtiero Marchesi, Mailand, Italien
Speisekarte. Gestaltung Giorgio Lucini, Mailand
Umschlag: 208 × 295 mm, offen 416 × 295 mm, 4seitig.
Chromokarton einseitig. Seiten 1 und 4 Offset 4farbig
und braun. Laminiert, gerillt, gefalzt
Innenteil: 205 × 292 mm, offen 410 × 292 mm, 4seitig.
Mattgestrichenes Papier. Buchdruck grau und rot. Ge-
falzt und in den Umschlag eingelegt

13a–b Gualtiero Marchesi, Milan, Italy
Menu-card. Designed by Giorgio Lucini, Milan
Cover: 208 × 295 mm, open 416 × 295 mm, 4 pages.
One-sided cast-coated card. Pages 1 and 4: 4-colour
offset printing plus brown. Laminated, scored, folded
Contents: 205 × 292 mm, open 410 × 292 mm, 4 pages.
Letterpress printing in grey and red. Folded and in-
serted into the cover

13a

13b

14a–b   L'Olivo, Park Hotel, Sienne, Italie
Carte de menu. Création: Service de publicité du Park Hotel. Impression: Rilievografia, Milan
Couverture: 212×300   mm,   ouvert 424×300 mm, 4 pages. Carton mat à structure gaufrée. Dorure à la feuille. Rainé, plié
Intérieur: 210×292   mm,   ouvert 420×292 mm, 8 pages. Chromo double face. Impression typo noir. Deux cahiers de 4 pages pliés et insérés dans la couverture. Deux fentes estampées en demi-cercle pour permettre l'insertion de la carte des spécialités
Carte des spécialités: 131×177 mm, 2 pages. Papier offset couleur. Lignes noires préimprimées, texte dactylographié. Estampé
La grande tradition typographique italienne se retrouve dans la présentation. Contraste intéressant entre les papiers: à la cuve mat pour la couverture et brillant pour l'intérieur.

14a–b   L'Olivo, Park Hotel, Siena, Italien
Speisekarte. Gestaltung Werbeabteilung Park Hotel. Druck Rilievografia, Mailand
Umschlag: 212×300   mm,   offen 424× 300 mm, 4seitig. Matter strukturgeprägter Karton. Goldfolienprägung. Gerillt, gefalzt
Innenteil: 210×292 mm, offen 420×292 mm, 8seitig. Chromokarton zweiseitig. Buchdruck schwarz. 2mal zu 4 Seiten gefalzt und in den Umschlag eingelegt. 2 halbrunde gestanzte Schlitze ermöglichen das Einstecken der Spezialitätenkarte
Spezialitätenkarte: 131×177 mm, 2seitig. Offsetpapier farbig. Vorgedruckte schwarze Linien, Text Schreibmaschine. Formgestanzt
In der Typografie ist die Tradition der italienischen Buchkünstler spürbar. Interessant der Kontrast zwischen dem büttenartigen und matten Umschlag und dem Spiegelglanzkarton des Innenteils

14a–b   L'Olivo, Park Hotel, Siena, Italy
Menu-card. Designed by the advertising department of the Park Hotel. Printed by Rilievografia, Milan
Cover: 212×300 mm, open 424×300 mm, 4 pages. Card with embossed texture and matt finish. Gold embossing. Scored, folded
Contents: 210×292   mm,   open 420×292 mm, 8 pages. Two-sided cast-coated card. Letterpress printing in black. Two 4-page folds, inserted into the cover. Two semi-circular die-cut slots enable insertion of the 'Specialities' card. 'Specialities' card: 131×177 mm, 2 pages. Coloured offset paper. Pre-printed black lines, typed text. Die-cut
The typography evokes in spirit the tradition of Italian book illuminators. A note of interest is the contrast between the imitation hand-made paper with matt finish for the cover on one hand and the high-gloss card for the contents on the other hand.

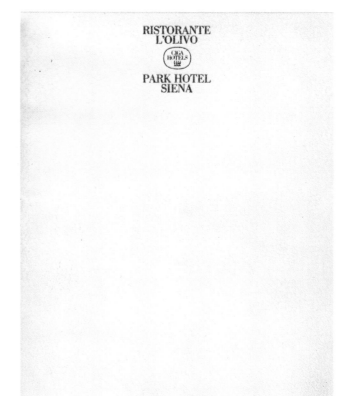

RISTORANTE
L'OLIVO
CIGA HOTELS

PARK HOTEL
SIENA

A LA CARTE

14a

CARNI
MEATS

Scaloppine di Vitella al Funghetto	
Veal Scaloppine with Mush-rooms	8.500
Scaloppa alla Milanese	
Veal Cutlet Milanese Style	8.000
Nodino alla Sassi	
Veal Chop Sassi Style	8.500
Bistecca alla Fiorentina (2 persone)	
Beefsteak Florentine	18.000
Pollo alla griglia	
Grilled Chicken	7.500
Filetto di Bue / Fillet of Beef	11.000
Saltimbocca alla Romana / Veal Saltimbocca a la Romaine	8.000
Grigliata mista / Mixed Grill	11.000
Costoletta Marciano / Veal Chop Marciano	8.500
Fegato di Vitello / Veal Liver	8.000
Lombatina di Vitella / Sirloin Steak	9.500
Braciola di Maiale / Pork Chop	8.000
Trippa alla Fiorentina / Tripe Florentine	7.500

LEGUMI
VEGETABLES

Legumi o Insalata di stagione	
Vegetables or Salads in Season	2.500

LO CHEF CONSIGLIA
CHEF'S SUGGESTIONS

RISOTTO CON PUNTE D'ASPARAGI

TAGLIOLINI VERDI AL PROSCIUTTO GRATINATI

RIBOLLITA DEL PODERE

FEGATO DI VITELLO IN TEGAME

ROSETTE AL BURRO CON CARCIOFI

COSTATA TOSCANA AI FERRI

LEGUMI MISTI DEL GIORNO

14b

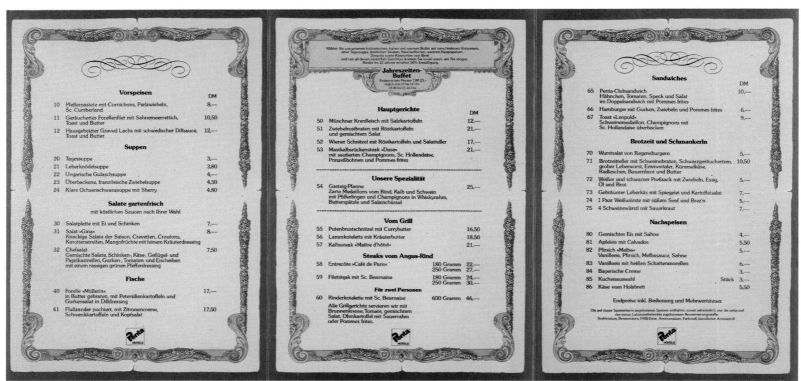

15b

15a–c Münchner Kindl-Stuben,
Penta Hotel, Munich, RFA
Carte de menu. Propre création
220 × 323 mm, ouvert 660 × 323 mm, 6
pages. Papier couché. Offset 4 couleurs et brun. Laminage mat, rainé deux
fois, plis roulés
En couverture, reproduction de la carte
originale de l'ancien établissement
Münchner Kindl-Keller (1909).

15a–c Münchner Kindl-Stuben,
Penta Hotel, München, Bundesrepublik
Deutschland
Speisekarte. Eigene Gestaltung
220 × 323 mm, offen 660 × 323 mm,
6seitig. Kunstdruckpapier. Offset 4far-
big und braun. Mattlaminiert. 2mal gerillt, Wickelfalz
Seite 1 zeigt eine Reproduktion der Ori-
ginalkarte des ehemaligen Münchner
Kindl-Kellers, 1909, Seite 6 eine Reproduktion mit Informationstext über die
Unionsbrauerei München.

15a–c Münchner Kindl-Stuben,
Penta Hotel, Munich, West Germany
Menu-card. Designed by the Penta
Hotel, Munich
220 × 323 mm, open 660 × 323 mm, 6
pages. Art paper; 4-colour offset printing plus brown. Laminated, with matt
finish. Twice scored, reverse accordion
fold
Page 1 illustrates a reproduction of the
original card of the former 'Münchner-
Kindl-Keller', 1909; page 6 depicts a reproduction with informative text about
the 'Unionsbrauerei München'.

15c

15a

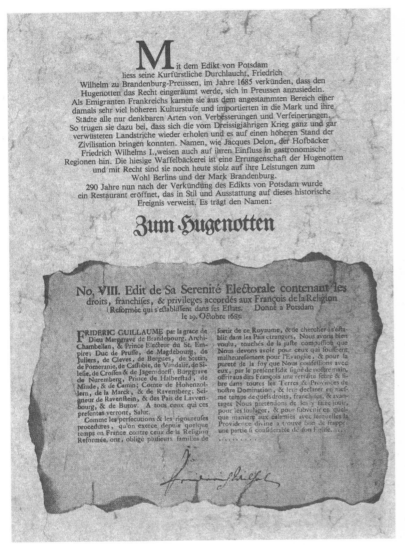

16a

16b

16a–b   Zum Hugenotten, Hotel Inter-Continental, Berlin-Ouest
Carte de menu. Création: Repro-Studio Gert Fortmann, Berlin
230 × 328 mm, ouvert 460 × 328 mm, 8 pages. Imitation parchemin. Offset 4 couleurs et brun. Plié en deux fois 4 pages et encarté dans une reliure en cuir. En page 1, courte présentation historique et illustration de l'Edit de Potsdam (1685), par lequel le Grand Electeur invita les huguenots à s'établir à Brandebourg. Le cadre guirlande des pages intérieures se répète en inversion gauche-droite.

16a–b   Zum Hugenotten, Hotel Inter-Continental, West-Berlin
Speisekarte. Gestaltung Repro-Studio Gert Fortmann, Berlin
230 × 328 mm, offen 460 × 328 mm, 8seitig. Pergamentimitation. Offset 4farbig und braun. Gefalzt und zweimal zu 4 Seiten in Ledermappe eingelegt Seite 1 kurze geschichtliche Einführung und Abbildung des Edikts von Potsdam 1685, mit dem der Große Kurfürst die Hugenotten zur Ansiedlung in Brandenburg einlud. Seite 8 kleines Hugenotten-Lexikon. Die einrahmende Ranke der Innenseite wird auf der gegenüberliegenden Seite jeweils spiegelverkehrt wiederholt.

16a–b   Zum Hugenotten, Hotel Inter-Continental, West Berlin
Menu-card. Designed by Repro-Studio Gert Fortmann, Berlin
230 × 328 mm, open 460 × 328 mm, 8 pages. Vellum imitation; 4-colour offset printing plus brown. Folded to two 4-page folds, inserted into the leather folder
Page 1: a short historical introduction to and illustration of the Edict of Potsdam, 1685, with which the Great Elector invited the Huguenots to settle in Brandenburg. Page 8: a short Huguenot encyclopaedia. The surrounding climber on the inside page is repeated in mirror image on the opposite page.

17 Brasserie de l'Hôtel Inter-Continental, Cologne, RFA
Carte de menu
Couverture: 250×373 mm, ouvert 500×373 mm, 4 pages. Chromo une face. Offset, page 1 trois tons de brun, pages 2–4 en brun. Laminé deux faces, rainé, plié
Intérieur: 247×370 mm, ouvert 496×370 mm, 4 pages. Papier couleur structuré à la cuve. Offset en deux tons de brun. Plié et agrafé deux fois dans le pli avec la couverture
Ancien motif modernisé. Les ornements et l'écriture rappellent les portes de verre dépoli ou gravé des auberges d'autrefois. Dans les pages intérieures le logo Inter-Continental est transformé en logo «brasserie». Les deux représentent les armoiries de Cologne.

17 Brasserie, Hotel Inter-Continental, Köln, Bundesrepublik Deutschland
Speisekarte
Umschlag: 250×373 mm, offen 500×373 mm, 4seitig. Chromokarton einseitig. Offset, Seite 1: 3 Brauntöne, Seiten 2–4: 1 Braunton. Beidseitig laminiert, gerillt, gefalzt
Innenteil: 247×370 mm, offen 496×370 mm, 4seitig. Büttenstrukturpapier farbig. Offset, 2 Brauntöne. Gefalzt und mit dem Umschlag 2mal drahtgeheftet
Altes Motiv auf moderne Art verwendet. Ornament und Schrift erinnern an geätzte oder geschliffene Glastüren alter Gaststätten. Im Innenteil wird das Inter-Continental-Signet zu einem Brasserie-Signet abgewandelt. Beide zeigen das Kölner Wappen.

17 Brasserie, Hotel Inter-Continental, Cologne, West Germany
Menu-card
Cover: 250×373 mm, open 500×373 mm, 4 pages. One-sided cast-coated card. Offset printing on page 1 in shades of brown, on pages 2–4 in brown. Laminated on both pages, scored, folded
Contents: 247×370 mm, open 496×370 mm, 4 pages. Coloured paper with finish of hand-made paper. Offset printing in 2 shades of brown. Folded and 2-wire stitched to the cover.
An old subject used in modern manner. Ornamentation and lettering call to mind etched or cut-glass doors of old inns. On the inside pages, the Inter-Continental logo is adapted to a brasserie logo. Both depict the coat of arms of Cologne.

17

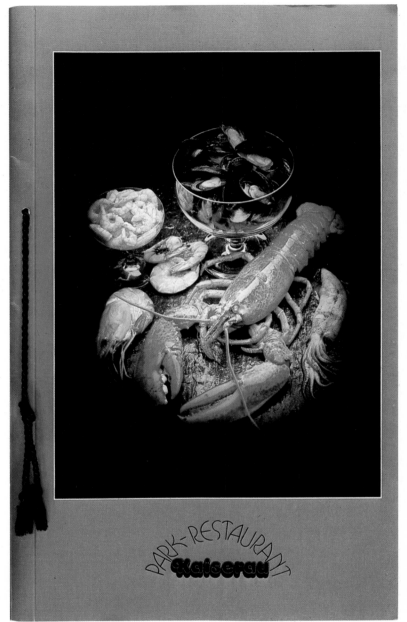

18a

18b

18a–b Park-Restaurant, Kaiserau, RFA
Carte de menu. Création: C.P. Dieckmann, éditeur spécialisé dans les cartes de menu, Bielefeld
Couverture: 257 × 420 mm, ouvert 514 × 420 mm, 4 pages. Chromo deux faces. Page 1 offset 4 couleurs et or, pages 2–3 offset noir et or, page 4 or. Laminage grain deux faces, rainé trois fois, plié, percé deux fois Intérieur: 257 × 420 mm, 12 pages. Imitation parchemin. Offset noir et or. Plié, percé deux fois et assemblé à la couverture par un cordon noir
Menus présentés en allemand et en français. Sur la carte des consommations, reproduction réduite du graphisme original.

18a–b Park-Restaurant, Kaiserau, Bundesrepublik Deutschland
Speisekarte. Gestaltung C. P. Dieckmann, Spezialverlag für besondere Speisekarten, Bielefeld
Umschlag: 257 × 420 mm, offen 514 × 420 mm, 4seitig. Chromokarton zweiseitig. Seite 1 Offset 4farbig und gold, Seiten 2–3 Offset schwarz und gold, Seite 4 gold. Beidseitig prägelaminiert, 3mal gerillt, gefalzt, 2mal gelocht
Innenteil: 257 × 420 mm, 12seitig. Pergamentimitation. Offset schwarz und gold. Gefalzt, 2mal gelocht und durch schwarze Kordel mit dem Umschlag verbunden
Speisenangebot 2sprachig Deutsch und Französisch. Für die Getränke werden die verkleinerten Originalschriftzüge verwendet.

18a–b Park-Restaurant, Kaiserau, West Germany
Menu-card. Designed by C.P. Dieckmann, publishers specializing in menu-cards, Bielefeld
Cover: 257 × 420 mm, open 514 × 420 mm, 4 pages. Two-sided cast-coated card. Page 1: 4-colour offset printing plus gold, pages 2–3: offset printing in black and gold, page 4: in gold. Two-sided grain-laminated finish, 3 times scored, folded, twice punched
Contents: 257 × 420 mm, 12 pages. Paper with vellum imitation, offset printing in black und gold. Folded, twice punched and attached to the cover with a black cord
Menus in both French and German. The original lettering, reduced in size, is used for the wine list.

WEINKARTE
HOTEL EISENHUT

19a

Stammwappen der Familie
Eisenhut.

20

19a–c Hotel Eisenhut, Rothenburg ob der Tauber, RFA
Carte des vins. Création: Mme Georg Pirner. Illustrations: Anton Hoffmann, Munich. Impression: Schneider-Druck, Rothenburg ob der Tauber
Couverture: 250×270 mm, ouvert 500×270 mm, 4 pages. Papier structuré «peau de crocodile». Page 1 impression typo noir, blanc et rouge. Armoiries estampées. Rainé trois fois, plié, percé trois fois
Intérieur: 243×262 mm, 14 pages. Imitation parchemin, impression typo noir. Rainé une fois, assemblé par feuillets, percé trois fois et relié à la couverture par un cordon jaune or

19a–c Hotel Eisenhut, Rothenburg ob der Tauber, Bundesrepublik Deutschland
Weinkarte. Gestaltung Frau Georg Pirner. Illustrationen Anton Hoffmann, München. Druck Schneider-Druck, Rothenburg ob der Tauber
Umschlag: 250×270 mm, offen 500×270 mm, 4seitig. Papier mit Elefantenhautstruktur. Seite 1 Buchdruck schwarz, weiß, rot. Wappen geprägt. 3mal gerillt, gefalzt, 3mal gelocht
Innenteil: 243×262 mm, 14seitig. Pergamentimitation. Buchdruck schwarz. 1mal gerillt, als Einzelblätter zusammengetragen, 3mal gelocht und durch goldgelbe Kordel mit dem Umschlag verbunden

19a–c Hotel Eisenhut, Rothenburg ob der Tauber, West Germany
Wine list. Designed by Frau Georg Pirner. Printed by Schneider-Druck, Rothenburg ob der Tauber. Illustrations by Anton Hoffmann, Munich
Cover: 250×270 mm, open 500×270 mm, 4 pages. Paper with elephant-grain. Page 1: letterpress printing in black, red and white. Embossed crest. Three times scored, folded, 3 times punched
Contents: 243×262 mm, 14 pages. Paper with vellum imitation. Letterpress printing in black. Once scored, bound as single pages, 3 times punched and attached to the cover with a golden-yellow cord

20 Carte de vœux de l'Hotel Eisenhut
105×148 mm, ouvert 210×148 mm, 4 pages. Chromo. Page 1 impression typo noir

20 Grußkarte Hotel Eisenhut
105×148 mm, offen 210×148 mm, 4seitig. Chromokarton. Seite 1 Buchdruck schwarz

20 Greetings-card, Hotel Eisenhut
105×148 mm, open 210×148 mm, 4 pages. Cast-coated card. Page 1: letterpress printing in black

Willkommen Gast!

Manch alt Geschlecht

Hat hier beim Tauberwein gezecht.

Im Herrenstueblein und im Tennen

Wirst Du noch heut gut weilen koennen.

16. Jahrhundert
(Alter Eisenhut-Hausspruch)

HOTEL EISENHUT
GEORG PIRNER
EIGENTÜMERIN FRAU GEORG PIRNER

19b

19c

21 Steigenberger Kurhaushotel, Bad Kissingen, RFA
Carte de menu. Création: Société hôtelière A. Steigenberger, Francfort-sur-le-Main, d'après reproduction de tableaux d'Otto Rückert de Munich. Les originaux sont exposés dans le restaurant
Couverture: 245 × 420 mm, ouvert 490 × 420 mm, 4 pages et rabats au format de la couverture, contrecollés. Chromo une face. Offset 4 couleurs. Pli fenêtre, 4 fentes estampées
Intérieur: 242 × 420 mm, 4 pages. Carton offset. Offset orange. Pages 2 et 3 contre-collées, fixées à la couverture par les plis. 2 × 4 fentes estampées
Carte du jour: papier machine à écrire, texte dactylographié. En principe interchangeable, mais le grand format rend indispensable le collage des feuilles.

21 Steigenberger Kurhaushotel, Bad Kissingen, Bundesrepublik Deutschland
Speisekarte. Gestaltung A. Steigenberger Hotelgesellschaft KGaA, Frankfurt am Main, unter Verwendung von Reproduktionen nach Ölgemälden von Prof. Otto Rückert, München. Die Originale befinden sich im Restaurant
Umschlag: 245 × 420 mm, offen 490 × 420 mm, 4seitig und Klappen im Format des Umschlags gegengeklebt. Chromokarton einseitig. Offset 4farbig. Fensterfalz, 4 gestanzte Schlitze
Innenteil: 242 × 420 mm, 4seitig. Offsetkarton. Offset orange. Seiten 2 und 3 gegengeklebt und durch Fälze auf dem Umschlag angeklebt. 2 × 4 gestanzte Schlitze
Tageskarten: Schreibmaschinenpapier, Text Schreibmaschine. Im Prinzip auswechselbar, das große Format erfordert aber ein Einkleben

21 Steigenberger Kurhaushotel, Bad Kissingen, West Germany
Menu-card. Designed by the A. Steigenberger Hotelgesellschaft KGaA, Frankfurt, using reproductions after oil-paintings by Prof. Otto Rückert, Munich. The originals hang in the restaurant
Cover: 245 × 420 mm, open 490 × 420 mm, 4 pages plus flaps, the size of the cover, glued against the cover. One-sided cast-coated card. 4-colour offset printing. Gate fold, 4 die-cut slots
Contents: 242 × 420 mm, 4 pages. Offset card. Offset printing in orange. Pages 2 and 3 glued together and joined to the cover with folds. 2 × 4 die-cut slots
Cards for 'Menu of the Day' on typewriting-paper, typed text. In principle interchangeable, however, the large size necessitates pasting in.

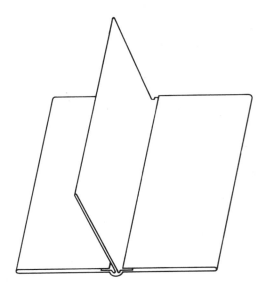

21

22 Restaurant Français, Steigenberger Hotel Frankfurter Hof, Francfort-sur-le-Main, RFA
Carte de menu. Création d'après une gravure de William Hamilton. L'original est exposé dans le restaurant
Couverture: 212×328 mm, ouvert 424×328 mm, 4 pages. Chromo double face. Page 1 impression typo 4 couleurs et rose clair, pages 2 et 3 impression typo noir et or. Rainé, plié
Intérieur: 210×328 mm, ouvert 630×328 mm, 6 pages. Papier couché mat. Impression typo or. Plis roulés. Deux pages collées ensemble et fixées à la page 3 de la couverture. 4 fentes estampées par page
Carte du jour: 175×281 mm, 2 pages. Papier machine à écrire. Texte dactylographié. Rappel du cadre rose clair de la couverture. Les cartes du jour sont soit insérées dans les fentes soit fixées par deux pinces
Texte et légende de l'illustration trilingues allemand-anglais-français. Menus bilingues français-allemand.

22 Restaurant Français, Steigenberger Hotel Frankfurter Hof, Frankfurt am Main, Bundesrepublik Deutschland
Speisekarte. Gestaltung unter Verwendung eines Stiches von William Hamilton. Der Stich befindet sich im Restaurant
Umschlag: 212×328 mm, offen 424×328 mm, 4seitig. Chromokarton zweiseitig. Seite 1 Buchdruck 4farbig und hellrosa, Seiten 2–3 Buchdruck schwarz und gold. Gerillt, gefalzt
Innenteil: 210×328 mm, offen 630×328 mm, 6seitig. Papier mattgestrichen. Buchdruck gold. Wickelfalz. Zwei Seiten zusammengeklebt und auf dritte Umschlagseite aufgeklebt. 4 Schlitze je Seite
Tageskarten: 175×281 mm, 2seitig. Schreibmaschinenpapier. Text Schreibmaschine. Übernahme des hellrosa Ornaments vom Umschlag. Die Tageskarten werden entweder in die Schlitze eingeschoben oder mit zwei Klemmen festgehalten. Text und Bildlegenden 3sprachig Deutsch, Französisch, Englisch. Speisenfolge 2sprachig Französisch, Deutsch

22 Restaurant Français, Steigenberger Hotel Frankfurter Hof, Frankfurt, West Germany
Menu-card. Designed after an engraving by William Hamilton. The engraving hangs in the restaurant
Cover: 212×328 mm, open 424×328 mm, 4 pages. Two-sided cast-coated card. Page 1: 4-colour letterpress printing plus pale pink, pages 2–3: letterpress printing in black and gold. Scored, folded
Contents: 210×328 mm, open 630×328 mm, 6 pages. Paper with matt finish. Letterpress printing in gold. Reverse accordion fold. Two pages glued back to back and glued to the third cover page; 4 die-cut slots per page
'Menu of the Day' cards: 175×281 mm, 2 pages. Typewriting-paper. Typed text. Adoption of the pale pink border from the cover. The cards for 'Menu of the Day' are either inserted into the slots or secured with two paper-clips. Text and picture captions in German, French and English. Menus in French and German.

22

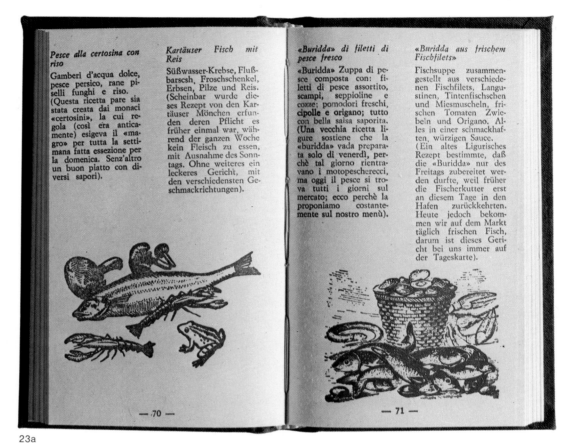

23a

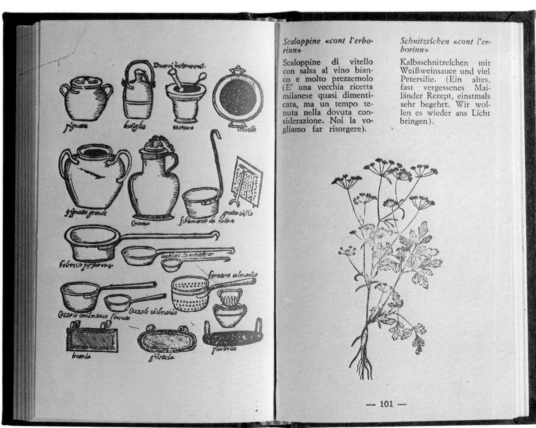

23b

23a–b Cagliostro, Munich, RFA
Carte de menu en forme de petit livre relié. Impression: Tipografia adriatica, Cattolica, Italie
Couverture: 90×148 mm, reliure toile, dorure à la feuille
Intérieur: 83×142 mm, 154 pages. Papier offset jaunâtre. Impression typo brun. Cousu fil, tranchefil
Textes sur l'origine, les ingrédients et la préparation des différents plats, bilingues italien-allemand. Gravures anciennes et photos illustrent ce petit volume.

23a–b Cagliostro, München, Bundesrepublik Deutschland
Speisekarte in Form eines gebundenen Büchleins. Druck Tipografia adriatica, Cattolica, Italien
Umschlag: 90×148 mm, Leineneinband, Goldfolienprägung
Innenteil: 83×142 mm, 154 Seiten. Offsetpapier gelblich. Buchdruck braun. Fadengeheftet, Kapitalband
Texte über Herkunft, Zutaten, Zubereitung der einzelnen Speisen 2sprachig Italienisch, Deutsch. Alte Stiche und Fotos illustrieren das Bändchen.

23a–b Cagliostro, Munich, West Germany
Menu-card in the size of a small bound book. Printed by Tipografia adriatica, Cattolica, Italy
Cover: 90×148 mm, cloth-bound cover, gold embossing
Contents: 83×142 mm, 154 pages. Offset paper with yellow tint. Letterpress printing in brown. Thread-sewn, headband
Texts on origin, ingredients and preparation of the individual dishes in Italian and German. Old prints and photographs illustrate the small book.

ATLANTIC

à la carte

24a

	DM
Cantaloupe melon with sorbet of beet root	20.50
Lobster salad with mushrooms and spinach	32.00
Tureen of young pigeons with Waldorf salad	26.00
Jellied fresh salmon Atlantic, sauce verte	21.00
Stuffed quail with asparagus salad	32.00
Iced cream of cucumbers with quail egg	9.00
Potato soup with stuffed morels	12.50
Herb-cream soup Royal	9.50
Frog legs à la mode du chef	29.00
Loup de mer in Chablis	39.50
Pike dumplings with scampi-sauce on leaf spinach	36.50
Fillets of sole Excellence	37.00
Fillet of salmon with leek in red butter	36.00
Soufflé of turbot in lobster sauce	42.00
Waterzooi of sea food 'Gent	36.00
Hamburg spring-chicken Périgord, Parisienne potatoes, lettuce with yoghourt dressing	34.00
Calf's sweetbread in Fleurie, mashed celery	29.00
Lamb cutlets with orange and green pepper, Celery, croquettes potatoes	34.00
Fillet tips Malaysia, Ginger rice	30.50
Stuffed medaillons of veal Newburg, Green noodles with pine kernels	34.00
Fillet of pork with vegetables In roquefort cream, "spätzle"	32.00

24b

24a–b Atlantic Hotel Kempinski, Hambourg, RFA
Carte de menu. Création: Karsten Drehmel
Couverture: 210×440 mm, ouvert 420×440 mm, 4 pages. Chromo une face. Impression typo noir et or. Rainé, plié. Page 3: 4 fentes estampées
Carte des spécialités: 160×390 mm, 2 pages. Bristol. Page 1 impression typo noir. Insérée dans la couverture
Carte du jour: 160×150 mm, 2 pages. Papier offset. Page 1 impression typo or. Texte dactylographié. Insérée dans la couverture.

24a–b Atlantic Hotel Kempinski, Hamburg, Bundesrepublik Deutschland
Speisekarte. Gestaltung Karsten Drehmel
Umschlag: 210×440 mm, offen 420×440 mm, 4seitig. Chromokarton einseitig. Buchdruck schwarz und gold. Gerillt, gefalzt. Seite 3: vier gestanzte Schlitze
Spezialitätenkarte: 160×390 mm, 2seitig. Bristolkarton. Seite 1 Buchdruck schwarz. Eingesteckt
Tageskarte: 160×150 mm, 2seitig. Offsetpapier. Seite 1 Buchdruck gold. Text Schreibmaschine. Eingesteckt

24a–b Atlantic Hotel Kempinski, Hamburg, West Germany
Menu-card. Designed by Karsten Drehmel
Cover: 210×440 mm, open 420×440 mm, 4 pages. One-sided cast-coated card. Letterpress printing in black and gold. Scored, folded. Page 3: 4 die-cut slots
'Specialities' card: 160×390 mm, 2 pages. Bristol board. Page 1: letterpress printing in black. Inserted
'Menu of the Day' card: 160×150 mm, 2 pages. Offset paper. Page 1: letterpress printing in gold. Typed text. Inserted

25

25 Schweizer Stuben, Wertheim-Bettingen, RFA
Carte de menu. Propre création
Couverture: 285×335 mm, ouvert 570×335 mm, 4
pages. Carton offset. Pages 1 et 4 offset 4 couleurs et
bleu foncé. Plié
Intérieur: 278×330 mm, ouvert 556×330 mm, 4
pages. Carton offset. Offset gris clair, gris foncé et
rouge. Rainé, plié et encarté dans la couverture
Présentation des mets bilingue français-allemand.

25 Schweizer Stuben, Wertheim-Bettingen, Bundesrepublik Deutschland
Speisekarte. Eigene Gestaltung
Umschlag: 285×335 mm, offen 570×335 mm, 4sei-
tig. Offsetkarton. Seiten 1 und 4 Offset 4farbig und
dunkelblau. Gefalzt
Innenteil: 278×330 mm, offen 556×330 mm, 4seitig.
Offsetkarton. Offset hellgrau, dunkelgrau und rot. Gerillt, gefalzt und in den Umschlag eingelegt. Speisenangebot 2sprachig Französisch, Deutsch

25 Schweizer Stuben, Wertheim-Bettingen, West
Germany
Menu-card. Designed by Schweizer Stuben, Wert-
heim-Bettingen
Cover: 285×335 mm, open 570×335 mm, 4 pages.
Offset card. Pages 1 and 4: 4-colour offset printing plus
dark blue. Folded
Contents: 278×330 mm, open 556×330 mm, 4
pages. Offset card. Offset printing in pale grey, dark
grey and red. Scored, folded and inserted into the
cover
Menus in French and German

26a

26a–b Fuchs'nstub'n, Zum Franziskaner, Munich, RFA
Carte de menu. Création: Stefan Hulbe & Claus Oliv, Grafic Design
260 × 400 mm, ouvert 567 × 400 mm, 6 pages. Papier couché. Offset 4 couleurs. Laminé grain deux côtés, estampé, rainé deux fois, pli fenêtre
Les titres en bavarois font «couleur locale». En fond apparaissent partout les couleurs bavaroises, bleu et blanc.

26a–b Fuchs'nstub'n, Zum Franziskaner, München, Bundesrepublik Deutschland
Speisekarte. Gestaltung stefan hulbe & claus oliv, grafic design
260 × 400 mm, offen 567 × 400 mm, 6seitig. Kunstdruckpapier. Offset 4farbig. Beidseitig prägelaminiert, formgestanzt, 2mal gerillt, Fensterfalz
Bayerische Titel sorgen für Lokalkolorit. Im Hintergrund erscheinen die bayerischen Farben Blau-Weiß.

26a–b Fuchs'nstub'n, Zum Franziskaner, Munich, West Germany
Menu-card. Designed by stefan hulbe & claus oliv, graphic design
260 × 400 mm, open 567 × 400 mm, 6 pages. Art paper; 4-colour offset printing. Two-sided grain-laminated finish, die-cut, twice scored, gate fold Bavarian headings lend a touch of the local spirit. The background is taken up by the Bavarian colours: blue and white.

26b

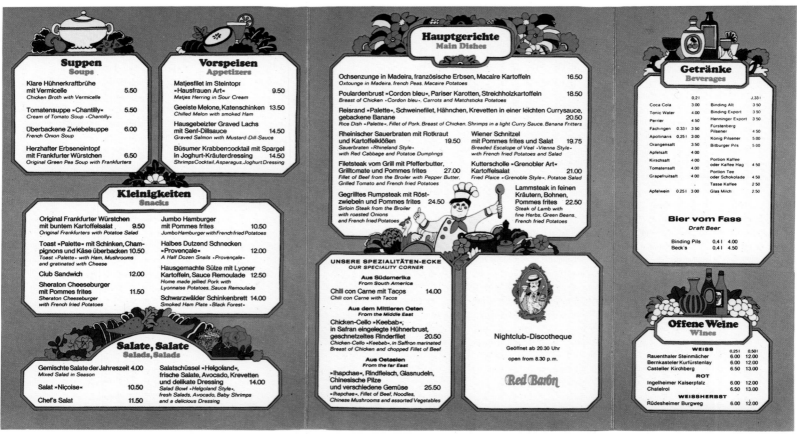

Suppen — Soups

Klare Hühnerkraftbrühe mit Vermicelle — 5.50
Chicken Broth with Vermicelle

Tomatensuppe »Chantilly« — 5.50
Cream of Tomato Soup »Chantilly«

Überbackene Zwiebelsuppe — 6.00
French Onion Soup

Herzhafter Erbseneintopf mit Frankfurter Würstchen — 6.50
Original Green Pea Soup with Frankfurters

Vorspeisen — Appetizers

Matjesfilet im Steintopf »Hausfrauen Art« — 9.50
Matjes Herring in Sour Cream

Geeiste Melone, Katenschinken — 13.50
Chilled Melon with smoked Ham

Hausgebeizter Graved Lachs mit Senf-Dillsauce — 14.50
Graved Salmon with Mustard-Dill-Sauce

Büsumer Krabbencocktail mit Spargel in Joghurt-Kräuterdressing — 14.50
Shrimps Cocktail, Asparagus, Joghurt Dressing

Kleinigkeiten — Snacks

Original Frankfurter Würstchen mit buntem Kartoffelsalat — 9.50
Original Frankfurters with Potatoe Salad

Toast »Palette« mit Schinken, Champignons und Käse überbacken — 10.50
Toast »Palette« with Ham, Mushrooms and gratinated with Cheese

Club Sandwich — 12.00

Sheraton Cheeseburger mit Pommes frites — 11.50
Sheraton Cheeseburger with French fried Potatoes

Jumbo Hamburger mit Pommes frites — 10.50
Jumbo Hamburger with French fried Potatoes

Halbes Dutzend Schnecken »Provençale« — 12.00
A Half Dozen Snails »Provençale«

Hausgemachte Sülze mit Lyoner Kartoffeln, Sauce Remoulade — 12.50
Home made jellied Pork with Lyonnaise Potatoes, Sauce Remoulade

Schwarzwälder Schinkenbrett — 14.00
Smoked Ham Plate »Black Forest«

Salate, Salate — Salads, Salads

Gemischte Salate der Jahreszeit — 4.00
Mixed Salad in Season

Salat »Niçoise« — 10.50

Chef's Salat — 11.50

Salatschüssel »Helgoland«, frische Salate, Avocado, Krevetten und delikate Dressing — 14.00
Salad Bowl »Helgoland Style«, fresh Salads, Avocado, Baby Shrimps and a delicious Dressing

Hauptgerichte — Main Dishes

Ochsenzunge in Madeira, französische Erbsen, Macaire Kartoffeln — 16.50
Oxtongue in Madeira, french Peas, Macaire Potatoes

Poulardenbrust »Cordon bleu«, Pariser Karotten, Streichholzkartoffeln — 18.50
Breast of Chicken »Cordon bleu«, Carrots and Matchsticks Potatoes

Reisrand »Palette«, Schweinefilet, Hähnchen, Krevetten in einer leichten Currysauce, gebackene Banane — 20.50
Rice Dish »Palette«, Fillet of Pork, Breast of Chicken, Shrimps in a light Curry Sauce, Banana Fritters

Rheinischer Sauerbraten mit Rotkraut und Kartoffelklößen — 19.50
Sauerbraten »Rhineland Style« with Red Cabbage and Potatoe Dumplings

Filetsteak vom Grill mit Pfefferbutter, Grilltomate und Pommes frites — 27.00
Fillet of Beef from the Broiler with Pepper Butter, Grilled Tomato and French fried Potatoes

Gegrilltes Rumpsteak mit Röstzwiebeln und Pommes frites — 24.50
Sirloin Steak from the Broiler with roasted Onions and French fried Potatoes

Wiener Schnitzel mit Pommes frites und Salat — 19.75
Breaded Escalope of Veal »Vienna Style« with French fried Potatoes and Salad

Kutterscholle »Grenobler Art« Kartoffelsalat — 21.00
Fried Plaice »Grenoble Style«, Potatoe Salad

Lammsteak in feinen Kräutern, Bohnen, Pommes frites — 22.50
Steak of Lamb with fine Herbs, Green Beans, French fried Potatoes

UNSERE SPEZIALITÄTEN-ECKE — OUR SPECIALITY CORNER

Aus Südamerika — From South America

Chili con Carne mit Tacos — 14.00
Chili con Carne with Tacos

Aus dem Mittleren Osten — From the Middle East

Chicken-Cello »Keebab«, in Safran eingelegte Hühnerbrust, geschnetzeltes Rinderfilet — 20.50
Chicken-Cello »Keebab«, in Saffron marinated Breast of Chicken and chopped Fillet of Beef

Aus Ostasien — From the far East

»Ihapchae«, Rindfleisch, Glasnudeln, Chinesische Pilze und verschiedene Gemüse — 25.50
»Ihapchae«, Fillet of Beef, Noodles, Chinese Mushrooms and assorted Vegetables

Nightclub-Discotheque

Geöffnet ab 20.30 Uhr

open from 8.30 p.m.

Red Barón

Getränke — Beverages

	0.2 l		0.33 l
Coca Cola	3.00	Binding Alt	3.50
Tonic Water	4.00	Binding Export	3.50
Perrier	4.50	Henninger Export	3.50
Fachingen 0.33 l	3.50	Fürstenberg Pilsener	4.50
Apollinaris 0.25 l	3.00	König Pilsener	5.00
Orangensaft	3.50	Bitburger Pils	5.00
Apfelsaft	3.50		
Kirschsaft	4.00	Portion Kaffee oder Kaffee Hag	4.50
Tomatensaft	4.00	Portion Tee oder Schokolade	4.50
Grapefruitsaft	4.00		
		Tasse Kaffee	2.50
Apfelwein 0.25 l	3.00	Glas Milch	2.50

Bier vom Fass — Draft Beer

Binding Pils	0,4 l	4.00
Beck's	0,4 l	4.50

Offene Weine — Wines

	0.25 l	0.50 l
WEISS		
Rauenthaler Steinmächer	6.00	12.00
Bernkasteler Kurfürstenlay	6.00	12.00
Casteller Kirchberg	6.50	13.00
ROT		
Ingelheimer Kaiserpfalz	6.00	12.00
Chatelroi	6.50	13.00
WEISSHERBST		
Rüdesheimer Burgweg	6.00	12.00

27b

27a–b Palette, Frankfurt-Sheraton Hotel, Francfort-sur-le Main, RFA
Carte de menu. Création: Susan Fitze, Zurich. Impression: Hauserpresse, Francfort/Main
250×360 mm, ouvert 647×360 mm, 6 pages. Carton offset. Page 1 offset 4 couleurs et couleurs spéciales ocre et orange, pages 2–6 offset 3 couleurs brun, ocre et orange. Texte en typo noir. Laminé deux faces, rainé deux fois, plis roulés
Les trois couleurs ocre, brun et orange se retrouvent sur toute la carte. L'ocre et l'orange sont également employés pour les deux cartes de petits déjeuners (ill. 75) créant ainsi un style propre à l'établissement.

27a–b Palette, Frankfurt-Sheraton Hotel, Frankfurt am Main, Bundesrepublik Deutschland
Speisekarte. Gestaltung Susan Fitze, Zürich. Druck Hauserpresse, Frankfurt am Main
250×360 mm, offen 647×360 mm, 6seitig. Offsetkarton. Seite 1 Offset 4farbig und Sonderfarben ocker und orange, Seiten 2–6 Offset 3farbig braun, ocker und orange. Texteindruck Buchdruck schwarz. Beidseitig laminiert, 2mal gerillt, Wickelfalz
Die drei Farben Ocker, Braun und Orange sind über die ganze Karte durchgezogen. Ocker und Orange werden auch bei der Frühstückskarte (Abb. 75) verwendet und bilden dadurch einen hauseigenen Stil.

27a–b Palette, Frankfurt-Sheraton Hotel, Frankfurt, West Germany
Menu-card. Designed by Susan Fitze, Zurich. Printed by Hauserpresse, Frankfurt
250×360 mm, open 647×360 mm, 6 pages. Cast-coated card. Page 1: 4-colour offset printing plus ochre and orange, pages 2–6: 3-colour offset printing in brown, ochre and orange. Text: letterpress printing in black. Laminated on two sides, twice scored, reverse accordion fold
The three colours ochre, brown and orange run throughout the whole card. Ochre and orange are also used for the 'Breakfast' card (ill. 75) and come to represent the familiar 'housecolours'.

27a

28 Maxwell's, Frankfurt-Sheraton Hotel, Francfort-sur-le Main, RFA
Carte de menu. Création: Susan Fitze, Zurich. Impression: Hauserpresse, Francfort/Main
Couverture: 280×380 mm, ouvert 560×380 mm, 4 pages. Papier à structure «peau de crocodile», vert. Page 1 impression typo vert et or. Rainé, plié
Intérieur: 270×375 mm, ouvert 540×375 mm, 4 pages. Papier structure à la cuve. Impression typo 2 couleurs vert et or. Plié et agrafé deux fois dans le pli avec la couverture.

28 Maxwell's, Frankfurt-Sheraton Hotel, Frankfurt am Main, Bundesrepublik Deutschland
Speisekarte. Gestaltung Susan Fitze, Zürich. Druck Hauserpresse, Frankfurt am Main
Umschlag: 280×380 mm, offen 560×380 mm, 4seitig. Papier mit Elefantenhautstruktur, grün. Seite 1 Buchdruck grün und gold. Gerillt, gefalzt
Innenteil: 270×375 mm, offen 540×375 mm, 4seitig. Papier mit Büttenstruktur. Buchdruck 2farbig gold und grün. Gefalzt und mit dem Umschlag zweimal drahtgeheftet
Siehe Abb. 66

28 Maxwell's, Frankfurt-Sheraton Hotel, Frankfurt, West Germany
Menu-card. Designed by Susan Fitze, Zurich. Printed by Hauserpresse, Frankfurt
Cover: 280×380 mm, open 560×380 mm, 4 pages. Paper with elephant-grain, green. Page 1: letterpress printing in green. Scored, folded
Contents: 270×375 mm, open 540×375 mm, 4 pages. Paper with texture of hand-made paper. Letterpress printing in gold and green. Folded and 2-wire stitched to the cover.
See ill. 66

BEILAGEN
VEGETABLES

Butterkarotten glaciert
Buttered glazed Carrots
5.—

Frische Champignons
in Butter gedünstet
Fresh sauteed Mushrooms
7.—

Gemüseplatte mit pochiertem Ei
Selection of fresh Garden greens with poached Egg
12.—

Je nach Jahreszeit
bieten wir Ihnen eine Auswahl
an frischen Gemüsen
Additional fresh Vegetables are being offered
in Season

Von unserem Buffet bieten wir
Ihnen
eine reichhaltige Auswahl frischer Salate
From our Buffet
we recommend a wide Variety of fresh Salads
6.50

KÄSE · CHEESE
Auswahl von in- u. ausländischem Käse
Choice of domestic and imported Cheese
8.50

Bedienungsgeld und Steuern
sind im Preis inbegriffen

All inclusive Prices

Copyright by Sheraton Management Corporation

200. 7. 79.

28

29a–b   Kockska Krogen, Savoy Hotel, Malmö, Suède
Carte de menu. Création: Blanking, Malmö. Impression: Malmö Centraltryckeri
148 × 220 mm, ouvert 585 × 220 mm, 8 pages. Carton offset couleur. Impression typo noir. Rainé trois fois, plis roulés
Carte réalisée avec les moyens les plus simples. En page 6, le personnel est présenté nominalement.

29a–b   Kockska Krogen, Savoy Hotel, Malmö, Schweden
Speisekarte. Gestaltung Blanking, Malmö. Druck Malmö Centraltryckeri
148 × 220 mm, offen 585 × 220 mm, 8seitig. Offsetkarton farbig. Buchdruck schwarz. 3mal gerillt, Wickelfalz
Mit einfachsten Mitteln realisierte Karte. Auf Seite 6 wird das gesamte Personal namentlich vorgestellt.

29a–b   Kockska Krogen, Savoy Hotel, Malmö, Sweden
Menu-card. Designed by Blanking, Malmö. Printed by Malmö Centraltryckeri
148 × 220 mm, open 585 × 220 mm, 8 pages. Coloured offset card. Letterpress printing in black. Three times scored, reverse accordion fold
Extremely simple means are used to realize this card. On page 6: all the personnel are introduced by name.

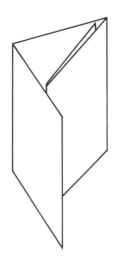

29a

29b

30a–b Savoy Hotel, Malmö, Suède
Carte de menu. Création: Blanking, Malmö. Impression: Malmö Centraltryckeri
Couverture: 230 × 320 mm, ouvert 460 × 320 mm, 4 pages. Chromo mat une face. Page 1 gaufré, illustration offset 4 couleurs sur papier couché mat, contre-collé. Rainé, plié, sur pages 2 et 3 deux angles estampés, cassés et collés permettent l'insertion des pages intérieures
Intérieur: 228 × 314 mm, ouvert 456 × 314 mm, 4 pages.
Papier offset. Offset noir et rouge. Plié
Présentation des mets bilingue français-suédois.

30a–b Savoy Hotel, Malmö, Schweden
Speisekarte. Gestaltung Blanking, Malmö. Druck Malmö Centraltryckeri
Umschlag: 230 × 320 mm, offen 460 × 320 mm, 4seitig. Matter Chromokarton einseitig. Seite 1 Blindprägung, Illustration Offset 4farbig auf mattes Kunstdruckpapier, kaschiert. Gerillt, gefalzt, auf den Seiten 2 und 3 zwei Ecken formgestanzt, eingeschlagen, angeklebt zum Einstecken des Innenteils
Innenteil: 228 × 314 mm, offen 456 × 314 mm, 4seitig.
Offsetpapier. Offset schwarz und rot. Gefalzt
Speisenangebot 2sprachig Französisch, Schwedisch

30a–b Savoy Hotel, Malmö, Sweden
Menu-card. Designed by Blanking, Malmö. Printed by Malmö Centraltryckeri
Cover: 230 × 320 mm, open 460 × 320 mm, 4 pages. One-sided cast-coated card with matt finish. Page 1: blind embossing, illustration in 4-colour offset printing on art paper with matt finish, mounted. Scored, folded; on pages 2 and 3: two die-cut corners, turned over and partly glued down to facilitate insertion of the inside pages
Contents: 228 × 314 mm, open 456 × 314 mm, 4 pages.
Offset paper. Offset printing in red and black. Folded
Menus in French and Swedish.

30b

30a

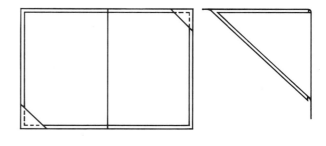

31 Bruegel, Oostkerke-Damme, Belgique
Carte de menu. Création: J. Zutternon
Couverture: 280×370 mm plus deux
rabats de 67 mm, ouvert 414×370 mm,
4 pages. Chromo une face. Impression
typo olive et orange. Rainé trois fois,
plié. Les rabats contiennent les pages
intérieures. Sur chaque rabat la place
est prévue pour écrire à la main le menu
du jour
Intérieur: 280×370 mm, ouvert
560×370 mm, 4 pages. Carton offset.
Pages 2 et 3 offset noir et rouge. Rainé,
plié

31 Bruegel, Oostkerke-Damme, Belgien
Speisekarte. Gestaltung J. Zutternon
Umschlag: 280×370 mm und 2 Klappen zu 67 mm, offen 414×370 mm,
4seitig. Chromokarton einseitig. Buchdruck olive und orange. 3mal gerillt, gefalzt. Die Klappen halten den Innenteil
und bieten Platz für das Tagesmenu,
das handschriftlich eingetragen wird
Innenteil: 280×370 mm, offen
560×370 mm, 4seitig. Offsetkarton.
Seiten 2–3 Offset schwarz und rot. Gerillt, gefalzt

31 Bruegel, Oostkerke-Damme, Belgium
Menu-card. Designed by J. Zutternon
Cover: 280×370 mm, plus 2 flaps of
67 mm, open 414×370 mm, 4 pages.
One-sided cast-coated card. Letterpress printing in olive and orange.
Three times scored, folded. The flaps
hold the contents in place and provide
space for the 'Menu of the Day' which is
written by hand.
Contents: 280×370 mm, open
560×370 mm, 4 pages. Offset card.
Pages 2–3: offset printing in black and
red. Scored, folded

RESTAVRANT

BRVEGEL

OOSTKERKE - DAMME

BELGIQUE

31

Diverse Provenienzen
PROVENANCES DIVERSES

Fürstentum Liechtenstein

			Flasche/Bouteille 7 dl
531	Grüner Veltliner	1976	26.—
532	Riesling×Sylvaner	1976	26.—
	Hausbrunn/Hofweingarten		

Deutsche Weine
VINS DU RHIN ET DE LA MOSELLE

541	Zeller Schwarze Katz, leicht süss	1974	26.—
	Peter Josef Hauth		
542	Liebfraumilch, leicht süss	1975	26.—
	Sonderabfüllung		
543	Rüdesheimer Bischofsberg, Riesling leicht süss	1975	36.—
	Originalabfüllung Schloss Groenensteyn		
544	Johannisberger Klauser Berg, Riesling Kabinett	1973	36.—
	Landgräfl. Hessisches Weingut		

BOCKSBEUTEL

545	Würzburger Stein, Silvaner	1978	39.—
	Staatliche Hofkellerei Würzburg		

32a   32b

32a–b   Kronenhalle, Zurich, Suisse
Carte des vins. Impression: Neue Zürcher Zeitung, Zurich
198×268 mm, ouvert 396×268 mm, 16 pages. Imitation cuve. Page 1 impression typo noir, rouge, jaune et or, pages 3–15 typo noir et rouge. Plié, agrafé deux fois, renforcé dans le pli
La première page de couverture est une reproduction de l'ancienne version originale.

32a–b   Kronenhalle, Zürich, Schweiz
Weinkarte. Druck Neue Zürcher Zeitung, Zürich
198×268 mm, offen 396×268 mm, 16seitig. Maschinenbütten. Buchdruck, Seite 1 schwarz, rot, gelb, gold. Seite 3–15 schwarz und rot. Gefalzt, 2mal drahtgeheftet, im Falz verstärkt
Erste Umschlagseite unter Verwendung der alten Originalfassung

32a–b   Kronenhalle, Zurich, Switzerland
Wine list. Printed by Neue Zürcher Zeitung, Zurich
198×268 mm, open 396×268 mm, 16 pages. Machine mould-made paper. Letterpress printing on page 1: in black, red, yellow, gold, on pages 3–15: in black and red. Folded, 2-wire stitched, reinforced in the fold
The first cover-page uses the old original version.

Atlantis Hotel ❧ Zürich   Döltschistube

Atlantis Hotel ❧ Zürich   Döltschistube

Kalte Teller – klein aber fein
Cold dishes
Assiettes froides

1 Délices des Grisons — Fr. 11.—
Luftgetrocknetes Bündnerfleisch und Rohschinken
Air dried swiss beef and ham

2 Hors d'œuvre sur assiette — Fr. 12.—
Reichhaltiger Hors d'œuvre-Teller
With air dried swiss beef, salami, sardines, ham and salads

3 Döltschi-Teller — Fr. 11.—
Bündnerfleisch und Hobelkäse
Air dried swiss beef and cheese
Viande des Grisons et fromage en copeaux

4 Buure-Teller — Fr. 11.—
Mit rassigem Bauernschinken, Speck, Appenzellerkäse
Cold ham with smoked bacon and cheese
Assiette paysanne, jambon, lard et fromage

5 Roastbeef mit Sauce Tartare — Fr. 12.—
Cold roastbeef with tartar sauce

6 Wurst-Käse-Salat — Fr. 6.50
Zubereitet mit bester Lyonerwurst, Käse, Zwiebeln, Gurken, Tomaten
Lyon-sausage and cheese salade, with onions, gherkins and tomatoes
Salade de saucisse avec oignons et fromage

Käse – Cheese
Choix de fromages

60 Ganze Portion 110 g — Fr. 5.—

Dessert-Portion:

1 Sorte/1 choice/1 sorte	Fr. 2.50
2 Sorten/2 choices/2 sortes	Fr. 4.—
3 Sorten/3 choices/3 sortes	Fr. 5.—

15 % Service inbegriffen / Service included
Service compris

11710

---

7 Hauspastete garniert — Fr. 9.—
Cumberlandsauce, Selleriesalat
Chef's pâté with Cumberland sauce
Pâté Maison garni

15 Birchermüesli — Fr. 4.50

mit Rahm/ — Fr. 5.—
with whipped cream/à la crème

Auf Teller angerichtet –
Warm dishes
Service sur assiette

16 St. Galler Rostbratwurst — Fr. 6.50
mit goldbrauner Butterrösti
Swiss sausage with hashed potatoes
Saucisse de St. Gall avec Rösti

19 Truthahnschnitzel «Djakarta» — Fr. 11.—
An rassiger Currysauce mit Früchten garniert
Scalloped turkey, fried in butter, served with curry sauce
Escalopes de dinde au curry

21 Omelette nature 3 Eier — Fr. 5.50
Omelette mit Schinken oder Pilzen — Fr. 7.—
Omelette with ham or mushrooms
Omelette aux champignons ou au jambon

22 Toast «Uetliberg» — Fr. 7.50
Feingeschnittenes Schweinefleisch an Champignons-Rahmsauce
Sliced pork with mushrooms in cream sauce
Emincé de porc aux champignons sur toast

Suppen und Consommé
Soups
Potages

26 Bouillon mit Mark oder mit Ei — Fr. 3.—
Beef broth with bone marrow or with an egg
Bouillon à la moelle ou à l'œuf

27 Klare Ochsenschwanzsuppe — Fr. 3.50
Clear oxtail soup/Oxtail clair

28 Schoppa da gluotta — Fr. 3.—
Bündner Gerstensuppe
Barley soup with ham and cream
Potage grisonnais

30 Tomatencrèmesuppe — Fr. 3.—
Tomato cream soup
Crème de tomates

Aus der Pfanne
From the pan
De la casserole

34 Wienerschnitzel — Fr. 16.50
Kalbfleischschnitzel paniert, Pommes frites

Fischgerichte
Fish dishes
Les poissons

50 Eglifilets mit Mandeln — Fr. 13.—
Fresh fish filets, from the lake, fried in

Atlantis Hotel ⅋ Zürich — Döltschistube

33b

33a–b Döltschistube, Atlantis Hotel, Zurich, Suisse
Carte de menu. Création: Agence de publicité Adolf Wirz, Zurich
Carte de menu: 210 × 330 mm, ouvert 388 × 330 mm, 4 pages. Chromo double face. Offset 4 couleurs plus chamois et brun. Texte typo. Laminé deux faces, rainé, plié, estampé
Présentation des mets trilingue allemand-anglais-français
Carte des desserts: 192 × 330 mm, ouvert 370 × 330 mm, 4 pages. Chromo double face. Offset 4 couleurs plus chamois et jaune. Texte typo. Laminé deux faces, rainé, plié, estampé
Ces deux cartes forment un tout mais elles peuvent aussi être présentées séparément.

33a–b Döltschistube, Atlantis Hotel, Zürich, Schweiz
Speisekarte. Gestaltung Werbeagentur Adolf Wirz, Zürich
Speisekarte: 210 × 330 mm, offen 388 × 330 mm, 4seitig. Chromokarton zweiseitig. Offset 4farbig sowie chamois und braun. Text Buchdruck. Zweiseitig laminiert, gerillt, gefalzt, formgestanzt
Speisenangebot 3sprachig Deutsch, Englisch, Französisch
Dessertkarte: 192 × 330 mm, offen 370 × 330 mm, 4seitig. Chromokarton zweiseitig. Offset 4farbig sowie chamois und gelb. Text Buchdruck. Zweiseitig laminiert, gerillt, gefalzt, formgestanzt
Speise- und Dessertkarte bilden eine Einheit, können aber auch einzeln verwendet werden.

33a–b Döltschistube, Atlantis Hotel, Zurich, Switzerland
Menu-card. Designed by Adolf Wirz advertising agency, Zurich
Menu-card: 210 × 330 mm, open 388 × 330 mm, 4 pages. Two-sided cast-coated card. 4-colour offset printing plus chamois and brown. Text: letterpress printing. Laminated on both sides, scored, folded, die-cut
Menus in German, English and French
Dessert-card: 192 × 330 mm, open 370 × 330 mm, 4 pages. Two-sided cast-coated card; 4-colour offset printing plus chamois and yellow. Text: letterpress printing. Laminated on both sides, scored, folded, die-cut
Menu and dessert card form a unity; they may, however, also be used individually.

34 Hotel Löwen, Sihlbrugg, Suisse
Carte de menu. Création: Agence de
publicité Bouchard, Zoug
Couverture: 230×355 mm, ouvert
460×355 mm, 4 pages. Chromo deux
faces. Page 1 impression typo 4 couleurs. Laminé, rainé, plié
Intérieur: 230×355 mm, ouvert
460×355 mm, 8 pages. Papier chiné à
la cuve. Typo noir. Agrafé trois fois dans
le pli avec la couverture. Cordon aux
couleurs zurichoises, bleu et blanc
Présentation des mets bilingue français-allemand. Les pages intérieures
sont ornées d'un cadre fin aux angles
biseautés. La même couverture, sans
cordon, est utilisée pour la version
«Auberge de campagne». Intérieur en
chromo au lieu du papier à la cuve.

34 Hotel Löwen, Sihlbrugg, Schweiz
Speisekarte. Gestaltung Werbeagentur
Bouchard, Zug
Umschlag: 230×355 mm, offen
460×355 mm, 4seitig. Chromokarton
zweiseitig. Seite 1 Buchdruck 4farbig.
Laminiert, gerillt, gefalzt
Innenteil: 230×355 mm, offen
460×355 mm, 8seitig. Büttenpapier
meliert. Buchdruck schwarz. Mit dem
Umschlag 3mal drahtgeheftet. Kordel
in den Zürcher Farben Blau-Weiß
Speisenangebot 2sprachig Franzö-
sisch, Deutsch. Die Innenseiten sind
durch einen feinen Linienrahmen mit
abgeschrägten Ecken begrenzt. Der
gleiche Umschlag wird für die Version
«Landgasthof» verwendet, ohne Kordel,
Innenteil auf Chromokarton statt auf
Büttenpapier.

34 Hotel Löwen, Sihlbrugg, Switzerland
Menu-card. Designed by Bouchard advertising agency, Zug
Cover: 230×355 mm, open
460×355 mm, 4 pages. Two-sided
cast-coated card. Page 1: 4-colour letterpress printing. Laminated, scored,
folded
Contents: 230×355 mm, open
460×355 mm, 8 pages. Marbled hand-
made paper. Letterpress printing in
black; 3-wire stitched to the cover.
Cord in the colours of Zurich
Menus in French and German. The inside pages are delineated with a fine
line-border with bevelled edges. The
same cover is used for the 'Country inn'
version, however, without a cord; contents on cast-coated paper instead of
hand-made paper.

HOTEL LÖWEN SIHLBRUGG

SPEISEKARTE

34

35a–c   Beef Club, Mövenpick, Berne, Suisse
Carte de menu. Création: Service de publicité Mövenpick
270 × 355 mm, ouvert 530 × 355 mm, 6 pages. Chromo double face. Offset noir et rouge. Laminé deux faces, rainé, plis roulés
Grand effet à peu de frais. A la page 5, texte sur la race de bœuf Angus, le choix et la qualité des morceaux utilisés

35a–c   Beef Club, Mövenpick, Bern, Schweiz
Speisekarte. Gestaltung Werbeabteilung Mövenpick
270 × 355 mm, offen 530 × 355 mm, 6seitig. Chromokarton zweiseitig. Offset schwarz und rot. Beidseitig laminiert, gerillt, Wickelfalz
Große Wirkung mit wenig Aufwand. Auf Seite 5 Text über Angus-Rinder, die Auswahl und die Qualität der verwendeten Stücke

35a–c   Beef Club, Mövenpick, Berne, Switzerland
Menu-card. Designed by the advertising department of Mövenpick
270 × 355 mm, open 530 × 355 mm, 6 pages. Two-sided cast-coated card. Offset printing in black and red. Laminated on two sides, scored, reverse accordion fold
Great effect at little expense. On page 5: text about Angus cattle, as well as the selection and quality of the cuts of meat.

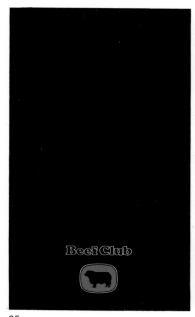

35a

35b

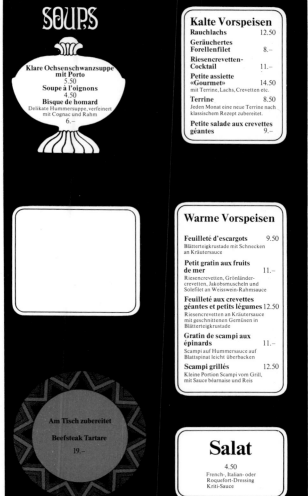

35c

51

Enjoy your Swiss meal!

Order No. 1
Barley soup from the Grisons
"Bratwurst" *(Swiss sausage)*
with onion gravy
"Rösti" *(hashbrown potatoes Swiss style)*
Tossed salad
Chocolate log cake
Price Fr. 11.90
including tip

Order No. 2
Grisons-Platter
"Geschnetzeltes" Zürich style
(cut bits of meat)
"Rösti" *(hashbrown potatoes Swiss style)*
Tossed salad
"Kirschtorte" from Zug
Price Fr. 19.50

Guten Appetit
zu einer richtigen Schweizer Mahlzeit!

Menu I
Bündner Gerstensuppe
Bratwurst mit Zwiebelsauce
Rösti
Gemischter Salat
Schoggi-Rolle
Preis Fr. 11.90
Service inbegriffen

Menu II
Bündner Teller
Zürcher Geschnetzeltes
Rösti
Gemischter Salat
Zuger Kirschtorte
Preis Fr. 19.50

We wish you an enjoyable meal
with our tasty Swiss-dishes!

Menu I
Barley soup from the Grisons
Fried sausage with onion sauce
"Rösti" *(fried potatos)*
Mixed salad
Chocolate roll
Price Fr. 11.90

Menu II
Plate of Grisons cold meats
Thinly sliced veal Zürich style
"Rösti" *(fried potatos)*
Mixed salad
"Kirschtorte" from Zug
Price Fr. 19.50

Buon appetito
mangiando veramente alla svizzera!

Lista I
Minestra d'orzo alla grigionese
Salsiccia arrostita
con salsa di cipolla
«Rösti» *(patate arrostite alla svizzera)*
Insalata mista
Rotolo di cioccolata
Prezzo fr. 11.90
Servizio compreso

Lista II
Piatto di affettato grigionese
«Geschnetzeltes» *(pezzettini di carne con salsa di zurighese)*
«Rösti» *(patate arrostite alla svizzera)*
Insalata mista
Torta di Zug al Kirsch
Prezzo fr. 19.50

Bon appétit
avec un repas suisse authentique!

Menu I
Velouté des Grisons, à l'orge
Saucisse de veau, sauce à l'oignon
Roestis
Salade panachée
Douceur au chocolat
Prix fr. 11.90
Service compris

Menu II
Assiette des Grisons
Eminçé à la zurichoise
Roestis
Salade panachée
Tarte zougoise au Kirsch
Prix fr. 19.50

Gute Mahlzeit
zu einem richtigen Schweizer Essen!

Menu I
Bratwurst mit Zwiebelsauce
«Rösti» *(Gröstel)*
Gemischter Salat
Schoggi-Rolle
Preis Fr. 11.90
Service inbegriffen

Menu II
Zürcher Geschnetzeltes
«Rösti» *(Gröstel)*
Gemischter Salat
Zuger Kirschtorte
Preis Fr. 19.50

Menu I Fr. 11.90 incl. Service

We wish you an enjoyable meal
with our tasty Swiss dishes!

Menu I
Barley soup from the Grisons
Fried sausage with onion sauce
"Rösti" *(rägti)*
Mixed salad
Chocolate roll
Price Fr. 11.90

Menu II
Plate of Grisons cold meats
Thinly sliced veal Zürich style
"Rösti" *(rägti)*
Mixed salad
"Kirschtorte" from Zug
Price Fr. 19.50
incl. service charges

Eet smakelijk
met een echt zwitsers etentje!

1e Menu
Bündner Gerstesoep
Braadworst met uiensaus
„Rösti" *(geraspte, gebakken aardappels)*
Gemengde sla
Chocolade cake
Prijs Fr. 11.90
Bediening inbegrepen

2e Menu
Bündnerschotel *(gerookt vlees)*
Zürcher „Geschnetzeltes" *(in reepjes gesneden, gebakken vlees)*
„Rösti" *(geraspte, gebakken aardappels)*
Gemengde sla
Zuger Kirsch-taart
Prijs Fr. 19.50

Bom apetite
para uma verdadeira refeição suiça!

Menu I
Sopa de cevada dos Grisões
Salsicha com molho de cebola
«Rösti» *(batata alourada)*
Salada mista
Torta de chocolate
Preço Fr. 11.90
Serviço incluido

Menu II
Prato de carnes dos Grisões
Carne cortada com molho
à maneira de Zurique
«Rösti» *(batata alourada)*
Salada mista
Bolo com kirsch de Zug
Preço Fr. 19.50

Buen provecho
con una típica comida suiza!

Minuta I
Sopa grisona de cebada
Salchicha asada con salsa de cebolla
«Rösti» *(patatas picadas y asadas)*
Ensalada mixta
Rollo de chocolate
Precio Fr.s. 11.90
Servicio comprendido

Minuta II
Plato de fiambres grisonas
«Geschnetzeltes» *(carne picada con salsa a la zuriguesa)*
«Rösti» *(patatas picadas y asadas)*
Ensalada mixta
Tarta de Zug al Kirsch
Precio fr.s. 19.50

Menu II Fr. 19.50 incl. Service

Hakiki İsviçre yemekleri için
afiyet olsun!

I. Yemek listesi
Bündner usulü mercimek çorbası
Soğan soslu beyaz kızarmış sosis
«Rösti» *(rägti)*
Karışık salata
Çukulatalı rulo
Fiatı Fr. 11.90

II. Yemek listesi
Bündner usulü soğuk et çesitleri
Zürih usulü soslu kuşbaşı
«Rösti» *(rägti)*
Karışık salata
Zug usulü kiraz pastası
Fiatı Fr. 19.50
servis.içinde

Smaklig måltid
med riktigt schweizisk mat!

Meny I
Bündner korngrymssoppa
Stekt korv med löksås
»Rösti«
Blandad sallad
Chokladrulle
Pris Fr. 11.90
Service inberäknad

Meny II
1 tallrik Bündner-kött
Småskuret kalvkött i gräddsås
»Rösti«
Blandad sallad
Zuger Kirsch-tårta
Pris Fr. 19.50

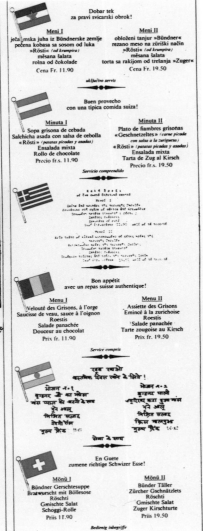

Dobar tek
za pravi svicarski obrok!

Meni I
ječa mska juha iz Bündnerske zemlje
pečena kobasa sa sosom od luka
»Rösti« *(od krumpira)*
mešana salata
rolna od čokolade
Cena Fr. 11.90
ukljuheiro servis

Meni II
obloženi tanjur »Bündner«
rezano meso na zuriški način
»Rösti« *(od krumpira)*
mešana salata
torta sa rakijom od trešanja »Zuger«
Cena Fr. 19.50

Buen provecho
con una típica comida suiza!

Minuta I
Sopa grisona de cebada
Salchicha asada con salsa de cebolla
«Rösti» *(patatas picadas y asadas)*
Ensalada mixta
Rollo de chocolate
Precio Fr.s. 11.90
Servicio comprendido

Minuta II
Plato de fiambres grisoñas
«Geschnetzeltes» *(carne picada con salsa a la zuriguesa)*
«Rösti» *(patatas picadas y asadas)*
Ensalada mixta
Tarta de Zug al Kirsch
Precio fr.s. 19.50

Bon appétit
avec un repas suisse authentique!

Menu I
Velouté des Grisons, à l'orge
Saucisse de veau, sauce à l'oignon
Roestis
Salade panachée
Douceur au chocolat
Prix fr. 11.90
Service compris

Menu II
Assiette des Grisons
Eminçé à la zurichoise
Roestis
Salade panachée
Tarte zougoise au Kirsch
Prix fr. 19.50

En Guete
zumene richtige Schwizer Esse!

Mönü I
Bünder Gerschtesuppe
Bratwurscht mit Böllesose
Röschti
Gmischte Salat
Schoggi-Rolle
Priis 11.90

Mönü II
Bünder Täller
Zürcher Gschnätzlets
Röschti
Gmischte Salat
Zuger Kirschturte
Priis 19.50

36a

36a–b Hotel St. Gotthard, Zurich, Suisse
Carte de menu. Création: CEM Management AG, Zurich
148 × 210 mm, ouvert 590 × 420 mm.
Papier offset. Offset 4 couleurs et brun.
Plis parallèles et croisés

36a–b Hotel St. Gotthard, Zürich, Schweiz
Speisekarte. Gestaltung CEM Management AG, Zürich
148 × 210 mm, offen 590 × 420 mm. Offsetpapier. Offset 4farbig und braun. Parallel- und Kreuzbruch

36a–b Hotel St. Gotthard, Zurich, Switzerland
Menu-card. Designed by CEM Management AG, Zurich
148 × 210 mm, open 590 × 420 mm. Offset paper, 4-colour offset printing plus brown. Parallel fold and right-angle fold

Cette carte, pliée comme une carte routière, présente deux mets typiques suisses en vingt langues. Au dos, neuf expressions importantes, également en vingt langues, permettent au client de se faire comprendre. La carte peut être emportée.

Die als Landkarte konzipierte Speisekarte bietet zwei typische Schweizer Gerichte in 20 Sprachen an. Auf der Rückseite dienen neun wichtige Sätze in ebenfalls 20 Sprachen dem Gast zur Verständigung. Die Karte darf mitgenommen werden.

The menu-card which was conceived as a map offers two typical Swiss dishes in 20 languages. On reverse page: nine important sentences in 20 languages aid the guest to communicate better. The card may be taken away.

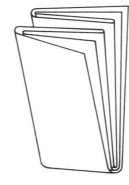

1 Menina! O senhor!
... traga-me, faça favor, o menu suiço nº 1... nº 2
2 ... e para beber um vinho tinto suiço... uma cerveja fresca suiça... uma garrafa de água
mineral
3 ... podia trazer-me mais um pouco de pão?
4 ... obrigado, foi magnifico!
5 ... faça favor de me trazer um café preto... e ainda um kirsch.

1 ¡Señorita! ¡Camarero!
... por favor, tráigame el menú suizo número uno... número dos
2 ... y un vino tinto suizo... una cerveza suiza bien fresca... un agua mineral
3 ... ¿quiere traerme un poco más de pan?
4 ... ¡gracias, estaba estupendo!
5 ... por favor, tráigame un café sin leche... y una copita de Kirsch

1 Küçük hanım! Garson!
... bana lütfen 1 numaralı listedeki Isviçre yemeklerini getirirmisiniz... 2 Numaralı
2 ... ve içmek için lütfen bir kırmızı Isviçre şarabı verebilirmisiniz... bir soğuk Isviçre
birası... bir maden suyu
3 ... lütfen bana biraz daha ekmek verebilirmisiniz?
4 ... teşekkür ederim, yemeyiniz çok güzeldi!
5 ... Lütfen bana bir mokka kahvesi... ve bir

1 Fröken! Hovmästaren!
...jag skall be att få den schweiziska menyn nr 1... nr 2
2 ... och att dricka ett rött schweiziskt vin... ett kallt schweiziskt öl... ett mineralvatten
3 ... kann jag få litet till bröd?
4 ... tack, det var utmärkt!
5 ... var snäll och ge mig en kaffe utan grädde... och kirsch

1 Gospodjice! Konobar!
... donesite mi molim švicarski meni br. 1... br. 2
2 ... a za piće crveno švicarsko vino... svježe švicarsko pivo... mineralnu vodu
3 ... mogu li dobiti još malo hleba?
4 ... hvala, to je bilo izvrsno!
5 ... molim donesite mi crnu kavu... sa rakijom od trešanja (»Kirš«)

1 ¡Señorita! ¡Camarero!
... por favor, tráigame el menú suizo número uno... número dos
2 ... y un vino tinto suizo... una cerveza suiza bien fresca... un agua mineral
3 ... ¿quiere traerme un poco más de pan?
4 ... ¡gracias, estaba estupendo!
5 ... por favor, tráigame un café sin leche... y una copita de Kirsch

1 S'il vous plaît! Garçon!
... j'aimerais le menu suisse no 1... no 2
2 ... et comme boisson un vin rouge suisse... une bière suisse fraîche... eau au minérale
3 ... pourrais-je avoir un peu de pain?
4 ... merci, c'était excellent!
5 ... apportez-moi un café noir et un kirsch s.v.p.

1 Fröulein! Herr Ober!
... bringed s mer bitte s Mönü Nr. 1... Nr. 2
2 ... und zum Trinke en rote Schwizer Wy... en wiisse Wy... ä frisches Schwizer Bier... äs Mineralwasser
3 ... chani no chli Brot ha?
4 ... danke, sisch fein gsi
5 ... bitte, bringed s mer no en schwarze Kafi und en Kirsch dezue

36b

37a–c   Seiler Hotels, Zermatt, Suisse
Carte de menu. Création: M. Knezy, Zurich
178×343 mm, ouvert 530×343 mm, 6 pages. Carton
offset. Offset 4 couleurs. Rainé deux fois, plis roulés
Présentation des mets quadrilingue allemand-fran-
çais-anglais-japonais. Les illustrations et les signes
du zodiaque de la première page indiquent que cette
carte est employée durant la saison d'hiver.

37a–c   Seiler Hotels, Zermatt, Schweiz
Speisekarte. Gestaltung M. Knezy, Zürich
178×343 mm, offen 530×343 mm, 6seitig. Offsetkar-
ton. Offset 4farbig. 2mal gerillt, Wickelfalz
Speisenangebot 4sprachig Deutsch, Französisch,
Englisch, Japanisch. Die Illustrationen und die Tier-
kreiszeichen auf der ersten Seite zeigen, daß diese
Karte während der Wintersaison aufgelegt wird.

37a–c   Seiler Hotels, Zermatt, Switzerland
Menu-card. Designed by M. Knezy, Zurich
178×343 mm, open 530×343 mm, 6 pages. Offset
card. 4-colour offset printing. Twice scored, reverse
accordion fold
Menus in German, French, English and Japanese. The
illustrations and the signs of the zodiac on the first
page show that this card is used during the winter
season.

37a

37b

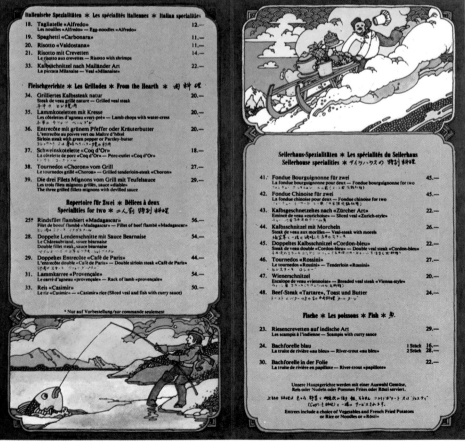

37c

38 Legazpi, Las Hadas, Manzanillo, Mexique
Carte de menu. Création: Elite SA, Mexico. Impression: Lito Offset Andina SA, Mexico
253 × 330 mm, ouvert 506 × 330 mm, 8 pages. Imitation parchemin chiné. Page 1 impression typo or, pages 2–7 bleu foncé et or, logo en bleu clair
Carte conçue simplement, sans illustration, avec présentation des mets claire en caractères bien ordonnés, en espagnol sur la page de gauche, en anglais sur la page de droite.

39 El Terral, Las Hadas, Manzanillo, Mexique
Carte de menu. Création: Elite SA, Mexico. Impression: Lito Offset Andina SA, Mexico
243 × 330 mm, ouvert 486 × 330 mm, 8 pages. Papier à la cuve. Page 1 offset or, pages 2–7 noir et bleu. Plié, agrafé deux fois dans le pli
Conçue comme la carte précédente (ill. 38), également bilingue, en espagnol à gauche, en anglais à droite.

38 Legazpi, Las Hadas, Manzanillo, Mexiko
Speisekarte. Gestaltung Elite SA, Mexiko. Druck Lito Offset Andina SA, Mexiko
253 × 330 mm, offen 506 × 330 mm, 8seitig. Pergamentimitation meliert. Buchdruck, Seite 1 gold, Seiten 2–7 dunkelblau und gold, Signet hellblau Einfache Karte, ohne Bildelemente, mit klarem Speisenangebot in Schriftlösung. Speisenangebot auf der linken Seite Spanisch, auf der rechten Seite Englisch

39 El Terral, Las Hadas, Manzanillo, Mexiko
Speisekarte. Gestaltung Elite SA, Mexiko. Druck Lito Offset Andina SA, Mexiko
243 × 330 mm, offen 486 × 330 mm, 8seitig. Büttenpapier. Offset, Seite 1 gold, Seiten 2–7 schwarz und blau. Gefalzt, 2mal drahtgeheftet
Der Karte Abb. 38 angepaßte Gestaltung, ebenfalls Speisenangebot 2sprachig, linke Seite Spanisch, rechte Seite Englisch

38 Legazpi, Las Hadas, Manzanillo, Mexico
Menu-card. Designed by Elite SA, Mexico. Printed by Lito Offset Andina SA, Mexico
253 × 330 mm, open 506 × 330 mm, 8 pages. Marbled paper with vellum imitation. Letterpress printing on page 1: in gold, on pages 2–7: in dark blue and gold, colophon in pale blue
Simple card without pictorial elements, clear compilation of menus resolved through use of lettering. Menus in Spanish on the left, in English on the right.

39 El Terral, Las Hadas, Manzanillo, Mexico
Menu-card. Designed by Elite SA, Mexico. Printed by Lito Offset Andina SA, Mexico
243 × 330 mm, open 486 × 330 mm, 8 pages. Hand-made paper. Offset printing on page 1: in gold, on pages 2–7: in black and blue; 2-wire stitched
Design adapted to that of card in ill. 38 with the menus also in Spanish on the left, in English on the right.

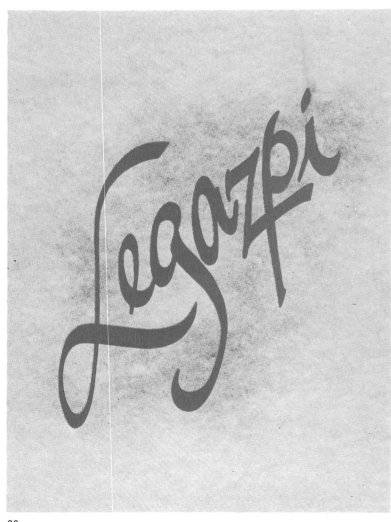

38

39

THE PARKER HOUSE, 1898

EATS & DRINKS

40a

EAT AND DRINK TO THE LAST HURRAH!

APPETIZERS

These tempting treats from land and sea will whet your tastes while we prepare a memorable feast. Ask whomever is waiting on you to select a plate just for you.

Bay Oysters on their Shell	Marinated Baby Shrimp
Little Neck Clams	Melon with Prosciutto
3.25	3.95

SOUPS

Great kettles are made every day and come to you fresh by the cup or the bowlful.

SOUP OF THE DAY
Cup .95   Bowl 1.50

Sun.	Chicken Noodle	Wed.	Ministrone
Mon.	Lentil	Thurs.	Split Pea
Tues.	Beef Barley	Fri.	Broccoli
	Sat.	Bisque	

STEWS & CHOWDERS

They're a meal by another name, our blend of fruits from the sea, the garden or the range, so rich they offer their juices for broth.

ALWAYS AVAILABLE

Stew of the Day Cup 1.25 Bowl 2.50	Hearty Chili Cup 1.25 Bowl 2.50

New England Clam Chowder
Cup .95   Bowl 1.50

The magnificent Miss Lillian Russell. Compliments of Bettmann Archive.

ENTREES

All Entrees include choice of Potato or Fresh Vegetable, Choice of Sauce and our Famous Parker House Rolls.

BEEF

	8 oz.	12 oz.
BEEF BROCHETTE Served on a bed of Rice.	7.25	8.95
NEW YORK SIRLOIN With the Sauce of your Choice.	7.95	10.95
LONDON BROIL Tender Beef sliced as you like it.	6.75	8.25
PRIME RIB OF BEEF Aged Beef, slowly cooked and carved to order.	7.75	10.25

BREAST OF CHICKEN 6.75
Gently Sauteed, Choice of Sauce.

FISH

	6 oz.	9 oz.
SCALLOPS Delectable morsels from the sea.	6.95	8.50
BOSTON SCHROD Parker House favorite.	6.50	7.95
SOLE MEUNIERE Native, fresh, and gently sauteed.	6.95	8.25
BROILED SWORDFISH One of our finest local delights.	8.25	9.50

VEAL CORDON BLEU 8.75
Tender Veal stuffed with imported Ham and Cheese.

THE FINISHING TOUCH

• Sauce Bearnaise • Sauce Choron • Herb Butter • Peppersauce • Mustard Sauce • Au Jus

The great John L. Sullivan. Compliments of Bettmann Archive.

SANDWICHES

KING OF CLUBS	4.50
BACON AND CHEDDAR BURGER	4.25
REUBEN GRILL	3.95
GASTRONOMICALDELICATESSEN-EPICUREAN'S DELIGHT A mound of Roast Beef, Ham, Turkey, Cheese, slices of Tomato, Onion and Egg. Served with Russian Dressing on Light Rye.	4.75
HAM AND BOURSIN Imported Boursin Cheese spread on Light Rye, heaped with shaved Ham, Broccoli and shredded Cheddar.	4.75

SALAD FOR YOUR MAKING

A mountain of greenery awaits you in the center of the room. There are vegetables, too, and trimmings like croutons, cheese and more. Not to mention dressings to dress up your own green scheme. It's up to you, so up you go. You have to make it yourself. So make a Salad to remember and we'll give it your very own name.

With your Entree .95   As a Feast 4.25
with Parker House Rolls

SIDE ORDERS

Onion Rings	French Fries
Potato Salad	Baked Potato
Cole Slaw	Vegetable of the Day

1.25

All Prices Subject to State Tax.

DESSERTS

Assorted Parker House Cakes and Tortes	1.75
Boston Cream Pie 1.75 Assorted Ice Creams	1.25
Apple Pie 1.25 A la Mode	2.00

BEVERAGES

A Pot of Fresh Roasted Coffee	.75
Decaffeinated Coffee, Imported Tea, Milk	.75
Our Famous Irish Coffee	2.25
Or Choose from our other International Coffees	

PH-GP52660-12/79-250

40b

40a–b   The Last Hurrah!, Parker House, Boston, USA
Carte de menu. Création et impression: Grigg Printing Co., Littleton, Massachusetts
210 × 383 mm, ouvert 420 × 383 mm, 4 pages. Papier structuré toile. Offset rouge et noir. Plié
La division en cases rend cette carte facile à consulter.

40a–b   The Last Hurrah!, Parker House, Boston, USA
Speisekarte. Gestaltung und Druck Grigg Printing Co., Littleton, Massachusetts
210 × 383 mm, offen 420 × 383 mm, 4seitig. Papier mit Leinenstruktur. Offset rot und schwarz. Gefalzt
Verschiedene Linienelemente unterteilen die Karte und machen sie gut übersichtlich.

40a–b   The Last Hurrah!, Parker House, Boston, USA
Menu-card. Designed and printed by Grigg Printing Co., Littleton, Massachusetts
210 × 383 mm, open 420 × 383 mm, 4 pages. Paper with linen finish. Offset printing in red and black. Folded
Various linear elements subdivide the card and render it easy to take in at a glance.

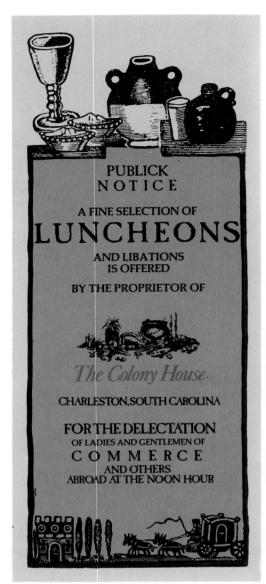

41a

41a–b   The Colony House, Charleston, Caroline du Sud, USA
Carte de menu. Création: Design Unlimited/Culinary Concepts, Hempstead, New York
140 × 324 mm, ouvert 420 × 324 mm, 6 pages. Papier

coloré structuré à la cuve. Offset brun et noir. Plis roulés
Le restaurant se situe dans un ancien dépôt datant du début du XIXe siècle et les éléments décoratifs de la carte rappellent le style de l'époque.

41a–b   The Colony House, Charleston, South Carolina, USA
Speisekarte. Gestaltung Design Unlimited/Culinary Concepts, Hempstead, New York
140 × 324 mm, offen 420 × 324 mm, 6seitig. Papier mit

Büttenstruktur, bunt. Offset braun und schwarz. Wickelfalz
Das Restaurant befindet sich in einem alten Lagerhaus aus den Anfängen des 19. Jahrhunderts. Die Gestaltung übernimmt Stilelemente aus jener Zeit.

41a–b   The Colony House, Charleston, South Carolina, USA
Menu-card. Designed by Design Unlimited/Culinary Concepts, Hempstead, New York
140 × 324 mm, open 420 × 324 mm, 6 pages. Coloured

paper with texture of hand-made paper. Offset printing in brown and black. Reverse accordion fold
The restaurant is housed in an old warehouse dating from the early 19th century. The design adopts stylistic elements of that period.

41b

42a–e   The Left Bank, Treadway Inn, Wilkes-Barre, Pennsylvanie, USA
Carte de menu. Création: Design Unlimited/Culinary Concepts, Hempstead, New York
Couverture: 280 × 280 mm, ouvert 560 × 280 mm, 4 pages. Carton structuré. Page 1 gaufrage à chaud, pages 2 et 3 offset ocre et brun. Estampé, percé deux fois
Intérieur: 280 × 280 mm, 8 pages. Papier couleur structuré. Offset noir, brun et rouge. Estampé, percé deux fois et relié à la couverture par un fil or élastique. Les formes estampées laissent apparaître une partie de la page suivante ou précédente. Les éléments ainsi visibles s'intègrent dans le graphisme de chaque page.

42a–e   The Left Bank, Treadway Inn, Wilkes-Barre, Pennsylvania, USA
Speisekarte. Gestaltung Design Unlimited/Culinary Concepts, Hempstead, New York
Umschlag: 280 × 280 mm, offen 560 × 280 mm, 4seitig. Strukturkarton. Seite 1 Farbfolienprägung weiß, Seiten 2–3 Offset ocker und braun. Gestanzt, 2mal gelocht
Innenteil: 280 × 280 mm, 8seitig. Strukturpapiere bunt. Offset schwarz, braun und rot. Gestanzt, 2mal gelocht und durch elastischen Goldfaden mit dem Umschlag verbunden
Die ausgestanzten Formen ergeben Durchblicke auf die folgenden und vorhergehenden Seiten. Die so sichtbaren Elemente werden in die Gestaltung der jeweiligen Seite einbezogen.

42a–e   The Left Bank, Treadway Inn, Wilkes-Barre, Pennsylvania, USA ▷
Menu-card. Designed by Design Unlimited/Culinary Concepts, Hempstead, New York
Cover: 280 × 280 mm, open 560 × 280 mm, 4 pages. Grained card. Page 1: coloured foil embossing in white, pages 2 and 3: offset printing in ochre and brown. Die-cut, twice punched
Contents: 280 × 280 mm, 8 pages. Coloured paper with grained texture. Offset printing in black, brown and red. Die-cut, twice punched and attached to the cover with an elastic gold-thread
The punched-out shapes provide glimpses of the following and preceding pages. The visible elements are thus incorporated into the design of each page.

42a

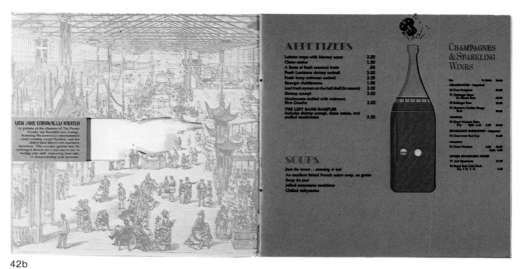

42b

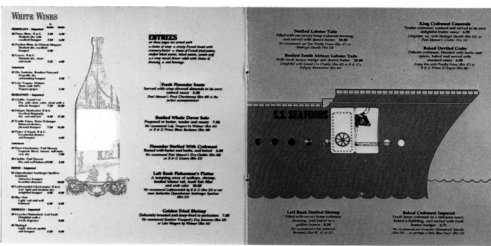

42c

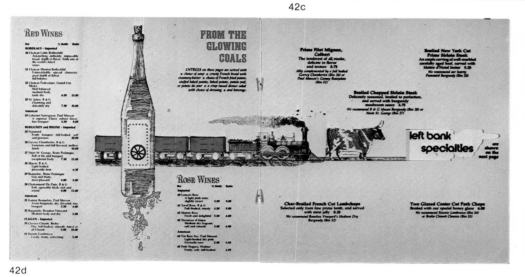

42d

42e

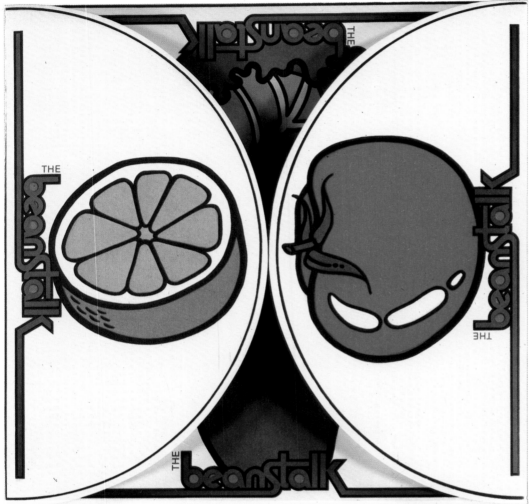

43a

43b

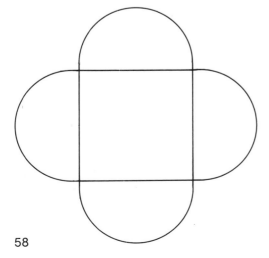

43a–b   The Beanstalk, Rockefeller Center, New York, N.Y., USA
Carte de menu. Création: Design Unlimited/Culinary Concepts, Hempstead, New York
265×265 mm, ouvert 535×535 mm, 2 pages. Chromo double face. Offset 4 couleurs. Laminé deux faces, estampé, rainé, plié. 4 découpes estampées en demi-cercle
Détail des constituants de chaque met. Les quatre entailles permettent l'insertion d'une petite carte «spécialités du jour». Forme originale, conception moderne.

43a–b   The Beanstalk, Rockefeller Center, New York, N.Y., USA
Speisekarte. Gestaltung Design Unlimited/Culinary Concepts, Hempstead, New York
265×265 mm, offen 535×535 mm, 2seitig. Chromokarton zweiseitig. Offset 4farbig. Beidseitig laminiert, formgestanzt, gerillt, gefalzt. 4 halbrunde gestanzte Schlitze
Ausführliche Aufzählung der Zutaten zu jedem Gericht. Die vier Stanzschlitze erlauben das Einschieben eines Kärtchens mit den Tagesspezialitäten. Originelle Form für eine modern gestaltete Karte

43a–b   The Beanstalk, Rockefeller Center, New York, N.Y., USA
Menu-card. Designed by Design Unlimited/Culinary Concepts, Hempstead, New York
265×265 mm, open 535×535 mm, 2 pages. Two-sided cast-coated card. 4-colour offset printing. Laminated on two sides, die-cut, scored, folded. Four semi-circular die-cut slots
Detailed compilation of ingredients to each dish. The 4 die-cut slots permit the insertion of a small menu-card for 'Specialities of the Day'. Inventive form for a card of modern design.

44   Greentrees, Ambridge, Pennsylvanie, USA
Carte de menu. Création: Design Unlimited/Culinary
Concepts, Hempstead, New York
218 × 355 mm, ouvert 436 × 355 mm, 4 pages. Chromo
double face. Offset beige, deux verts et mauve. Laminé
deux faces, plié
De la page 2 à la page 4, les titres sont en vert clair, les
menus en vert foncé ornés de cadres beiges et vert
clair. La carte elle-même est verte, en accord avec le
nom de l'établissement.

44   Greentrees, Ambridge, Pennsylvania, USA
Speisekarte. Gestaltung Design Unlimited/Culinary
Concepts, Hempstead, New York
218 × 355 mm, offen 436 × 355 mm, 4seitig. Chromo-
karton zweiseitig. Offset beige, 2 grün, mauve. Beid-
seitig laminiert, gefalzt
Auf den Seiten 2–4 sind die Titel hellgrün, die Speisen
selbst dunkelgrün, dazu beige und hellgrüne Rahmen.
Die Karte ist dem Titel des Lokals entsprechend in
Grün gehalten.

44   Greentrees, Ambridge, Pennsylvania, USA
Menu-card. Designed by Design Unlimited/Culinary
Concepts, Hempstead, New York
218 × 355 mm, open 436 × 355 mm, 4 pages. Two-
sided cast-coated card. Offset printing in beige, two
greens, mauve. Laminated on two sides, folded
On pages 2 to 4 the headings are in pale green, the
menu text is in dark green, the borders are in beige and
pale green. Living up to the name of the restaurant, the
card is kept in green.

44

45a–b Humphrey's, Half Moon Inn, San Diego, Californie, USA
Carte de menu. Création: Kaufman & Lansky, San Diego
215 × 215 mm, ouvert 430 × 215 mm, 8 pages. Chromo double face. Offset noir et vert. Page 1 dorure à la feuille. Laqué, plié, agrafé deux fois
L'ornementation linéaire varie d'un titre à l'autre et crée l'unité avec la couverture.

45a–b Humphrey's, Half Moon Inn, San Diego, California, USA
Speisekarte. Gestaltung Kaufman & Lansky, San Diego
215 × 215 mm, offen 430 × 215 mm, 8seitig. Chromokarton zweiseitig. Offset schwarz und grün. Seite 1 Goldfolienprägung. Lackiert, gefalzt, 2mal drahtgeheftet
Die Linienornamente variieren von einem Titel zum andern und bringen eine Verbindung zum Umschlag.

45a–b Humphrey's, Half Moon Inn, San Diego, California, USA
Menu-card. Designed by Kaufman & Lansky, San Diego
215 × 215 mm, open 430 × 215 mm, 8 pages. Two-sided cast-coated card. Offset printing in black and green. Page 1: gold embossing. Varnished, folded, 2-wire stitched
The linear ornamentation varies from one title to another and creates the link to the cover.

45a

45b

46

46 Samantha's, Mariott Hotels, Orlando, Floride, USA
Carte de menu. Création: Peggy Dunnagan, Rollins Press, Orlando, Floride
Couverture: 270 × 248 mm, ouvert 270 × 496 mm, 4 pages. Papier structure toile, recto blanc, verso rose. Offset une face, brun, rouge et noir. Plié, estampé
Intérieur: 270 × 248 mm, ouvert 270 × 496 mm, 8 pages. Papier teinté structuré toile. Offset brun et rouge. Plié, estampé et encarté dans la couverture
Dans les pages intérieures les cadres sont en harmonie avec les éléments décoratifs de la couverture. Texte explicatif sur les mets.

46 Samantha's, Mariott Hotels, Orlando, Florida, USA
Speisekarte. Gestaltung Peggy Dunnagan, Rollins Press, Orlando, Florida
Umschlag: 270 × 248 mm, offen 270 × 496 mm, 4seitig. Papier mit Leinenprägung, einseitig weiß, Rückseite rosa. Offset einseitig, braun, rot und schwarz. Gefalzt, formgestanzt
Innenteil: 270 × 248 mm, offen 270 × 496 mm, 8seitig. Papier mit Leinenstruktur, getönt. Offset braun und rot. Gefalzt, formgestanzt und in den Umschlag eingesteckt
Im Innenteil Rahmen in Anlehnung an Dekorationselemente des Umschlags. Erklärende Texte zu den Gerichten

46 Samantha's, Mariott Hotels, Orlando, Florida, USA
Menu-card. Designed by Peggy Dunnagan, Rollins Press, Orlando, Florida
Cover: 270 × 248 mm, open 270 × 496 mm, 4 pages. Paper with linen-grain finish: white on one side, pink on the reverse. One-sided offset printing in brown, red and black. Folded, die-cut
Contents: 270 × 248 mm, open 270 × 496 mm, 8 pages. Paper with linen texture, tinted. Offset printing in brown and red. Folded, die-cut and inserted into the cover
On the inside pages, the borders take up the decorative elements of the cover. Explanatory text to the various dishes.

47a-b   Golden Cape, Hawaï, USA
Carte de menu. Création: Design Unlimited/Culinary
Concepts, Hempstead, New York
Couverture: 240×406 mm, ouvert 480×406 mm, 4
pages. Plastique structuré. Page 1 dorure à la feuille.
Percé deux fois
Intérieur: 220×387 mm, ouvert 365×387 mm, 8
pages. Imitation parchemin. Offset bordeaux et brun.
Plis asymétriques, à la manière d'un répertoire. Agrafé
deux fois, percé deux fois et relié à la couverture par un
fil or élastique
Un texte réparti sur trois pages intérieures est con-
sacré aux chefs de tribu hawaïens et à leurs capes de
plumes: cet artisanat aurait relevé d'une tradition déjà
très ancienne lorsque le capitaine Cook aborda l'île
pour la première fois.

47a-b   Golden Cape, Hawaii, USA
Speisekarte. Gestaltung Design Unlimited/Culinary
Concepts, Hempstead, New York
Umschlag: 240×406 mm, offen 480×406 mm, 4sei-
tig. Kunststoff, strukturiert. Seite 1 Goldfolienprägung.
2mal gelocht
Innenteil: 220×387 mm, offen 365×387 mm, 8seitig.
Pergamentimitation. Offset weinrot und braun. Unsym-
metrisch gefalzt, so daß Griffregister entsteht. 2mal
drahtgeheftet, 2mal gelocht und durch elastischen
Goldfaden mit dem Umschlag verbunden
Ein über drei Innenseiten laufender Text ist den hawai-
ischen Häuptlingen und ihren Federmänteln gewid-
met, deren Herstellung schon uralte Handwerkskunst
war, als Captain Cook erstmals Fuß auf die Insel setzte.

47a-b   Golden Cape, Hawaii, USA
Menu-card. Designed by Design Unlimited/Culinary
Concepts, Hempstead, New York
Cover: 240×406 mm, open 480×406 mm, 4 pages.
Textured plastic. Page 1: gold embossing. Twice
punched
Contents: 220×387 mm, open 365×387 mm, 8
pages. Vellum imitation. Offset printing in wine-red and
brown. Asymmetrically folded, thus creating a thumb
index. 2-wire stitched, twice punched and attached to
the cover with an elastic gold-thread
The running text, which continues across three inside
pages, is dedicated to the Hawaiian chieftains and
their feather cloaks, the making of which was already
an ancient craft by the time Captain Cook set foot on
the island for the first time.

47a

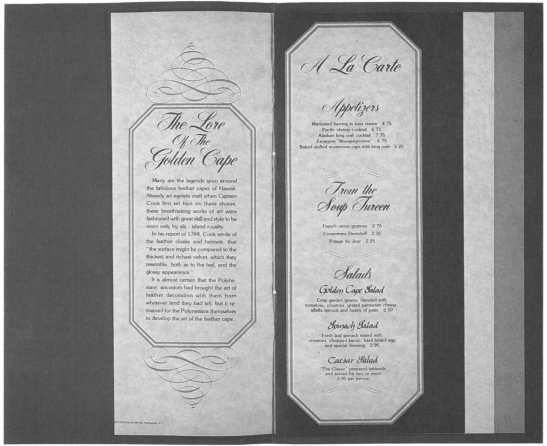

47b

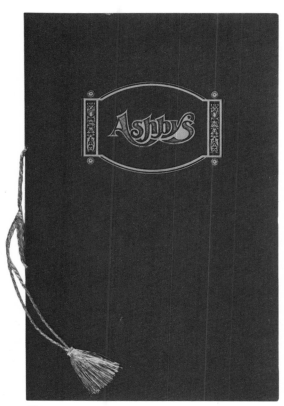

48a

48a–b   Ashby's, Hilton, Washington D.C., USA
Carte de menu. Création: Design Unlimited/Culinary
Concepts, Hempstead, New York
Couverture: 265×420 mm, ouvert 530×420 mm, 4
pages. Plastique structuré. Page 1 dorure à la feuille,
plaque de métal estampée et enchâssée, percé deux
fois
Intérieur: 245×403 mm, ouvert 490×806 mm, 8
pages. Pergamin à la cuve. Impression typo vert et or.
Pli anglais, percé deux fois et relié à la couverture par
un cordon or

48a–b   Ashby's, Hilton, Washington, D.C., USA
Speisekarte. Gestaltung Design Unlimited/Culinary
Concepts, Hempstead, New York
Umschlag: 265×420 mm, offen 530×420 mm, 4sei-
tig. Kunststoff, strukturiert. Seite 1 Goldfolienprägung,
Schriftzug als eingelassene geprägte Metallplatte,
2mal gelocht
Innenteil: 245×403 mm, offen 490×806 mm, 8seitig.
Pergamentbütten. Buchdruck grün, gold. Englischer
Falz, 2mal gelocht und durch Goldkordel mit dem Um-
schlag verbunden

48a–b   Ashby's, Hilton, Washington D.C., USA
Menu-card. Designed by Design Unlimited/Culinary
Concepts, Hempstead, New York
Cover: 265×420 mm, open 530×420 mm, 4 pages.
Textured plastic. Page 1: gold embossing, lettering
embedded as embossed metal plaque, twice punched
Contents: 245×403 mm, open 490×806 mm, 8
pages. Hand-made paper. Letterpress printing in
green and gold. English fold, twice punched and at-
tached to the cover with a gold cord

Ashby's

For many years the name "Ashby's" symbolized a tradition of warm hospitality exemplified by hearty fare, fine spirits, and an always ready welcome. In creating Ashby's at the Washington Hilton, we have let ourselves be guided by these traditions as we strive to create even higher standards of service and hospitality.

Appetizers

Fresh Melon
Flavored with port wine **2.25**   With prosciutto ham **3.25**

A Cocktail of Shrimp
On crushed ice, with cocktail sauce and lemon **4.25**

Fresh Clams or Oysters
On the half shell, bedded in ice, with the appropriate condiments **3.95**

Imported Smoked Scottish Salmon
Without question the very finest **4.75**

Lump Crabmeat Cocktail
With a specially flavored cocktail sauce **4.75**

Chopped Chicken Livers
Garnished with the traditional egg and onion **2.50**

Quiche Windsor
Prepared with mushrooms and herbs, plus a touch of tomato **2.50**

Snails Ashby
Braised in herbed brandy butter, and served without the shells **3.95**

Baked Bay Scallops
Served in a shell, with a light garlic butter sauce **3.50**

Marinated Fresh Mushrooms
With artichoke hearts, steeped in the chef's special marinade **2.75**

The Soups

Cream of Stilton
Imported Stilton cheese adds its distinctive flavor **1.50**

Classic French Onion Soup
Baked in an earthenware crock, crusted with three kinds of cheeses **1.75**

Today's Soup
The Chef invites your inquiry **1.50**

Chilled Spinach Soup Victoria
Flavored with a hint of curry and coconut **1.50**

48b

49a

49b

49a–b   Miller Brothers, The Baltimore Hilton Hotel, Baltimore, Maryland, USA
Carte de menu. Création: Design Unlimited/Culinary Concepts, Hempstead, New York
Couverture: 265 × 428 mm, ouvert 530 × 428 mm, 4 pages. Imitation cuir sur carton ³/₁₀. Page 1 dorure à la feuille et coquillage estampé et enchâssé
Intérieur: 240 × 407 mm, ouvert 480 × 814 mm, 8 pages. Papier couleur structuré à la cuve. Offset ocre et brun. Pli anglais
L'avantage du pli anglais: impression d'un seul côté pour une carte de 4 pages. Un papier plus léger peut également être utilisé sans que le texte transparaisse. A l'intérieur, reprise de la coquille Saint-Jacques de la page 1 comme élément décoratif. L'intérieur est simplement glissé dans la couverture.

49a–b   Miller Brothers, The Baltimore Hilton Hotel, Baltimore, Maryland, USA
Speisekarte. Gestaltung Design Unlimited/Culinary Concepts, Hempstead, New York
Umschlag: 265 × 428 mm, offen 530 × 428 mm, 4seitig. Kunstledereinband auf ³/₁₀-Karton. Seite 1 Goldfolienprägung und geprägte Muschel eingelassen
Innenteil: 240 × 407 mm, offen 480 × 814 mm, 8seitig. Papier mit Büttenstruktur, farbig. Offset ocker und braun. Englischer Falz
Der Vorteil beim englischen Falz ist der nur einseitige Druck; dadurch entsteht eine 4seitige Karte. Es kann ein leichteres Papier verwendet werden, ohne daß der Text durchscheint. Im Innenteil Verwendung der Jakobsmuschel aus dem Schriftzug der Seite 1 als dekoratives Element. Der Innenteil ist lose in den Umschlag eingelegt.

49a–b   Miller Brothers, The Baltimore Hilton Hotel, Baltimore, Maryland, USA
Menu-card. Designed by Design Unlimited/Culinary Concepts, Hempstead, New York
Cover: 265 × 428 mm, open 530 × 428 mm, 4 pages. Simulated leather mounted on to card ³/₁₀. Page 1: gold embossing and embossed, shell-shaped metal plaque embedded
Contents: 240 × 407 mm, open 480 × 814 mm, 8 pages. Coloured paper with the texture of hand-made paper. Offset printing in ochre and brown. English 8-page fold
The advantage with the English 8-page fold is the printing process on one side only, providing a 4-sided card. A lighter paper may be used with the text shining through. On the inside pages: use of the scallop-shaped shell, taken from the lettering as decorative element.

50a–c   Top of the M, The Mandarin, Singapour
Carte de menu. Création: Overseas Union Advertising
Couverture: 260×380 mm, ouvert 520×380 mm, 4
pages. Reliure velours. Page 1 piqué, ouatiné sur bois
aggloméré 5/10, plaque métallique gravée et enchâssée
Intérieur: 243×374 mm, ouvert 486×374 mm, 12
pages. Papiers à la cuve. Pages 1 et 2 vergé Ingres
bordeaux contre-collé sur papier à la cuve blanc,
estampage à la feuille d'argent. Autres pages offset
noir. Plié, agrafé trois fois dans le pli et assemblé à la
couverture par un cordon rouge
Présentation des mets bilingue français-anglais. La
qualité du papier et de la typographie contrastent avec
la reliure et le cordon de nylon.

50a–c   Top of the M, The Mandarin, Singapur
Speisekarte. Gestaltung Overseas Union Advertising
Umschlag: 260×380 mm, offen 520×380 mm, 4sei-
tig. Samteinband. Seite 1 gesteppt, wattiert auf 5/10-
Holzpappe, mit eingelassener gravierter Metallplatte
Innenteil: 243×374 mm, offen 486×374 mm, 12seitig.
Büttenpapier. Seiten 1–2 weinrot Vergé Ingres auf das
weiße Bütten kaschiert, Silberfolienprägung, übrige
Seiten Offset schwarz. Gefalzt, 3mal drahtgeheftet und
durch rote Kordel mit dem Umschlag verbunden
Speisenangebot 2sprachig Französisch, Englisch. Die
Qualität des Papiers und der Typographie kontrastiert
mit dem Einband und der Nylonkordel.

50a–c   Top of the M, The Mandarin, Singapore
Menu-card. Designed by Overseas Union Advertising
Cover: 260×380 mm, open 520×380 mm, 4 pages.
Velvet cover. Page 1: quilted, lined with wadding on to
5/10 mm board made of wood pulp with engraved metal
plaque embedded
Contents: 243×374 mm, open 486×374 mm, 12
pages. Hand-made paper. Pages 1 and 2: wine-red laid
Ingres paper mounted on to the white hand-made
paper, silver embossing, remaining pages in black
offset printing. Folded, 3-wire stitched and attached to
the cover with a red cord
Menus in French and English. The quality of the paper
and typography contrasts with the cover and nylon
cord.

50a

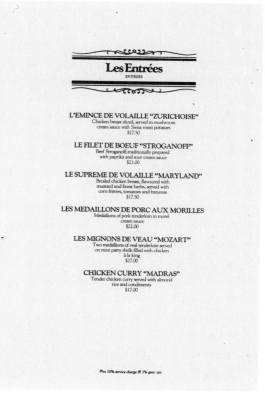

50b

Les Poissons Et Crustaces
FISH AND SHELLFISH

LE SUPREME D'IKAN KURAU "RIVIERA"
Panfried ikan kurau with Parisian
potatoes, artichokes and tomatoes
$18.00

LA BROCHETTE DE FRUITS DE MER
"ARMORICAINE"
Seafood skewer with sauce Americaine
$24.00

LES FILETS DE SOLE "MARGUERY"
Poached fillets of Dover sole and
seafood served with white wine sauce
$26.00

LES COQUILLES ST. JACQUES AU SAFRAN
Deep sea scallops simmered with saffron
in brandy and white wine
$17.50

LES CREVETTES GEANTES A L'ANETH
King prawns with dill
$21.00

Plus 10% service charge & 3% govt. tax

Les Entrées
ENTREES

L'EMINCE DE VOLAILLE "ZURICHOISE"
Chicken breast sliced, served in mushroom
cream sauce with Swiss roesti potatoes
$17.50

LE FILET DE BOEUF "STROGANOFF"
Beef Stroganoff, traditionally prepared
with paprika and sour cream sauce
$21.00

LE SUPREME DE VOLAILLE "MARYLAND"
Broiled chicken breast, flavoured with
mustard and finest herbs, served with
corn fritters, tomatoes and bananas
$17.50

LES MEDAILLONS DE PORC AUX MORILLES
Medallions of pork tenderloin in morel
cream sauce
$22.00

LES MIGNONS DE VEAU "MOZART"
Two medallions of veal tenderloin served
on mini patty shells filled with chicken
à la king
$27.00

CHICKEN CURRY "MADRAS"
Tender chicken curry served with almond
rice and condiments
$17.00

Plus 10% service charge & 3% govt. tax

50c

51a–b   Volcano House, Sheraton Hotels in the Pacific, Honolulu, Hawaï, USA
Carte de menu. Création Dietrich Varez
Couverture: 260×350 mm, ouvert 520×350 mm, 4
pages. Plastique noir. Page 1 estampage de feuille de
métal rouge, coins arrondis
Intérieur: 240×330 mm, ouvert 480×330 mm, 4
pages. Papier structuré toile. Pages 2 et 3 offset noir et
rouge. Percé deux fois, assemblé à la couverture par
un cordon noir
Présentation des mets en anglais avec explication des
divers plats. Le fort cordon noir fait partie intégrante du
graphisme de l'intérieur.

51a–b   Volcano House, Sheraton Hotels in the Pa-
cific, Honolulu, Hawaii, USA
Speisekarte. Gestaltung Dietrich Varez
Umschlag: 260×350 mm, offen 520×350 mm, 4sei-
tig. Schwarzer Kunststoff. Seite 1 rote Metallfolienprä-
gung, abgerundete Ecken
Innenteil: 240×330 mm, offen 480×330 mm, 4seitig.
Papier mit Leinenstruktur. Seiten 2–3 Offset schwarz
und rot. 2mal gelocht, durch schwarze Kordel mit dem
Umschlag verbunden
Speisenangebot Englisch mit Erklärungen zu den ein-
zelnen Gerichten. Die kräftige schwarze Kordel wird im
Innenteil in die typographische Gestaltung einbezo-
gen.

51a–b   Volcano House, Sheraton Hotels in the Pacific, Honolulu, Hawaii, USA
Menu-card. Designed by Dietrich Varez
Cover: 260×350 mm, open 520×350 mm, 4 pages.
Black plastic. Page 1: red metal embossing, rounded
corners
Contents: 240×330 mm, open 480×330 mm, 4
pages. Paper with linen-grain finish. Pages 2 and 3:
offset printing in black and red. Twice punched, attached to the cover with a black cord
Menus in English with explanation to each dish. The
strong black cord is incorporated into the typographic
design of the inside pages.

51a

51b

52a

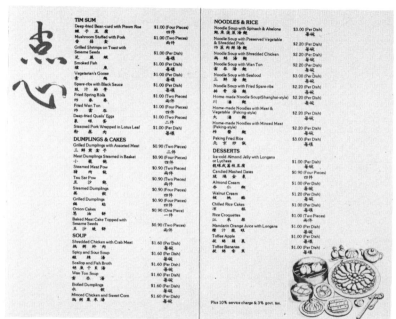

TIM SUM

Deep-fried Bean-curd with Prawn Roe	$1.00 (Four Pieces)
Mushroom Stuffed with Pork	$1.00 (Two Pieces)
Grilled Shrimps on Toast with Sesame Seeds	$1.00 (Per Dish)
Smoked Fish	$1.00 (Per Dish)
Vegetarian's Goose	$1.00 (Per Dish)
Spare-ribs with Black Sauce	$1.00 (Per Dish)
Fried Spring Rolls	$1.00 (Two Pieces)
Fried Wan Ton	$1.00 (Four Pieces)
Deep-fried Quails' Eggs	$1.00 (Two Pieces)
Steamed Pork Wrapped in Lotus Leaf	$1.00 (Per Dish)

DUMPLINGS & CAKES

Grilled Dumplings with Assorted Meat	$0.90 (Two Pieces)
Meat Dumplings Steamed in Basket	$0.90 (Four Pieces)
Steamed Meat Pow	$0.90 (Two Pieces)
Tau Sar Pow	$0.90 (Two Pieces)
Steamed Dumplings	$0.90 (Four Pieces)
Grilled Dumplings	$0.90 (Four Pieces)
Onion Cakes	$0.90 (One Piece)
Baked Meat Cake Topped with Sesame Seeds	$0.90 (Two Pieces)

SOUP

Shredded Chicken with Crab Meat	$1.60 (Per Dish)
Spicy and Sour Soup	$1.60 (Per Dish)
Scallop and Fish Broth	$1.60 (Per Dish)
Wan Ton Soup	$1.60 (Per Dish)
Boiled Dumplings	$1.60 (Per Dish)
Minced Chicken and Sweet Corn	$1.60 (Per Dish)

NOODLES & RICE

Noodle Soup with Spinach & Abalone	$3.00 (Per Dish)
Noodle Soup with Preserved Vegetable & Shredded Pork	$2.20 (Per Dish)
Noodle Soup with Shredded Chicken	$2.20 (Per Dish)
Noodle Soup with Wan Ton	$2.20 (Per Dish)
Noodle Soup with Seafood	$3.00 (Per Dish)
Noodle Soup with Fried Spare-ribs	$2.20 (Per Dish)
Home-made Noodle Soup(Shanghai-style)	$2.20 (Per Dish)
Home-made Noodles with Meat & Vegetable (Peking-style)	$2.20 (Per Dish)
Home-made Noodles with Minced Meat (Peking-style)	$2.20 (Per Dish)
Peking Fried Rice	$3.00 (Per Dish)

DESSERTS

Ice-cold Almond Jelly with Longans or Lychees	$1.00 (Per Dish)
Candied Mashed Dates	$0.90 (Four Pieces)
Almond Cream	$1.00 (Per Dish)
Walnut Cream	$1.20 (Per Dish)
Chilled Rice Cakes	$1.00 (Per Dish)
Rice Croquettes	$1.00 (Two Pieces)
Mandarin Orange Juice with Longans	$1.00 (Per Dish)
Toffee Apple	$1.00 (Per Dish)
Toffee Bananas	$1.00 (Per Dish)

Plus 10% service charge & 3% govt. tax.

52b

52a–b Pine Court, The Mandarin, Singapour
Carte de menu. Création: Overseas Union Advertising
Couverture: 134 × 224 mm, ouvert 268 × 224 mm, 4 pages. Chromo double face. Pages 1 et 4 sérigraphie or. Rainé, plié

Intérieur: 134 × 224 mm, ouvert 268 × 224 mm, 4 pages. Papier vergé à la cuve. Pages 2 et 3 offset noir. Plié, collé à la couverture
Présentation des mets bilingue anglais-chinois. Reproduction de calligraphie chinoise sur les pages intérieures.

52a–b Pine Court, The Mandarin, Singapur
Speisekarte. Gestaltung Overseas Union Advertising
Umschlag: 134 × 224 mm, offen 268 × 224 mm, 4seitig. Chromokarton zweiseitig rot. Seiten 1 und 4 Siebdruck gold. Gerillt, gefalzt

Innenteil: 134 × 224 mm, offen 268 × 224 mm, 4seitig. Büttenpapier vergé. Seiten 2–3 Offset schwarz. Gefalzt, im Rücken mit dem Umschlag zusammengeklebt
Speisenangebot 2sprachig Englisch, Chinesisch. Übernahme der chinesischen Kalligraphie auf die Innenseiten.

52a–b Pine Court, The Mandarin, Singapore
Menu-card. Designed by Overseas Union Advertising
Cover: 134 × 224 mm, open 268 × 224 mm, 4 pages. Two-sided cast-coated red card. Page 1 and 4: screen printing in gold. Scored, folded

Contents: 134 × 224 mm, open 268 × 224 mm, 4 pages. Laid hand-made paper. Pages 2–3: offset printing in black. Folded, the spine glued to the cover
Menus in English and Chinese. Adoption of Chinese calligraphy on the inside pages.

53a

53b

53a–b   The Mandarin, Hong Kong
Carte de menu. Création: P. Hawkes, Leo Burnett Ltd.
Couverture: 2 plats à 253×355 mm, reliés par des
gardes structurées contre-collées. Plein papier laminé
grain, couché 4 couleurs monté sur carton gris ¹²/₁₀
Intérieur: 252×350 mm, ouvert 504×350 mm, 8
pages. Papier couleur structuré à la cuve. Offset rouge
et brun foncé. Rainé, plié, agrafé deux fois dans le pli et
assemblé à la couverture par un cordon rouge

53a–b   The Mandarin, Hongkong
Speisekarte. Gestaltung P. Hawkes, Leo Burnett Ltd.
Umschlag: 2 Deckel à 253 × 355 mm mit gegengekleb-
tem, über beide Deckel laufendem strukturiertem Vorsatz zu einem 4seitigen Deckel verbunden. Pappband
mit 4farbigem Kunstdruck, prägelaminiert auf
¹²/₁₀-Graukarton aufgezogen
Innenteil: 252 × 350 mm, offen 504 × 350 mm, 8seitig.
Papier mit Büttenstruktur farbig. Offset rot und dunkelbraun. Gerillt, gefalzt, 2mal drahtgeheftet und durch
rote Kordel mit dem Umschlag verbunden

53a–b   The Mandarin, Hong Kong
Menu-card. Designed by P. Hawkes, Leo Burnett Ltd.
Cover: 2 separate covers of 253×355 mm combined
to a 4-page cover through use of textured end-paper
glued to and projecting over the two covers. Stiff paper
binding with grain-laminated finish, art paper mounted
on to ¹²/₁₀ grey card.
Contents: 252×350 mm, open 504×350 mm, 8
pages. Coloured paper with texture of hand-made
paper. Offset printing in red and dark brown. Scored,
folded, 2-wire stitched and attached to the cover with a
red cord

54 Yamazato, Hotel Okura, Tokyo, Japon
Carte de menu
Couverture: 208×294 mm, ouvert 416×294 mm, 4 pages. Chromo une face. Pages 1 et 4 (face mate) offset beige, olive et noir. Rainé, plié
Intérieur: 195×277 mm, ouvert 390×277 mm, 4 pages. Papier vergé à la cuve, pages 2 et 3 typo noir. Plié, assemblé à la couverture par un ruban jaune
Ce ruban, par sa largeur et sa couleur, est en harmonie avec la couverture. On remarque également le soin mis à la réalisation d'un nœud plat. Présentation des mets bilingue japonais-anglais.

54 Yamazato, Hotel Okura, Tokio, Japan
Speisekarte
Umschlag: 208×294 mm, offen 416×294 mm, 4seitig. Chromokarton einseitig. Seiten 1 und 4 (matte Seite) Offset beige, olive, schwarz. Gerillt, gefalzt
Innenteil: 195×277 mm, offen 390×277 mm, 4seitig. Büttenpapier vergé, Seiten 2–3 Buchdruck schwarz, Gefalzt, durch gelbes Band mit dem Umschlag verbunden
Das gelbe Band ist in Breite und Farbe schön auf den Umschlag abgestimmt. Der Knoten ist besonders sorgfältig und flach geknüpft. Speisenangebot 2sprachig Japanisch, Englisch

54 Yamazato, Hotel Okura, Tokyo, Japan
Menu-card
Cover: 208×294 mm, open 416×294 mm, 4 pages. One-sided cast-coated card. Pages 1 and 4 (matt side): offset printing in beige, olive, black. Scored, folded
Contents: 195×277 mm, open 390×277 mm, 4 pages. Laid handmade paper. Pages 2–3: letterpress printing in black. Folded, attached to the cover with a yellow ribbon
The yellow ribbon is effectively matched in width and colour to the cover. The knot is tied flat and with particular care. Menus in Japanese and English.

54

Cartes de grill-rooms et rôtisseries

Speisekarten für Grill-Room und Rôtisserie

Grill-room and rôtisserie menus

Entre la rôtisserie de riche tradition et le grill-room moderne et soigné, la distinction n'est pas aisée à faire si l'on s'en tient au style de la seule raison sociale. L'établissement lui-même, les spécialités offertes et la clientèle spécifique sont des facteurs permettant mieux de déterminer l'aspect d'une carte «dans le ton».

Die Karten dieses Kapitels stammen von zwei Arten von Lokalen, der Rôtisserie mit ihrer reichen Tradition und dem Grill-Room in seiner gepflegten neuzeitlichen Eleganz. Die Bezeichnungen sind etwas fließend, so daß sich der genaue Charakter des Lokals nicht ohne weiteres aus dem Namen ableiten läßt. Stil des Lokals, Angebot und Zielpublikum prägen das Aussehen der Karte entscheidend mit. Es ist besonders wichtig, den «richtigen Ton» des Lokals zu treffen.

The menus in this chapter come from two types of establishment: the rôtisserie with its noble tradition and the grill-room with its modern elegance and charm. These categories are a bit vague, so one cannot always be sure from the name which type of establishment is meant. Its style, clientèle and choice of dishes all determine the menu's appearance. It is especially important to convey the right ambience in each case.

55a–b Rôtisserie Rivoli, Hôtel Inter-Continental, Paris
Carte de menu. Création: Hotel Inter-Continental, New York
250 × 366 mm, ouvert 500 × 366 mm, 4 pages. Imitation parchemin. Impression typo brun et olive. Plié
La décoration de la première et de la dernière page est faite d'anciens motifs d'encadrement, partiellement agrandis et montés en miroir inversé (gauche-droite) pour l'intérieur.

55a–b Rôtisserie Rivoli, Hôtel Inter-Continental, Paris, Frankreich
Speisekarte. Gestaltung Hotel Inter-Continental, New York
250 × 366 mm, offen 500 × 366 mm, 4seitig. Pergamentimitation. Buchdruck braun und olive. Gefalzt
Gestaltung der ersten und letzten Seite unter Verwendung eines alten Rahmens, der teilweise vergrößert und spiegelverkehrt zusammenmontiert auf den Innenseiten wieder verwendet wird.

55a–b Rôtisserie Rivoli Hôtel Inter-Continental, Paris, France
Menu-card. Designed by the Hotel Inter-Continental, New York
250 × 366 mm, open 500 × 366 mm, 4 pages. Vellum imitation. Letterpress printing in brown and olive. Folded
Design of the first and last page using an old border which is repeated on the inside pages, partly enlarged and in mirror image.

ROTISSERIE
RIVOLI

LES HORS D'ŒUVRES

Le Saumon Fumé 45   Le Caviar Beluga 75
Le Jambon de Parme 28   Le Cocktail de Crevettes 28
La Terrine de Saumon et Brochet 30
L'Anguille Fumée 30
L'Avocat Castiglione 28

LES HORS D'ŒUVRES CHAUDS

La Croûte aux Morilles 18   Tartelette aux Œufs de Caille 20
Bouchée d'Escargots Vigneronne 32   Mousseline de Brochet Nantua 24

LES POTAGES

La Gratinée Lyonnaise 14   La Chaudrée des Pêcheurs 20
La Julienne au Pistou 14

LES POISSONS

Le Suprême de Turbot Oursinade 50
Le Loup Grillé Flambé au Fenouil 68
La Coquille St Jacques au Safran 65
Le Blanc de St Pierre au Poivre Rose 45
Fricassée de Sole et Écrevisses 70
La Sole Meunière aux Courgettes 45   La Truite au Bleu 36

LES SALADES

Salade César 18   Salade de Saison 10   Salade Malabar 10

LES LÉGUMES

La Bouquetière de Légumes 14
Les Épinards en Branche Elizabeth 12
La Purée du Jour 12   Les Endives au Jambon Gratinées 12
Les Haricots Verts Frais aux Herbes 12

LES ENTRÉES

Le Ris de Veau aux Crevettes Joinville 70
La Poularde Sautée au Vinaigre de Xérès 42
Le Canard aux Pêches Sauce Cassis (2 pers.) 90
Le Rognon de Veau Beaugé 70
Le Pintadeau Rôti Sauce Smitane 45
Le Tournedos Sauté à la Jambe de Bois 55
Le Filet au Poivre Flambé 55
Le Steak Diane à Votre Table 70

LES PLATS DU JOUR

LES GRILLADES

Carré d'Agneau au Feu de Bois Aubergines au Gratin (2 pers.) 110
La Côte de Bœuf Grillée Bordelaise (2 pers.) 130
L'Entrecôte Double Béarnaise (2 pers.) 120
La Tranche de Gigot d'Agneau à la Provençale 48
Le Cœur de Filet de Bœuf Vert Pré 55
Le Châteaubriand Sauce Choron (2 pers.) 130

LES FROMAGES

Le Plateau du Terroir 14

LES DESSERTS

Le Chariot de Pâtisseries 14
La Charlotte Amadita 18
Soufflé Glacé Framboise 18   Parfait Joséphine 14
Salade de Fruits au Kirsch 16
La Tarte des Demoiselles Tatin 14
La Tarte aux Pommes Chaudes 14
Les Glaces et Sorbets 12   Les Crêpes Suzette (2 pers.) 36
Le Café Irlandais 16   Le Café Jamaïcain 16
Expresso 4   Thé 4   Infusions 4
SERVICE 15 % NON COMPRIS

55b

55a–b   Rôtisserie Rivoli, Hôtel Inter-Continental, Paris
Carte de menu. Création: Hotel Inter-Continental, New York
250 × 366 mm, ouvert 500 × 366 mm, 4 pages. Imitation parchemin. Impression typo brun et olive. Plié
La décoration de la première et de la dernière page est faite d'anciens motifs d'encadrement, partiellement agrandis et montés en miroir inversé (gauche-droite) pour l'intérieur.

55a–b   Rôtisserie Rivoli, Hôtel Inter-Continental, Paris, Frankreich
Speisekarte. Gestaltung Hotel Inter-Continental, New York
250 × 366 mm, offen 500 × 366 mm, 4seitig. Pergamentimitation. Buchdruck braun und olive. Gefalzt
Gestaltung der ersten und letzten Seite unter Verwendung eines alten Rahmens, der teilweise vergrößert und spiegelverkehrt zusammenmontiert auf den Innenseiten wieder verwendet wird

55a–b   Rôtisserie Rivoli Hôtel Inter-Continental, Paris, France
Menu-card. Designed by the Hotel Inter-Continental, New York
250 × 366 mm, open 500 × 366 mm, 4 pages. Vellum imitation. Letterpress printing in brown and olive. Folded
Design of the first and last page using an old border which is repeated on the inside pages partly enlarged and in mirror image.

56   Grill des Ambassadeurs, Hôtel Métropole, Monte-Carlo
Carte de menu. Impression: Imprimerie de Monte-Carlo, Monte-Carlo
210 × 318 mm, ouvert 420 × 318 mm, 4 pages. Chromo une face couleur. Impression typo bordeaux. Rainé, plié
Page 3: quatre fentes estampées pour

l'insertion de petites cartes dactylographiées «Spécialités du jour», 74 × 30 mm
Carte simple, conception claire et répétition du sigle de l'établissement de page 1 sur les pages intérieures.

56   Grill des Ambassadeurs, Hôtel Métropole, Monte-Carlo
Speisekarte. Druck Imprimerie de Monte-Carlo, Monte-Carlo
210 × 318 mm, offen 420 × 318 mm, 4seitig. Chromokarton einseitig farbig. Buchdruck weinrot. Gerillt, gefalzt

Seite 3 vier gestanzte Schlitze zum Einstecken eines kleinen Tagesspezialitäten-Zettels in Schreibmaschine, 74 × 30 mm
Einfache Karte, übersichtlich gestaltet unter Verwendung des Hauszeichens von Seite 1 auf den Innenseiten

56   Grill des Ambassadeurs, Hôtel Métropole, Monte-Carlo
Menu-card. Printed by Imprimerie de Monte-Carlo, Monte-Carlo
210 × 318 mm, open 420 × 318 mm, 4 pages. One-sided cast-coated coloured card. Letterpress printing in wine-red. Scored, folded

Page 3: 4 die-cut slots to insert small typewritten menu for 'Specialities of the Day', 74 × 30 mm
Simple card, clearly designed, using on the inside pages the house logo from page 1.

GRILL
DES
AMBASSADEURS

HOTEL METROPOLE
MONTE-CARLO

57 Carlton Grill, Hôtel Carlton, Cannes, France
Carte de menu. Création et impression: Imprimerie de Noailles, P. Raybaud, Cannes, en collaboration avec la direction de l'hôtel
243×335 mm, 2 pages. Chromo double face. Typo 4 couleurs. Laqué
La décoration linéaire de la couverture, répétée au dos, suggère une tapisserie. Les menus, imprimés en petits caractères en médaillons sur fond jaune encadrés de blanc, ressortent clairement.

57 Carlton Grill, Hôtel Carlton, Cannes, Frankreich
Speisekarte. Gestaltung und Druck Imprimerie de Noailles, P. Raybaud, Cannes, in Zusammenarbeit mit der Hoteldirektion
243×335 mm, 2seitig. Chromokarton zweiseitig. Buchdruck 4farbig. Lackiert
Die Liniendekoration der Vorderseite erinnert an eine Tapete und wird auf der Rückseite wiederholt. Das Speisenangebot in kleinen Druckbuchstaben ist auf gelbem Hintergrund mit abgerundeten Ecken und weißem Rahmen und hebt sich klar ab.

57 Carlton Grill, Hôtel Carlton, Cannes, France
Menu-card. Designed and printed by Imprimerie de Noailles, P. Raybaud, Cannes, in collaboration with the management of the hotel
243×335 mm, 2 pages. Two-sided cast-coated card; 4-colour letterpress printing. Varnished
The linear decoration of the front page, reminiscent of wallpaper, is repeated on the back page. The menus, printed in small print on yellow background with curved corners and white border, stand out well.

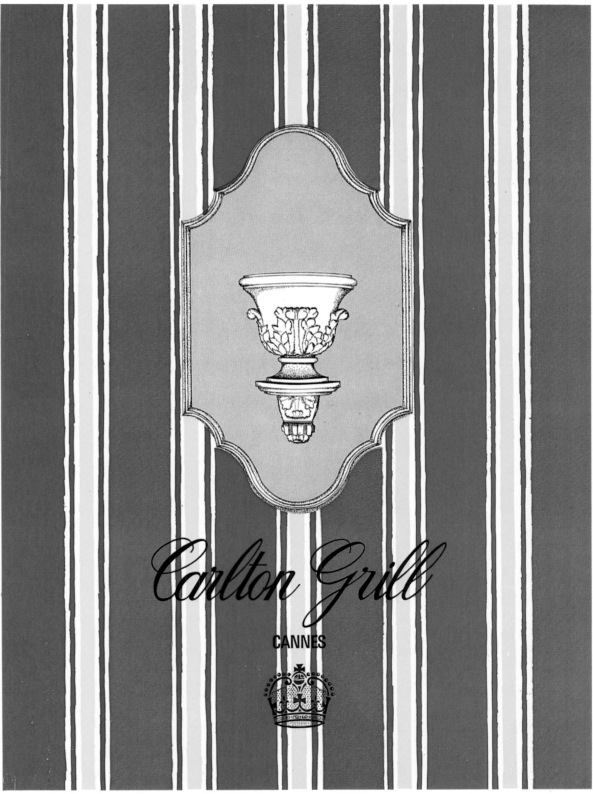

57

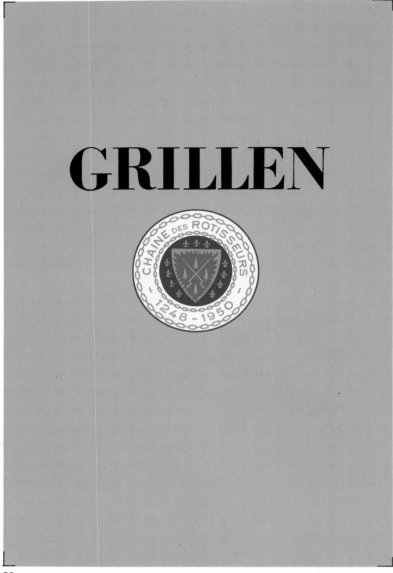

58a

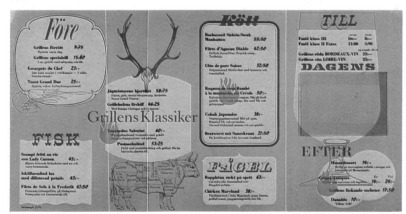

58b

58a–b Grillen, Hotel Savoy, Malmö, Suède
Carte de menu. Impression: m.c.t., Malmö
152 × 230 mm, ouvert 435 × 230 mm, 6 pages. Papier offset. Offset noir, brun et rouge. Rainé deux fois, plis roulés. En page 1, auto-collant de la Chaîne des Rôtisseurs en bleu, rouge et dorure à la feuille. En page 4, étui plastique pour l'insertion des cartes des spécialités du jour
L'œil est attiré sur les différents groupes de plats par des pavés de formes diverses. En page 5, bref texte sur la Chaîne des Rôtisseurs.

58a–b Grillen, Hotel Savoy, Malmö, Schweden
Speisekarte. Druck m.c.t., Malmö
152 × 230 mm, offen 435 × 230 mm, 6seitig. Offsetpapier farbig. Offset schwarz, braun und rot. 2mal gerillt, Wickelfalz. Seite 1 Kleber der Chaîne des Rôtisseurs blau, rot und Goldfolienprägung. Seite 4 Kunststofftasche zum Einschieben der Tagesspezialitäten-Kärtchen
Die Speisen sind durch optische Blickfänge in verschiedene Gruppen zusammengefaßt, wobei jede Gruppe eine andere Form hat. Auf Seite 5 kurzer Text über die Chaîne des Rôtisseurs

58a–b Grillen, Hotel Savoy, Malmö, Sweden
Menu-card. Printed by m.c.t., Malmö
152 × 230 mm, open 435 × 230 mm, 6 pages. Coloured offset paper. Offset printing in black, brown and red. Twice scored, reverse accordion fold. Page 1: stamp of the 'Chaîne des Rôtisseurs' in blue, red and with gold embossing. Page 4: plastic pocket to insert small menu-cards for 'Specialities of the Day'
Using visual focal points, the various dishes are grouped into different categories, whereby each group takes on a different form. On page 5: a short text on the 'Chaîne des Rôtisseurs'.

59a–c Rôtisserie, Atlantis Hotel, Zurich, Suisse
Carte de menu et carte des desserts. Création: Agence de publicité Adolf Wirz, Zurich
Carte de menu: 210 × 330 mm, ouvert 390 × 330 mm, 4 pages. Chromo double face. Offset 4 couleurs, plus chamois et bleu foncé, texte en typo. Laminé deux faces, rainé, plié, estampé
Carte des desserts: 192 × 330 mm, ouvert 370 × 330 mm, 4 pages. Chromo double face. Offset 4 couleurs, plus chamois et vert. Texte en typo. Laminé deux faces, rainé, plié, estampé et inséré dans la carte de menu
Les deux cartes forment un tout, mais peuvent également être présentées séparément, de par leur conception graphique.

59a–c Rôtisserie, Atlantis Hotel, Zürich, Schweiz
Speisekarte und Dessertkarte. Gestaltung Adolf Wirz, Werbeagentur, Zürich
Speisekarte: 210 × 330 mm, offen 390 × 330 mm, 4seitig. Chromokarton zweiseitig. Offset 4farbig sowie chamois und dunkelblau. Text Buchdruck. Zweiseitig laminiert, gerillt, gefalzt, formgestanzt
Dessertkarte: 192 × 330 mm, offen 370 × 330 mm, 4seitig. Chromokarton zweiseitig. Offset 4farbig sowie chamois und grün. Text Buchdruck. Zweiseitig laminiert, gerillt, gefalzt, formgestanzt und in die Speisekarte eingesteckt
Speise- und Dessertkarte bilden eine Einheit, können aber auch einzeln verwendet werden, die jeweilige Gestaltung der ersten Seiten ist entsprechend konzipiert.

59a–c Rôtisserie, Atlantis Hotel, Zurich, Switzerland
Menu-card and dessert card. Designed by Adolf Wirz advertising agency, Zurich
Menu-card: 210 × 330 mm, open 390 × 330 mm, 4 pages. Two-sided cast-coated card; 4-colour offset printing plus chamois and dark blue. Text in letterpress printing. Laminated on both sides, scored, folded, die-cut
Dessert card: 192 × 330 mm, open 370 × 330 mm, 4 pages. Two-sided cast-coated card; 4-colour offset printing plus chamois and green. Text in letterpress printing. Laminated on both sides, scored, folded, die-cut and inserted into the menu-card
Together menu-card and dessert card form a unity. The cards may, however, also be used independently, and the design of each first page is conceived accordingly.

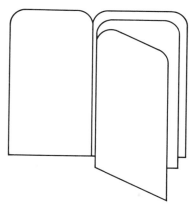

59a

59b

Hors d'œuvre froids

PATE RICHE MAISON A LA GELEE — Fr. 12.—
Hauspastete nach dem Rezept unseres Chefs
Chef's pâté with sauce cumberland

MEDAILLONS DE FOIE GRAS DE STRASBOURG — Fr. 25.—
Echte Strassburger Gänseleber mit Trüffel
Goose-liver from Strasbourg with truffle

SAUMON FUME D'ECOSSE TOAST ET BEURRE — Fr. 23.—
Frischer, schottischer Räucherlachs
Smoked salmon with toast and butter

Nos petites entrées

SAUMON FUME FRAIS TOAST ET BEURRE — Fr. 15.—

TRUITE FUMEE, SAUCE RAIFORT — Fr. 10.—

COCKTAIL DE CREVETTES ROSES — Fr. 12.50

DELICES DES GRISONS — Fr. 12.50
Luftgetrocknete Bündner Spezialitäten
Air-dried speciality from Grisons

ROASTBEEF AVEC SAUCE TARTARE — Fr. 16.50
Zartes Roastbeef mit Tartarsauce
Tender roastbeef with sauce tartar

Consommés et Potages

CONSOMME A LA MOELLE OU A L'ŒUF — Fr. 4.50
Kraftbrühe mit Mark oder Eigelb
Beef broth with an egg or bone marrow

OXTAIL CLAIR — Fr. 5.—
Ochsenschwanzsuppe

CREME DE TOMATES CHANTILLY — Fr. 4.50
Tomatencrèmesuppe mit Sahne
Tomato soup with wipped cream

Poissons

TRUITE DU VIVIER AU BLEU — Fr. 15.—
Frische Forelle «blau»
Fresh, poached river trout

TRUITE «BELLE MEUNIERE» — Fr. 15.—
Forelle nach Müllerinnenart
In butter fried trout with mushrooms

FILETS DE PERCHES AUX AMANDES — Fr. 15.—
Egglifilets mit Mandelsplittern
Perch filets from the Lake with almonds

SAUMON GRILLE OU POCHE SAUCE BEARNAISE OU HOLLANDAISE — Fr. 24.—
Grilliertes oder pochiertes Salmsteak
Fresh salmon, grilled or poached

SOLE D'OSTENDE GRILLEE — Fr. 24.—
Grillierte Seezunge
Grilled sole

Garnitures: pommes nature ou riz créole
Beilage: Salzkartoffeln oder Trockenreis

15% Service inbegriffen / Service compris / Service included 765

Grillades et Entrées

EMINCE DE VEAU ZURICHOISE — Fr. 22.—
Fein geschnetzeltes Kalbfleisch an einer zarten Rahmsauce mit Champignons und Butterrösti
Sliced veal with cream sauce and mushrooms

FOIE DE VEAU A L'ANGLAISE — Fr. 19.—
Kalbsleberschnitte mit Speck
Veal liver with grilled bacon

STEAK DE VEAU AUX MORILLES A LA CREME — Fr. 25.—
Kalbssteak an Morchelrahmsauce
Veal steak in morilcreamsauce

ENTRECOTE «CAFE DE PARIS» — Fr. 25.—
Sirloin steak with «café de Paris butter»

FILETS GULYAS «STROGANOFF» — Fr. 24.50

T-BONE STEAK 350 g — Fr. 30.—

COTE ET CHOPS D'AGNEAU SUR LE GRIL — Fr. 18.50
Grilled lamb chops

Délices à deux

CHATEAUBRIAND, SAUCE BEARNAISE 2 Personen — Fr. 58.—
Double filet steak with sauce béarnaise

Tous ces plats sont garnis avec tomate grillée et pommes au choix ou riz créole

Garnitures

VARIATION DE LEGUMES — Fr. 6.50
Gemüseplatte
Choice of vegetables

RÖSTI — Fr. 3.—
Hash browned potatoes

Salade de la voiture

C'est à vous de choisir
Wählen Sie von unserem Salatwagen
Salad of your choice

et les sauces

A L'ITALIENNE / *Italian*

A LA FRANCAISE / *French*

AU ROQUEFORT / *Roquefort*

Les fromages

«Prenez toujours un fromage pour terminer votre repas»
Ein Stückchen Käse – die Vollendung der Tafelfreuden
A piece of cheese complets your feast

15% Service inbegriffen Diese Karte liegt auf von 14.00–18.00 Uhr, 22.00–24.00 Uhr

Glaces

Vanille, Fraises, Citrons, Chocolats, Noix de Coco, Mocca — 3.—
Crème Chantilly — + –.70
Meringue glacée — 4.50
Meringue mit Vanilleglace und Schlagrahm
Café glacé — 4.50
Sorbet aux citrons — 4.50
Sorbet Vodka — 5.50
Sorbet champagne — 5.50

Frappés

Vanille, Fraises, Chocolat, Noix de Coco, Mocca — 3.—

Coupes

Coupe Danemark — 5.—
Vanilleglace mit warmer Schokoladensauce
Coupe Jacques — 5.—
Glace mit Fruchtsalat und Schlagrahm
Pêche Melba — 5.—
Vanilleglace mit Pfirsich, Himbeersauce und Mandelsplittern
Coupe «Atlantis» — 5.50
Kokosnussglace, Ananas und Kirsch
Banana Split — 5.50

Spécialités

Vacherin glacé Suchard — 4.50
Meringues, Schokoladenglace und Schlagrahm
Cassata napolitaine — 4.50
Tourte glacée «Atlantis» — 5.—
Soufflé glacé Grand Marnier — 5.—
Parfait glacé au noix — 5.—
Praliné parfait mit Nougat und Nüssen

Tourtes et Gâteaux

Tourte au Kirsch de Zoug — 3.—
Zuger Kirschtorte
Tourte aux noix — 3.—
Engadiner Nusstorte
Tourte forêt noir — 3.—
Schwarzwäldertorte
Tarte aux pommes à la mode — 3.—
Apfelkuchen mit Vanilleglace
Gugelhopf — 2.30
nach Grossmutters Rezept
Quarkkuchen — 3.—

Desserts

Macédoine de fruits — 4.50
Macédoine de fruits au Maraschino ou Kirsch — 5.50
Crème renversée au caramel — 3.—
Meringue Chantilly — 4.50
(der Klassiker unter den Meringues)
Sabayon au Marsala — 5.50
Crêpes Suzette (für 2 Personen) — 17.—
Pêches flambées (für 2 Personen) — 17.—
Bananes flambées (für 2 Personen) — 17.—
Friandises pro Portion — 4.—

15% Service inbegriffen Diese Karte liegt auf von 11.30–24.00 Uhr

Atlantis Hotel & Zürich — Rôtisserie

59c

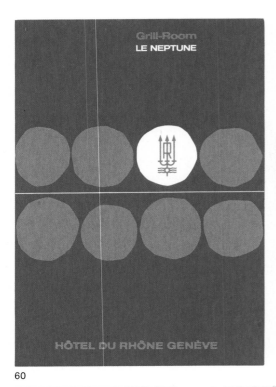

60

61a

Quelques plats de chez nous .
5   Viande séchée des Grisons . . . .
    Dried beef from the Grisons
32 Eminé de veau zurichoise avec rösti . . . .
    Eminé of veal Zurichoise style with rösti
36 Saltimbocca tessinoise . . . .
    Small escalopes of veal Tessinoise

Les poissons
T   Loup grillé aux fenouils, mousseline de légumes . . . .
    Grilled seabass with fennel and vegetables purée
T   Loup Val d'Esquiers (2 pers.) . . . .
    Seabass Val d'Esquiers (2 pers.)
21 Turbot aux algues à la vapeur . . . .
    Steamed turbot on seaweed
22 Omble chevalier Polignac . . . .
    Golden trout Polignac
23 Filets de sole Grand Véfour . . . .
    Fillets of sole Grand Véfour
25 Escalope de saumon au thym . . . .
    Escalopes of salmon with thyme
27 Cassolette de scampis au whisky . . . .
    Cassolette of scampis with whisky
28 Filets de sole Courtine . . . .
    Fillets of sole Courtine
29 Blanc de turbot en papillotte . . . .
    Fillets of turbot en papillotte
30 Blanquette de Saint-Jacques aux stigmates de safran . . .
    Blanquette of scallop with saffron stigmas

Les mets cuisinés
31 Côte de bœuf à la moëlle (2 pers.) . . . .
    Rib of beef with bone-marrow (2 pers.)
33 Mignons de veau périgourdine . . . .
    Mignon of veal Périgourdine
36 Piccata au citron vert . . . .
    Small escalopes of veal with lime
37 Médaillons de veau aux pruneaux . . . .
    Medallions of veal with prunes
39 Ris de veau au melon confit . . . .
    Sweet-bread of veal with melon confit
40 Entrecôte poêlée au poivre vert . . . .
    Sirloin steak sautéed with green pepper
41 Mignons de bœuf aux trois champignons . . . . . .
    Medallions of fillet of beef with mushrooms
42 Noisettes d'agneau aux haricots panachés . . . . .
    Fillet of lamb with mixed beans
43 Gratin de rognons de veau à la moutarde . . . . .
    Veal kidneys gratin with mustard
44 Navarin d'agneau aux primeurs . . . .
    Mutton stew with vegetables

Les grillades
46 Chateaubriand ou Porterhouse steak écossais (2 pers.) .
    Chateaubriand or Porterhouse steak (2 pers.)
47 Côtes d'agneau vert-pré . . . .
    Lamb chops vert-pré
48 Paillard de veau . . . .
    Paillard of veal
49 Tournedos, sauce béarnaise . . . .
    Fillet of beef, Béarnaise sauce
50 Côte de veau . . . .
    Veal chop
51 Entrecôte . . . .
    Sirloin steak

Les volailles
58 Poulet ou coquelet rôti à la broche . . . .
    Spit roasted chicken or baby rooster
60 Fricassée de poussin aux morilles à la crème . . . .
    Fricassée of baby chicken with creamed morel sauce
61 Magret de canard aux olives et navets . . . . . .
    Breast of duck with olives and turnips
62 Perdreau mijoté campagnard . . . .
    Simmered young partridge country style
63 Pintade au vinaigre d'estragon . . . .
    Guinea-fowl with tarragon vinegar

Les desserts
Choix de fromages . . . .
    Choice of cheese
La voiture des desserts . . . .
    Sweets from the trolley
Les différents sorbets . . . .
    Variety of sherbets
Glace aux pruneaux à l'armagnac . . . .
    Prune ice cream flavoured with Armagnac
Mousse au chocolat aux zestes d'orange . . . . . .
    Mousse of chocolate with orange zests
Soufflé glacé Grand-Marnier . . . .
    Iced soufflé Grand-Marnier

Sur commande au début du repas
    By special order at the beginning of the meal
Tartes aux pommes chaudes (2 pers.) . . . .
    Apple Tart (2 pers.)
Gratin de fruits exotiques (2 pers.) . . . .
    Gratin of exotic fruits (2 pers.)
Crêpes soufflées Baumanière (2 pers.) . . . .
    Soufflée pancakes Baumanière (2 pers.)

Service
included

61b

60   Grill-Room Le Neptune, Hôtel du Rhône, Genève,
Suisse
Carte de menu. Création et impression: Albert Gilodi
Couverture: 225 × 325 mm, ouvert 890 × 325 mm, 8
pages. Chromo une face. Offset rouge. Dorure à la
feuille, rainé trois fois, pli fenêtre, contre-collé
Intérieur: 215 × 318 mm, ouvert 430 × 318 mm, 4 pages.
Papier couché machine. Pages 2 et 3 offset noir et
rouge. Plié et collé à la couverture

60   Grill-Room Le Neptune, Hôtel du Rhône, Genf,
Schweiz
Speisekarte. Gestaltung und Druck Albert Gilodi
Umschlag: 225 × 325 mm, offen 890 × 325 mm, 8sei-
tig. Chromokarton einseitig. Offset rot. Goldfolienprä-
gung, 3mal gerillt, Fensterfalz, gegengeklebt
Innenteil: 215 × 318 mm, offen 430 × 318 mm, 4seitig.
Maschinengestrichenes Kunstdruckpapier. Seiten
2–3 Offset schwarz und rot. Gefalzt und im Rücken am
Umschlag angeklebt

60   Grill-Room Le Neptune, Hôtel du Rhône, Geneva,
Switzerland
Menu-card. Designed and printed by Albert Gilodi
Cover: 225 × 325 mm, open 890 × 325 mm, 8 pages.
One-sided cast-coated card. Offset printing in red.
Gold embossing, thrice scored, gate fold, two pages
mounted together
Contents: 215 × 318 mm, open 430 × 318 mm, 4 pages.
Machine-finished art paper. Pages 2–3: offset printing
in red and black. Folded and glued on the spine to the
cover

61a–b   Hôtel du Rhône, Genève, Suisse
Carte de menu. Création et impression: Albert Gilodi
Couverture: 225 × 320 mm, ouvert 665 × 320 mm, 6
pages. Chromo une face gris argent. Pages 1 et 6 offset
bleu. Page 1 estampage à la feuille d'argent, laminé,
rainé, première page avec pouce de répertoire estampé, plis roulés, pages 3 et 4 contre-collées
Intérieur: 217 × 312 mm, ouvert 434 × 312 mm, 4 pages.
Papier couché machine. Pages 1–3 offset noir, gris et
rouge. Rainé, plié et collé à la couverture, première
page avec pouce de répertoire

61a–b   Hôtel du Rhône, Genf, Schweiz
Speisekarte. Gestaltung und Druck Albert Gilodi
Umschlag: 225 × 320 mm, offen 665 × 320 mm, 6sei-
tig. Chromokarton einseitig silbergrau. Seiten 1 und 6
Offset blau. Seite 1 Silberfolienprägung, laminiert, gerillt, erste Umschlagseite mit Daumenregisterstan-
zung, Wickelfalz, Seite 4 auf Seite 3 kaschiert
Innenteil: 217 × 312 mm, offen 434 × 312 mm, 4seitig.
Maschinengestrichenes Kunstdruckpapier. Seiten
1–3 Offset schwarz, grau, rot. Gerillt, gefalzt, im Rücken
am Umschlag angeklebt, erste Seite mit Daumen-
registerstanzung

61a–b   Hôtel du Rhône, Geneva, Switzerland
Menu-card. Designed and printed by Albert Gilodi
Cover: 225 × 320 mm, open 665 × 320 mm, 6 pages.
One-sided cast-coated card in silver-grey. Pages 1 and
6: offset printing in blue. Page 1: silver embossing,
laminated, scored, first page with die-cut thumb index,
reverse accordion fold; page 4: mounted on to page 3
Contents: 217 × 312 mm, open 434 × 312 mm, 4 pages.
Machine-finished art paper. Pages 1–3: offset printing
in black, grey and red. Scored, folded, glued in the
spine to the cover, front cover with die-cut thumb
index

62a–b Grill-Room, Badrutt's Palace Hotel, St-Moritz, Suisse
Carte de menu. Création: BSSM, Zurich
Couverture: 297×210 mm, ouvert 594×210 mm, 4 pages. Chromo une face. Pages 1 et 4 offset 4 couleurs. Laminé, rainé, plié
Intérieur: 297×210 mm, ouvert 594×210 mm, 4 pages. Papier chiné à la cuve. Pages 2 et 3 impression typo gris et brun. Rainé, plié et assemblé à la couverture par un cordon gris
Présentation des mets en français avec brève explication sur la composition de certains plats.

62a–b Grill-Room, Badrutt's Palace Hotel, St. Moritz, Schweiz
Speisekarte. Gestaltung BSSM, Zürich
Umschlag: 297×210 mm, offen 594×210 mm, 4seitig. Chromokarton einseitig. Seiten 1 und 4 Offset 4farbig. Laminiert, gerillt, gefalzt
Innenteil: 297×210 mm, offen 594×210 mm, 4seitig. Büttenpapier meliert. Seiten 2–3 Buchdruck grau und braun. Gerillt, gefalzt und durch graue Kordel mit dem Umschlag verbunden
Speisenangebot Französisch mit einigen Erklärungen zu gewissen Gerichten

62a–b Grill-Room, Badrutt's Palace Hotel, St. Moritz, Switzerland
Menu-card. Designed by BSSM, Zurich
Cover: 297×210 mm, open 594×210 mm, 4 pages. One-sided cast-coated card. Pages 1 and 4: 4-colour offset printing. Laminated, scored, folded
Contents: 297×210 mm, open 594×210 mm, 4 pages. Marbled handmade paper. Pages 2–3: letterpress printing in grey and brown. Scored, folded and attached to the cover with a grey cord
Menus in French with short explanatory notes to certain dishes.

62a

GRILL-ROOM

★TURBOT DE LA MER DU NORD «MARCO POLO» . . . . 32.—
poché vin blanc, crevettes, champignons, truffes et tomates concassées, riz pilaw

DARNE DE SAUMON . . . . 30.—
poché au Pommery

TRUITE DU TORRENT EN PAPILLOTE . 22.—
Sauce aux herbes

LES ENTREES

COTE DE VEAU FARCIE «PROF. VORONOFF» 30.—
farci morilles, sauté, déglacé vin blanc et Cognac, sauce crème, dés de foie-gras

★PICCATA DE VEAU AUX ARTICHAUTS . 28.—

MEDAILLONS DE VEAU AUX CEPES . . . 30.—

ROGNON DE VEAU FLAMBE «SANTOS DUMONT» . . . . 60.—
(2 personnes)

★PORTERHOUSE STEAK sur feu de bois (3 pers.)
accompagné de primeurs

★COTE DE BOEUF «PALACE» (2 personnes) . 68.—
grillée, diablée, sauce Béarnaise

★FILET DE CHAROLAIS EN PAPILLOTE (2 pers.) 76.—
garni champignons, julienne de truffes langue et champignons, sauce château au foie-gras, pommes soufflées

★COEUR DE FILET DE BOEUF «DE FRANCE» 37.—
garni foie-gras, truffes, jambon crû, déglacé Cognac, morilles à la crème

FILET STEAK «DIANE» . . . . 28.—
filet de boeuf applati, moutardé, flambé fine champagne, persil haché et ciboulette. préparation à table

ENTRECÔTE AU POIVRE VERT «AGA KHAN» 26.—
flambé Cognac, demi-glace et crème au poivre vert, ris pilaw

★CARRE OU SELLE D'AGNEAU «SARLADAISE» s. g.
(2 personnes)
préparé Provençale, pommes haricots verts sautés

COTES D'AGNEAU «PERSEPOLIS» . . . 32.—
riz spécial Iranien

★POJARSKI DE VOLAILLE «HELENE BADRUTT» 28.—
d'après une vieille recette du Palace, sauce crème, julienne truffes, nouillettes

POULET «ROSA PONSELLE» . . . . . . 30.—
sauté à l'Estragon, Riz Pilaw

CANETON DE NANTES A L'ORANGE (2 pers.) 65.—
Préparation spéciale

SELLE DE CHEVREUIL «ALFRED HITCHCOCK» (2 personnes) . . . 68.—

★commander à l'avance / grande spécialité

LES LEGUMES ET SALADES

PETITS POIS, HARICOTS VERTS
ENDIVES BELGES, CELERI, CAROTTES
EPINARDS . . . . 7.—

ARTICHAUT . . . . 8.—
Sauce Hollandaise ou Vinaigrette

GRATIN D'EPINARDS
AUX CHAMPIGNONS (2 personnes) . . . 12.—

BROCCOLIS HOLLANDAISE . . . . 8.—

PUREE DE LEGUMES (2 personnes) . . . 15.—
Céleris, carottes, artichauts

BOUQUETIERE DE LEGUMES «PALACE» (2 pers.) 24.—

SALADE DE SAISON . . . . 6.—

SALADE MELEE . . . . 8.—

LES ENTREMETS

SOUFFLE PAULETTE GODDARD» (2 personnes) 30.—
vanille, fruits confits, sauce chocolat, glace vanille à part

PECHES FLAMBEES «PALACE» (2 personnes) . 28.—

FRAISES «ROMANOFF» . . . . 12.—

ANANAS ORIENTALE (2 personnes) . . . 24.—

OMELETTE NORVEGIENNE (2 personnes) . 24.—

SABAYON «PEDRO DOMECQ» (2 personnes) . 16.—

GRATIN DE FRAMBOISES «CHESA VEGLIA» 10.—

SOUFFLE GLACE AU GRAND MARNIER . 9.—

CERISES JUBILE (2 personnes) . . . . . 28.—

CREPES SUZETTE (2 personnes) . . . . 28.—

SORBET divers . . . . 7.—
champagne, liqueurs, à part

★DELICE AUX FRAISES «ENGADINOISE» (2 pers.) 30.—

MOUSSE AU CHOCOLAT «JOSEPHINE BAKER» . . . . 12.—

SERVICE COMPRIS

LE SPECIALITES DU GRILL — PALACE HOTEL ST. MORITZ

62b

From The Trawlers

IKAN TENGGIRI PAPILLOTE
*Butterfried fish fillet topped with mushrooms,
tomatoes and oysters* — $12.50

**GRILLED NOVA SCOTIA SALMON STEAK
"BEARNAISE"** — 18.50

FILLET OF IKAN KURAU "GRENOBLOISE"
*Charcoal broiled and topped with capers
and diced lemon in butter sauce* — 11.00

POMFRET "PRINCE MURAT"
Strips of pomfret butterfried with potatoes and artichoke — 16.50

LOBSTER AMERICAINE [*if available*]

**A WHOLE LOBSTER FROM THE
SURROUNDING WATERS** [*if available*]
*Check with the Captain for the best
preparation ....per oz.* — 2.25

From Our Copper Kettle

ORIGINAL FRENCH ONION SOUP — 4.00

PETITE BOUILLABAISSE "MARSEILLE"
The Classical French fish soup — 6.50

TURTLE SOUP "AMONTILLADO"
Served with chester straws — 4.50

SOUP KAMBING
Lamb chowder in traditional Malay style — 3.00

VICHYSSOISE
Served the Sultan's way — 3.50

From The Broiler

PORK CHOPS "WESTMORELAND"
Two chops with assorted pickles — $12.00

WHOLE SPRING CHICKEN — 13.50

A PAIR OF DOUBLE CUT LAMB CHOPS
Accompanied with mint sauce — 12.50

PRIME US SIRLOIN STEAK.........per oz. — 2.40

PRIME TENDERLOIN STEAK (8oz.) — 24.00

SURF AND TURF
*For the undecided Charcoal broiled lobster tail
and a filet mignon served with bearnaise sauce* — 22.00

VEAL STEAK "BEATRICE"
Served with morel cream sauce — 24.00

TROIS MEDALLION "GASTRONOME"
*Beef, veal and pork fillets topped with bearnaise,
mushroom sauce and tomatoes concasse* — 16.50

63

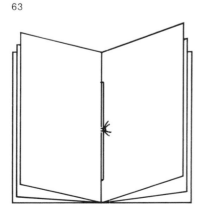

63 Feringgi Grill, Rasa Sanyang Hotel, Penang, Malaisie
Carte de menu. Création et impression: Syarikat Hai Chuan, Penang
Couverture: 110×165 mm, ouvert 220×165 mm, 4 pages. Chromo double face. Offset brun et noir. Page 1 dorure à la feuille, laqué
Intérieur: 110×165 mm, ouvert 220×165 mm, 8 pages. Papier couleur à structure gaufrée, fond en brun clair. Texte et illustrations offset brun foncé. Rainé, plié et assemblé à la couverture par du fil brun
Couverture et format font penser à un passeport. La structure gaufrée et le «fond de sécurité» de l'intérieur renforcent ce sentiment. Le fil de reliure est dans le ton d'impression.

63 Feringgi Grill, Rasa Sanyang Hotel, Penang, Malaysia
Speisekarte. Gestaltung und Druck Syarikat Hai Chuan, Penang
Umschlag: 110×165 mm, offen 220×165 mm, 4seitig. Chromokarton zweiseitig. Offset braun und schwarz. Seite 1 Goldfolienprägung. Lackiert
Innenteil: 110×165 mm, offen 220×165 mm, 8seitig. Papier mit Prägestruktur, farbig, Hintergrund hellbraun. Text und Illustrationen Offset dunkelbraun. Gerillt, gefalzt und mit braunem Faden in den Umschlag eingeheftet
Format und Umschlag erinnern an einen Reisepaß. Prägestruktur und «Sicherheitshintergrund» der Innenseiten verstärken diesen Eindruck. Der Faden ist im Ton des Drucks gehalten.

63 Feringgi Grill, Rasa Sanyang Hotel, Penang, Malaysia
Menu-card. Designed and printed by Syarikat Hai Chuan, Penang
Cover: 110×165 mm, open 220×165 mm, 4 pages. Two-sided cast-coated card. Offset printing in brown and black. Page 1: gold embossing, varnished
Contents: 110×165 mm, open 220×165 mm, 8 pages. Paper with textured finish, coloured, pale brown background. Text and illustration: offset printing in dark brown. Scored, folded and stitched to the cover with brown thread
The size and cover call to mind a passport. Grained texture and 'security background' of the inside pages emphasize this impression.

ASIA CHINESE GRILL ROOM

64a

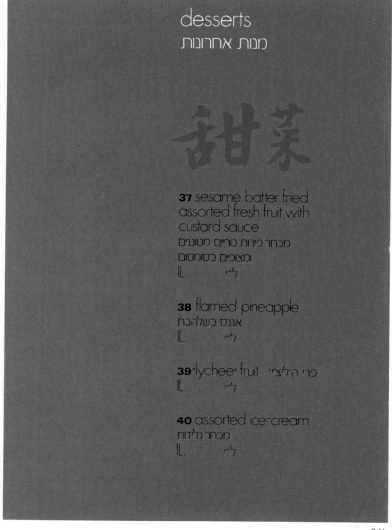

desserts
מנות אחרונות

37 sesame batter fried
assorted fresh fruit with
custard sauce
מבחר פירות טריים מטוגנים
ומצופים בסוכר
IL. לי'

38 flamed pineapple
אננס בשלהבת
IL. לי'

39 "lychee" fruit   פרי הליצ'י
IL. לי'

40 assorted ice-cream
מבחר גלידות
IL. לי'

64b

64a–b Asia Chinese Grill Room,
Ramada Continental, Tel Aviv, Israël
Carte de menu. Propre création
Couverture: 228×322 mm, ouvert
456×322 mm, 4 pages. Carton de
décoration noir. Pages 1 et 4 sérigraphie blanc et estampage noir. Rainé,
plié
Intérieur: 223×318 mm, ouvert
446×318 mm, 8 pages. Newschromo.
Offset ocre, noir et rouge. Rainé, plié et
assemblé à la couverture par un cordon
jaune
Présentation des mets en partie trilingue anglais-chinois-hébreu. La calligraphie chinoise du titre sert d'élément
décoratif.

64a–b Asia Chinese Grill Room,
Ramada Continental, Tel Aviv, Israel
Speisekarte. Eigene Gestaltung
Umschlag: 228×322 mm, offen
456×322 mm, 4seitig. Ausstattungs-
karton schwarz. Seiten 1 und 4 Siebdruck weiß und schwarze Folienprä-
gung. Gerillt, gefalzt
Innenteil: 223×318 mm, offen
446×318 mm, 8seitig. Newschromo.
Offset ocker, schwarz und rot. Gerillt,
gefalzt und durch gelbe Kordel mit dem
Umschlag verbunden
Speisenangebot teilweise 3sprachig
Englisch, Chinesisch, Hebräisch. Die
kalligraphierten chinesischen Titel wirken als dekorative Elemente.

64a–b Asia Chinese Grill Room,
Ramada Continental, Tel Aviv, Israel
Menu-card. Designed by the Ramada
Continental
Cover: 228×322 mm, open
456×322 mm, 4 pages. Black display
board. Pages 1 and 4: screen printing in
white and black foil embossing.
Scored, folded
Contents: 223×318 mm, open
446×318 mm, 8 pages. Super calen-
dered paper. Offset printing in ochre,
black and red. Scored, folded and at-
tached to the cover with a yellow cord
Menus partly in English, Chinese and
Hebrew.

The Chef's Recommendation

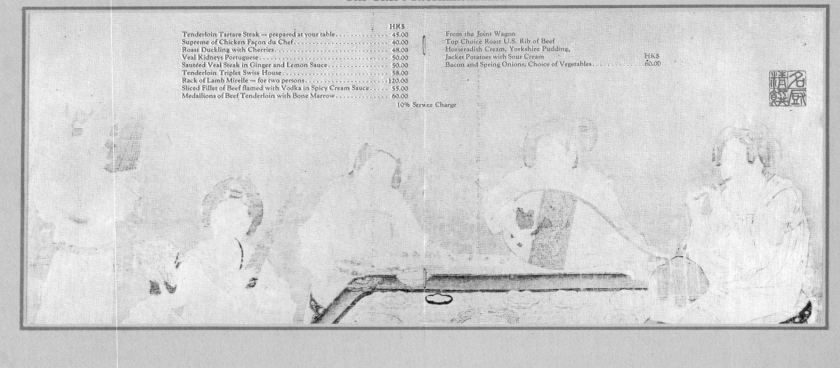

	HK$
Tenderloin Tartare Steak — prepared at your table	45.00
Supreme of Chicken Façon du Chef	40.00
Roast Duckling with Cherries	48.00
Veal Kidneys Portuguese	50.00
Sautéed Veal Steak in Ginger and Lemon Sauce	50.00
Tenderloin Triplet Swiss House	58.00
Rack of Lamb Mirelle — for two persons	120.00
Sliced Fillet of Beef flamed with Vodka in Spicy Cream Sauce	55.00
Medallions of Beef Tenderloin with Bone Marrow	60.00

From the Joint Wagon
Top Choice Roast U.S. Rib of Beef
Horseradish Cream, Yorkshire Pudding,
Jacket Potatoes with Sour Cream

	HK$
Bacon and Spring Onions, Choice of Vegetables	60.00

10% Service Charge

Hors d'Oeuvre

Cold	HK$
Selected Pacific Rock Oysters — per piece	4.00
Scampi Salad in Iced Melon	28.00
Shrimp Cocktail Mandarin	20.00
Smoked Scotch Salmon	40.00
Spiced Beef with Chives and Onion Sauce	19.00
The Mandarin Grill's Special Terrine	20.00

Hot	
Small Pancakes filled with Lobster	30.00
Escargots with Garlic and Herb Butter in Champignons	25.00
Spinach Rolls with Fresh Mushrooms	16.00
Gratinated Veal Sweetbread Soubisse	25.00

Finest Beluga Malossol Caviar and Truffled Gooseliver are available.

10% Service Charge

Soups

	HK$
Cold Senegalese Soup	12.00
Cold Gaspachuelo Andaluz	12.00
Consommé Célestine	12.00
Hong Kong Lobster Bisque	18.00
Onion Soup Mandarin	12.00
Turtle Soup Lady Curzon	18.00
Cream of Asparagus	12.00

10% Service Charge

The Mandarin Grill

65a

65a–c The Mandarin Grill, The Mandarin, Hong Kong
Carte de menu. Création: P. Hawkes, Leo Burnett Ltd.
Couverture: 278 × 280 mm, ouvert 560 × 280 mm, 4 pages. Couvrure à structure gaufrée, carton 30/10. Offset 4 couleurs plus brun et or. Dorure à la feuille en pages 1 et 4. Système de fixation permettant l'insertion de l'intérieur
Intérieur: 275 × 278 mm, ouvert 550 × 278 mm, 12 pages. Papier à structure toile. Pages 3–10 offset ocre, or, noir et rouge. Plié, agrafé deux fois dans le pli. 2 rabats estampés permettent de fixer l'intérieur à la couverture

65a–c The Mandarin Grill, The Mandarin, Hongkong
Speisekarte. Gestaltung P. Hawkes, Leo Burnett Ltd.
Umschlag: 278 × 280 mm, offen 560 × 280 mm, 4seitig. Pappband mit Strukturprägung, Karton 30/10. Offset 4farbig und braun und gold. Goldfolienprägung auf Seiten 1 und 4. Einhängevorrichtung unter dem Vorsatz für Einstecken des Innenteils
Innenteil: 275 × 278 mm, offen 550 × 278 mm, 12seitig. Papier mit Leinenstruktur. Seiten 3–10 Offset ocker, gold, schwarz, rot. Gefalzt, 2mal drahtgeheftet. 2 formgestanzte, über das Format hinausragende Klappen ermöglichen das Einhängen in den Umschlag.

65a–c The Mandarin Grill, The Mandarin, Hong Kong
Menu-card. Designed by P. Hawkes, Leo Burnett Ltd.
Cover: 278 × 280 mm, open 560 × 280 mm, 4 pages. Stiff paper binding with textured finish, card 30/10. 4-colour offset printing plus brown and gold. Gold embossing on pages 1 and 4. Attachment device under the endpaper for the insertion of inside pages
Contents: 275 × 278 mm, open 550 × 278 mm, 12 pages. Paper with linen grain finish. Pages 3–10: offset printing in ochre, gold, black and red. Folded, 2-wire stitched. Two die-cut flaps which protrude beyond the format facilitate insertion into the cover

Cartes de bars

Pour un tel lieu de rencontre tranquille, une carte discrète transmettra bien l'atmosphère feutrée propre aux clubs. Un ton d'exclusivité, une touche d'élégance et le but sera atteint. Boissons et cocktails y sont souvent internationaux si ce n'est franchement exotiques; il est par conséquent important d'insister sur ce que recherche la clientèle.

Karten für die Bar

Die Bar ist der Ort des Zusammentreffens, des gemütlichen Beisammenseins. In der gediegenen, oft diskreten Ausführung der Karte kommt – manchmal mit einer Note vornehmer Exklusivität – die Club-Atmosphäre der Bar zum Ausdruck.
Drinks und Cocktails sind international und somit Standardbestandteil des Angebots. Auf Einheimisches (für den ausländischen Gast also Exotisches) soll speziell hingewiesen werden.

Bar menus

A bar is a place for people to meet and be merry. The menu must be superior and discreet, with a note of exclusiveness, in order to express the clublike atmosphere. Drinks and cocktails are international and therefore standardized. Mention may, however, be made of local products which have an exotic flavour for foreign guests.

66a–c Maxwell's, Frankfurt-Sheraton Hotel, Francfort-sur-le-Main, RFA
Carte des consommations. Création: Susan Fitze, Zurich. Impression: Hauserpresse, Francfort/Main
Couverture: 194×284 mm, ouvert 382×284 mm, 4 pages. Papier brun à structure «peau de crocodile», une face. Impression typo, page 1 vert et or, page 4 vert. Rainé, plié
Intérieur: 187×278 mm, ouvert 374×278 mm, 8 pages. Papier vergé à la cuve. Impression typo vert clair et vert foncé. Rainé, plié, agrafé deux fois dans le pli avec la couverture
Pour la décoration de l'intérieur, reprise de caractères d'écriture et de motifs «Jugendstil» (voir ill. 28).

66a–c Maxwell's, Frankfurt-Sheraton Hotel, Frankfurt am Main, Bundesrepublik Deutschland
Getränkekarte. Gestaltung Susan Fitze, Zürich. Druck Hauserpresse, Frankfurt am Main
Umschlag: 191×284 mm, offen 382×284 mm, 4seitig. Papier mit Elefantenhautstruktur, einseitig, braun. Buchdruck, Seite 1 gold und grün, Seite 4 grün. Gerillt, gefalzt
Innenteil: 187×278 mm, offen 374×278 mm, 8seitig. Büttenpapier vergé. Buchdruck hell- und dunkelgrün. Gerillt, gefalzt und mit dem Umschlag zweimal drahtgeheftet
Bei der Gestaltung der Innenseiten wurden Schriftzug und Jugendstilembleme wieder aufgenommen. Siehe Abb. 28

66a–c Maxwell's, Frankfurt-Sheraton Hotel, Frankfurt, West Germany
Wine list. Designed by Susan Fitze, Zurich. Printed by Hauserpresse, Frankfurt
Cover: 191×284 mm, open 382×284 mm, 4 pages. Paper with texture of elephant-grain, one-sided, brown. Letterpress printing on page 1: in gold and green, on page 4: in green. Scored, folded
Contents: 187×278 mm, open 374×278 mm, 8 pages. Hand-made laid paper. Letterpress printing in pale green and dark green. Scored, folded, 2-wire stitched to the cover
The flow of the lettering and Art nouveau elements are taken up again for the design of the inside pages. See ill. 28

APERITIFS

	5 cl	
Martini, Rosso oder Bianco		6.—
Cinzano, Rosso oder Bianco		6.—
Dubonnet		6.—
Picon Rouge		7.—
Pernod*	4 cl	8.—
Campari* mit Soda	4 cl	8.50

Cognac

	4 cl
Courvoisier VSOP	9.50
Armagnac St. Vivant VSOP	10.—
Baron Otard VSOP	10.—
BISQUIT VSOP	10.—
Martell VSOP	10.—
Martell Cordon Bleu	18.—
Hennessy XO	19.—

WHISKY

(includes Soft Drinks)

SCOTCH:	4 cl
White Label	9.—
Black & White	9.—
Johnnie Walker Red Label	9.—
Ballantines	9.—
100 Pipers	9.—
Bell's 12 years old	11.50
John Haig's Dimple	12.50
Johnnie Walker Black Label	12.50
Chivas Regal	13.50
Chivas Regal »Royal Salute«	30.—

BOURBON:	
Four Roses	9.—
Old Grand Dad	9.50
Jack Daniels	13.—

CANADIAN:	
Canadian Club	9.—
Seagram's V.O.	9.—
Seagram's Crown Royal	13.—

IRISH:	
Tullamore Dew	9.—
John Jameson	9.—

PORT & SHERRY

	5 cl
Sandeman Port	6.50
Don Felix Sherry	6.50

66a

* mit Farbstoff

Bedienungsgeld und Steuern sind im Preis inbegriffen

All inclusive prices

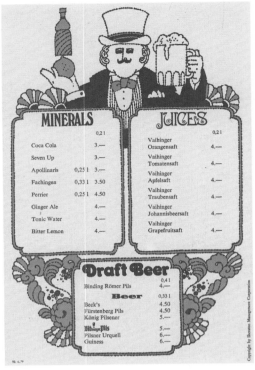

66b

66a–c   Maxwell's, Frankfurt-Sheraton Hotel, Francfort-sur-le-Main, RFA
Carte des consommations. Création: Susan Fitze, Zurich. Impression: Hauserpresse, Francfort/Main
Couverture: 191 × 284 mm, ouvert 382 × 284 mm, 4 pages. Papier brun à structure «peau de crocodile», une face. Impression typo, page 1 vert et or, page 4 vert. Rainé, plié
Intérieur: 187 × 278 mm, ouvert 374 × 278 mm, 8 pages. Papier vergé à la cuve. Impression typo vert clair et vert foncé. Rainé, plié, agrafé deux fois dans le pli avec la couverture
Pour la décoration de l'intérieur, reprise de caractères d'écriture et de motifs «Jugendstil» (voir ill. 28).

66a–c   Maxwell's, Frankfurt-Sheraton Hotel, Frankfurt am Main, Bundesrepublik Deutschland
Getränkekarte. Gestaltung Susan Fitze, Zürich. Druck Hauserpresse, Frankfurt am Main
Umschlag: 191 × 284 mm, offen 382 × 284 mm, 4seitig. Papier mit Elefantenhautstruktur, einseitig, braun. Buchdruck, Seite 1 gold und grün, Seite 4 grün. Gerillt, gefalzt
Innenteil: 187 × 278 mm, offen 374 × 278 mm, 8seitig. Büttenpapier vergé. Buchdruck hell- und dunkelgrün. Gerillt, gefalzt und mit dem Umschlag zweimal drahtgeheftet
Bei der Gestaltung der Innenseiten wurden Schriftzug und Jugendstilembleme wieder aufgenommen. Siehe Abb. 28

66a–c   Maxwell's, Frankfurt-Sheraton Hotel, Frankfurt, West Germany
Wine list. Designed by Susan Fitze, Zurich. Printed by Hauserpresse, Frankfurt
Cover: 191 × 284 mm, open 382 × 284 mm, 4 pages. Paper with texture of elephant-grain, one-sided, brown. Letterpress printing on page 1: in gold and green, on page 4: in green. Scored, folded
Contents: 187 × 278 mm, open 374 × 278 mm, 8 pages. Hand-made laid paper. Letterpress printing in pale green and dark green. Scored, folded, 2-wire stitched to the cover
The flow of the lettering and Art nouveau elements are taken up again for the design of the inside pages. See ill. 28

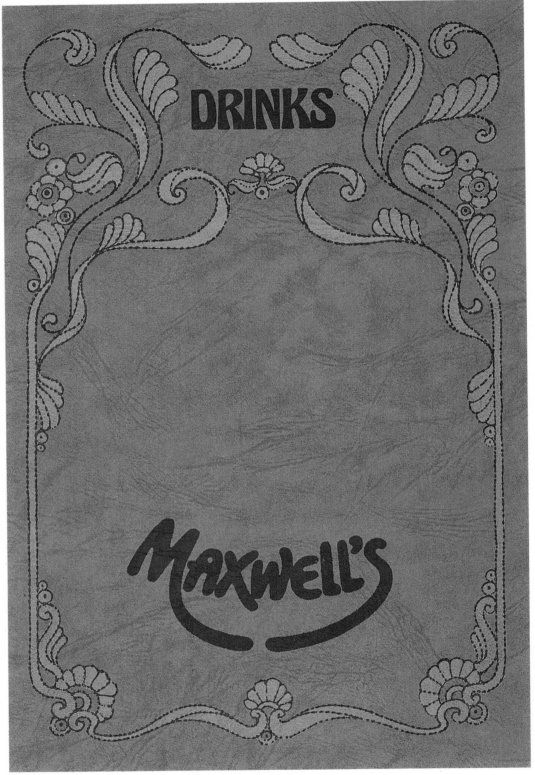

66c

67

67 Carousel Bar, The Mandarin, Manille, Philippines
Carte des consommations. Création: département de publicité de l'établissement
133 × 225 mm, ouvert 266 × 225 mm, 4 pages. Newschromo double face. Offset orange, rouge et noir. Pages 2 et 3 orange tramé et noir. Laminé deux faces, rainé, plié
La reproduction d'une ancienne affiche sur la première page rappelle les «saloons» et l'atmosphère des cirques d'alors.

67 Carousel Bar, The Mandarin, Manila, Philippinen
Getränkekarte. Gestaltung im hauseigenen Werbestudio
133 × 225 mm, offen 266 × 225 mm, 4seitig. Newschromo zweiseitig. Offset orange, rot, schwarz, Seiten 2–3 orange gerastert und schwarz. Zweiseitig laminiert, gerillt, gefalzt
Die Reproduktion eines alten Plakates auf Seite 1 erinnert an amerikanische Saloons und vermittelt einen Hauch früher Zirkusluft.

67 Carousel Bar, The Mandarin, Manila, The Philippines
Wine list. Designed by the restaurant's own advertising studio
133 × 225 mm, open 266 × 225 mm, 4 pages. Two-sided super-calendered paper. Offset printing in orange, red and black. Pages 2–3: orange silk-screen printing plus black. Laminated on both sides, scored, folded
The reproduction of an old poster on page 1 calls to mind American saloons and evokes a touch of the circus atmosphere in bygone days.

68

69

68 Bar, Hôtel Inter-Continental, Paris
Carte des consommations. Création et
impression: Akila-Pasquet, Pantin
200×105 mm, ouvert 400×105 mm, 4
pages. Carton offset couleur. Offset
brun. Laminé deux faces, rainé, plié

68 Bar, Hotel Inter-Continental, Paris,
Frankreich
Getränkekarte. Gestaltung und Druck
Akila-Pasquet, Pantin
200×105 mm, offen 400×105 mm,
4seitig. Offsetkarton farbig. Offset
braun. Zweiseitig laminiert, gerillt,
gefalzt

68 Bar, Hotel Inter-Continental, Paris,
France
Wine list. Designed and printed by
Akila-Pasquet, Pantin
200×105 mm, open 400×105 mm, 4
pages. Coloured offset card. Offset
printing in brown. Laminated on both
sides, scored, folded

69 Bistrothèque, Hôtel Inter-Continental, Paris
Carte des consommations. Création et
impression: Akila-Pasquet, Pantin
105×105 mm, ouvert 210×105 mm, 4
pages. Chromo une face gris argent.
Pages 2 et 3 impression typo gris-bleu.
Page 1 argenté à la feuille. Plié
Le petit format de cette carte reflète le
caractère privé de l'établissement.

69 Bistrothèque, Hotel Inter-Continental, Paris, Frankreich
Getränkekarte. Gestaltung und Druck
Akila-Pasquet, Pantin
105×105 mm, offen 210×105 mm,
4seitig. Chromokarton einseitig
silbergrau. Seiten 2–3 Buchdruck
graublau. Seite 1 Silberfolienprägung.
Gefalzt
Das kleine Format bringt den privaten
Charakter des Lokals zum Ausdruck.

69 Bistrothèque, Hotel Inter-Continental, Paris, France
Wine list. Designed and printed by
Akila-Pasquet, Pantin
105×105 mm, open 210×105 mm, 4
pages. One-sided cast-coated card in
silver-grey. Pages 2–3: letterpress
printing in blue-grey. Page 1: silver
embossing. Folded
The small size gives expression to the
rather private character of the wine-
bar.

70a–b The Library, The Mandarin, Singapour
Carte des consommations. Création: Overseas Union Advertising
100 × 206 mm, ouvert 300 × 206 mm, 6 pages. Chromo double face. Pages 1, 5 et 6 offset 4 couleurs et couleurs spéciales noir et gris, pages 2–4 offset noir et gris. Laminé deux faces, rainé deux fois, plis roulés
Conception intime à caractère exclusif des pages intérieures. Subtile harmonie du texte en négatif, des titres argent et des cadres.

70a–b The Library, The Mandarin, Singapur
Getränkekarte. Gestaltung Overseas Union Advertising
100 × 206 mm, offen 300 × 206 mm, 6seitig. Chromokarton zweiseitig. Seiten 1, 5 und 6 Offset 4farbig sowie Sonderfarben schwarz und grau, Seiten 2–4 Offset schwarz und grau. Zweiseitig laminiert, 2mal gerillt, Wickelfalz
Exklusiver intimer Charakter der Innenseiten. Fein abgestimmt der Negativtext, die silbernen «Titel» und die einrahmenden Linien

70a–b The Library, The Mandarin, Singapore
Wine list. Designed by Overseas Union Advertising
100 × 206 mm, open 300 × 206 mm, 6 pages. Two-sided cast-coated card. Pages 1, 5 and 6: 4-colour offset printing, plus additional colours black and grey; pages 2–4: offset printing in black and grey. Laminated on both sides, twice scored, reverse accordion fold
Exclusive and intimate character evoked on the inside pages. Precisely matched and harmonized negative text, as well as the silver 'titles' and delineating borders.

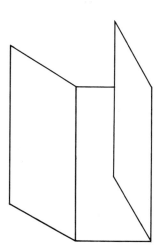

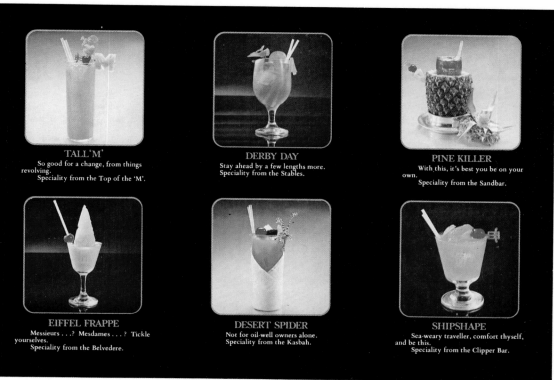

70a

The Library
Very exclusive. Very different. Very private.

FROM THE BAR:

Aperitifs	$5.80
Port & Sherry	$5.80
Vodka	$5.80
Gin	$5.80
Rum	$5.80

WHISKIES
Regular Brands

Scotch	$5.80
Canadian	$5.80
American	$5.80
Irish	$5.80

Premium Brands

Johnnie Walker Black Label	$6.90
Haigs Dimple Scotch	$6.90
Jack Da niels	$6.90
Chivas Regal	$7.50

COGNACS
Regular Brands

Three Stars	$6.50
V.S.O.P.	$6.90

Premium Brands

Hennessy X.O.	$14.50
Courvoisier Napoleon	$14.50
Martell Cordon Bleu	$14.50

EAUX-DE-VIE	$6.70
LIQUEURS	$6.70

Specially created for The Library

BEST SELLER — A tall, refreshing cocktail just right for members.	$6.90
BOOKWORM — A long, cool drink which will stick to you and put you in the mood.	$6.90

COCKTAILS

Martini Dry	$6.90
Whisky Sour	$6.90
Mai Tai — A Hawaiian speciality	$6.90

TALL COOLERS

The Tall "M"	$6.90
Singapore Sling	$6.90
Screwdriver	$6.90
Fizzes	$6.90
Collins	$6.90

FRUIT JUICES

Orange Juice	$4.50
Fruit Punch	$4.50

MINERAL WATERS

Perrier	$4.00
Vichy	$4.00
Soft Drinks	$4.00

BEERS

Local	$4.80
Imported	$6.00
Stout	$6.00

BAR DRINKS BY THE BOTTLE:

	½ btl	1 btl
WHISKIES		
Regular Brands	$ 70.00	$130.00
Premium Brands		
Johnnie Walker Black Label	$ 85.00	$150.00
Haigs Dimple Scotch	—	$150.00
Chivas Regal	—	$170.00
COGNACS		
Three Stars	—	$140.00
V.S.O.P.	$ 85.00	$160.00
Hennessy X.O.	$135.00	$260.00
Courvoisier Napoleon	$135.00	$260.00
Martell Cordon Bleu	—	$260.00
Otard X.O.	—	$260.00
Courvoisier Cour Imperiale	—	$260.00
GIN	$ 70.00	$130.00
VODKA	—	$130.00
RUM	—	$130.00

MIXERS	$ 2.00
IRISH COFFEE	$ 6.90
A PORTION OF COFFEE OR TEA	$ 4.00

CHAMPAGNE	½ btl	1 btl
100 Mercier Private Brut	$70.00	$130.00
101 Veuve Clicquot Brut	—	$160.00
108 Heidsieck Dry Monopole Rose	—	$170.00
111 Moët & Chandon Cuvée Dom Perignon	—	$195.00

MEMBERS' SPECIAL: $40.00 LESS, PER FULL BOTTLE
$20.00 LESS, PER HALF BOTTLE
NON-MEMBERS:
A first drink charge will be applied.

All prices subject to 10% service charge & 3% government tax.

TL/5/79/200

Mandarin Singapore
In the tradition of emperors.

TALL 'M'
So good for a change, from things revolving.
Speciality from the Top of the 'M'.

DERBY DAY
Stay ahead by a few lengths more.
Speciality from the Stables.

PINE KILLER
With this, it's best you be on your own.
Speciality from the Sandbar.

EIFFEL FRAPPE
Messieurs...? Mesdames...? Tickle yourselves.
Speciality from the Belvedere.

DESERT SPIDER
Not for oil-well owners alone.
Speciality from the Kasbah.

SHIPSHAPE
Sea-weary traveller, comfort thyself, and be this.
Speciality from the Clipper Bar.

70b

71

72

73

71 Crazy Bar, Passage, New Bar, Société des Hôtels Plaza, Atlantic, Park Réunis, Nice, France
Carte des consommations. Propre création
140 × 308 mm, ouvert 280 × 308 mm, 4 pages. Chromo une face. Impression typo, page 1 or, pages 2 et 3 brun. Laminé, plié
Couverture pleine d'effet obtenue en un seul passage sous presse avec un carton glacé noir une face.

71 Crazy Bar, Passage, New Bar, Société des Hôtels Plaza, Atlantic, Park Réunis, Nizza, Frankreich
Getränkekarte. Eigene Gestaltung
140 × 308 mm, offen 280 × 308 mm, 4seitig. Chromo-karton einseitig. Buchdruck, Seite 1 gold, Seiten 2–3 braun. Laminiert, gefalzt
Effektvoller Umschlag in einem Druckgang durch Verwendung eines einseitig schwarzen Chromokar-tons

71 Crazy Bar, Passage, New Bar, Société des Hôtels Plaza, Atlantic, Park Réunis, Nice, France
Wine list. Designed by the Société des Hôtels Plaza
140 × 308 mm, open 280 × 308 mm, 4 pages. One-sided cast-coated card. Letterpress printing on page 1: in gold, on pages 2–3: in brown. Laminated, folded
Effective cover achieved in one press-run by using one-sided black cast-coated card.

72 Belvedere Club, Hotel Inter-Continental, Co-logne, RFA
Carte des consommations
124 × 305 mm, ouvert 248 × 305 mm, 4 pages. Carton offset. Offset rouge et noir. Laminé deux faces, rainé, plié
Le fond brun foncé est obtenu par surimpression du rouge et du noir.

72 Belvedere Club, Hotel Inter-Continental, Köln, Bundesrepublik Deutschland
Getränkekarte
124 × 305 mm, offen 248 × 305 mm, 4seitig. Offsetkar-ton. Offset rot und schwarz. Zweiseitig laminiert, gerillt, gefalzt
Der dunkelbraune Untergrund wird durch Übereinan-derdrucken einer roten und einer schwarzen Voll-fläche erreicht.

72 Belvedere Club, Hotel Inter-Continental, Co-logne, West Germany
Wine list
124 × 305 mm, open 248 × 305 mm, 4 pages. Offset card. Offset printing in red and black. Laminated on both sides, scored, folded
The dark brown background is realized by super-imposed printing of solid plates in red and black.

73 Bar Dancing, Hotel Löwen, Sihlbrugg, Suisse
Carte des consommations. Création: Agence de publi-cité Bouchard, Zoug
140 × 297 mm, ouvert 417 × 297 mm, 6 pages. Chromo double face. Pages 1 et 5 impression typo 4 couleurs, pages 2–4 typo noir. Rainé deux fois, plis roulés
Les noms de l'établissement et du lieu, ainsi que les «3 étoiles», sont utilisés comme motifs décoratifs. Les pages intérieures sont délimitées par un fin filet aux angles biseautés.

73 Bar Dancing, Hotel Löwen, Sihlbrugg, Schweiz
Getränkekarte. Gestaltung Werbeagentur Bouchard, Zug
140 × 297 mm, offen 417 × 297 mm, 6seitig. Chromo-karton zweiseitig. Seiten 1 und 5 Buchdruck 4farbig, Seiten 2–4 Buchdruck schwarz. 2mal gerillt, Wickel-falz
Name des Lokals und des Ortes sowie die Dreistern-klasse des Hotels als Bildmotive verwendet. Die Innen-seiten sind durch einen feinen Linienrahmen mit abge-schrägten Ecken begrenzt.

73 Bar Dancing, Hotel Löwen, Sihlbrugg, Switzer-land
Wine list. Designed by Bouchard advertising agency, Zug
140 × 297 mm, open 417 × 297 mm, 6 pages. Two-sided cast-coated card. Pages 1 and 5: 4-colour letterpress printing, pages 2–4: letterpress printing in black. Twice scored, reverse accordion fold
The place-name and name of restaurant, as well as the hotel's three-star category are used as pictorial themes. The inside pages are delineated with a fine line border with bevelled corners.

74 Chinoiserie, Hyatt Regency, Singapour
Carte des consommations. Création: Agence de publicité Adolf Wirz, Zurich
Couverture: 185×375 mm, ouvert 370×375 mm, 4 pages. Papier brun à structure «peau de crocodile» contre-collé sur Newschromo. Pages 1 et 4 dorure à la feuille, pages 2 et 3 offset brun
Intérieur: 185×375 mm, ouvert 370×375 mm, 4 pages. Papier chiné à la cuve. Offset 4 couleurs. Plié, agrafé deux fois dans le pli avec la couverture
Le brun uni, choisi pour reproduire la peinture chinoise de l'intérieur de la couverture, contraste avec les éventails délicatement peints, décorant les pages intérieures

74 Chinoiserie, Hyatt Regency, Singapur
Getränkekarte. Gestaltung Adolf Wirz, Werbeagentur, Zürich
Umschlag: 185×375 mm, offen 370×375 mm, 4seitig. Elefantenhaut braun auf Newschromo kaschiert. Seiten 1 und 4 Goldfolienprägung, Seiten 2–3 Offset braun
Innenteil: 185×375 mm, offen 370×375 mm, 4seitig. Büttenpapier meliert. Offset 4farbig. Gefalzt und mit dem Umschlag 2mal drahtgeheftet
Die einfarbig braune Reproduktion einer chinesischen Malerei auf der Umschlaginnenseite kontrastiert mit den äußerst feinen Abbildungen bemalter Fächer im Innenteil.

74 Chinoiserie, Hyatt Regency, Singapore
Wine list. Designed by Adolf Wirz advertising agency, Zurich
Cover: 185×375 mm, open 370×375 mm, 4 pages. Brown elephant-grain mounted on to super-calendered paper. Pages 1 and 4: gold embossing, pages 2–3: offset printing in brown
Contents: 185×375 mm, open 370×375 mm, 4 pages. Marbled handmade paper. 4-colour offset printing. Folded and 2-wire stitched to the cover
The monochrome brown reproduction of a Chinese painting on the inside page of the cover contrasts with the extremely delicate pictures of painted fans on the inside pages.

74

DRINK LIST

APERITIFS $5.50
Campari, Dubonnet, Pernod, Pimm's No. 1, Cinzano, Martini, Cynar, Noilly Prat

MIXED DRINKS $5.50
Americano, Brandy Alexander, Bloody Mary, Collins, Black Russian, Champagne Cocktail, Dry Martini, Daiquiri, Fizzes, Gimlet, Gibson Manhattan, Margarita, Old Fashioned, Pink Lady, Rob Roy, Singapore Sling, Screwdriver, Stinger, Vodka Martini, White Lady, Whisky or Brandy Sour

SHERRY $5.50
Tio Pepe, Ammontillado, Dry Fly, Dry Sack, Bristol Cream

PORT $5.50
Cockburn's Fine Old Tawny, Harvey's Hunting Port Sandeman's Invalid, Sandeman's Vintage 1966

SCOTCH $5.50
Johnnie Walker Red Label, Cutty Sark, Teacher's J&B, Vat 69, White Horse, Black & White, Dewar's — White Label, Haig Gold Label, The Famous Grouse

PREMIUM SCOTCH $5.50
Johnnie Walker Black Label, Haig Dimple, Chivas Regal, Glenfiddich, Johnnie Walker Swing

SUPERIOR SCOTCH $18.00
Chivas Royal Salute 21 years

BOURBON $5.50
I.W. Harper, Jack Daniel's — Black Label, Jim Beam, Old Crow, Old Grand Dad

RYE $5.50
Canadian Club, Seagram's V.O., Crown Royal

GIN $5.50
Beefeater, Gordon's, Booth's High & Dry, Gilbey's Tanqueray

VODKA $5.50
Stolichnaya, Cossack, Smirnoff, Polish Wyborowa, Borzoi

Plus 10% Service Charge & 3% Cess

Les petites cartes

Sont classées dans cette catégorie les cartes de petit déjeuner, de petite collation, cartes pour la terrasse, pour le service en chambre, etc. Ces repas légers sont généralement pris dans une ambiance détendue, ce que le style de la carte devrait traduire. Fréquemment non conventionnelles, les solutions choisies ont un langage bien précis; par exemple, la carte du petit déjeuner apporte une sensation de fraîcheur matinale et transmet une vivacité propre à animer la journée nouvelle. Celles du bar de plage et de piscine ont avantage à être solides et résistantes à l'eau. Les cartes de menus pour enfants sont souvent conçues commes des jeux de pliage ou de coloriage, et que leur destinataire peut conserver. Pour le service en chambre, la carte doit contribuer à la création d'une atmosphère discrète et privée, donnant l'impression au client qu'il est vraiment «chez lui».

Die «kleine Karte»

In diesem Kapitel sind verschiedene «kleine Karten» aufgenommen worden: Frühstückskarte, Imbißkarte, Terrassenkarten, Karten für Schwimmbad, Zimmerservice usw. Kleine Mahlzeiten werden in einer ungezwungenen Atmosphäre eingenommen, was auch im Charakter der Karte zum Ausdruck kommen soll. Es sind oft unkonventionelle Lösungen. Die Frühstückskarte soll die Frische des Tages zeigen und lebendig wirken. Karten für Strandbar und Swimmingpool müssen solid und nässeunempfindlich sein. Kinderkarten können als Beschäftigungsspiele gestaltet werden, zum Falten, Ausmalen, zum Mitnehmen. Die Zimmerkarte muß den Eindruck erwecken, daß der Hotelgast sich in seinen eigenen vier Wänden fühlt, und eine diskrete private Atmosphäre ausstrahlen.

'Small menus'

This chapter deals with various 'small menus' such as those for breakfast, snacks, room service or use on the terrace or at the pool. Such light meals are taken in an informal atmosphere, and this should be brought out by the menu, which is often unconventional in form. A breakfast menu should have an invigorating effect, hinting at the dawn of a new day. Menus for the beach or pool must be solid and water-resistant. Children's menus should be designed with an eye to playfulness; they may have shapes that can be filled in with colour, or else be suitable for folding and taking away. Room service menus have to make the guest feel at home and convey an atmosphere of privacy and discretion.

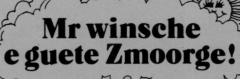

e glayne Zmoorge

1 Tasse Kaffee oder Tee oder Ovomaltine
1 Schlumbi und 1 Gipfel
(Sonntags Zopf)
10 gr Butter, 1 Confiture 2.90

e grosse Zmoorge

1 Portion Kaffee oder Tee oder Ovomaltine
1 dl Orangensaft
Gipfeli, Schwöbli, Schlumbi
(Sonntags Zopf)
Hausbrot
20 gr Butter, 2 Confituren
1 Ecke Streichkäse . . . . 5.—

e englisch Zmoorge

1 Portion Kaffee oder Tee oder Ovomaltine
1 Portion Cornflakes
2 Spiegeleier mit Speck oder Schinken
Toasts
20 gr Butter
2 Bitter-Orange Confituren 8.50

HOTEL BASEL
Postfach 581
4001 Basel
Münzgasse 12
Tel. 061/25 24 23

Diverses

Weichgekochtes Ei . . . . 1.—
2 Spiegeleier . . . . 3.—
2 Spiegeleier mit Schinken oder
Speck 4.50
Rührei 3.50
Fruchtsäfte, 1 dl
Orangen, Grapefruit, Tomaten 1.50
Joghurt nach Wahl 1.50
Schinken gekocht 50 gr 3.50
Bündnerfleisch 6.50
1 Portion Käse . . . . 3.—
1 Portion Cornflakes mit Milch
und Zucker . . . . 3.—
1 Portion Rice Crispies mit
Milch und Zucker . . . . 3.—
Birchermüsli 4.50

76   Hotel Basel, Bâle, Suisse
Carte des petits déjeuners. Création
CEM Management AG, Zurich
105 × 297 mm, ouvert 210 × 297 mm, 4
pages. Carton offset de couleur. Pages
2–3 offset noir. Laminé une face, plié
L'emploi du dialecte pour les titres
donne un air couleur locale. Séparation
entre le petit déjeuner continental et
celui à l'anglaise.

76   Hotel Basel, Basel, Schweiz
Frühstückskarte. Gestaltung CEM
Management AG, Zürich
105 × 297 mm, offen 210 × 297 mm,
4seitig. Offsetkarton farbig. Seiten 2–3
Offset schwarz. Einseitig laminiert, ge-
falzt
Lokalkolorit durch die Dialekttitel.
Unterteilung zwischen «kontinentalem»
und «englischem» Frühstück

76   Hotel Basel, Basle, Switzerland
Menu-card for breakfast. Designed by
CEM Management AG, Zurich
105 × 297 mm, open 210 × 297 mm, 4
pages. Coloured offset card. Pages
2–3: offset printing in black. Laminated
on one side, folded
Local spirit evoked by using dialect for
title-headings. Division between 'Continental' and 'English' breakfast.

76

77   Eurotel Villars, Villars-sur-Ollon, Suisse
Carte des petits déjeuners. Création et impression: Imprimerie Gerber, Steffisburg
138 × 238 mm, ouvert 276 × 238 mm, 4 pages. Carton offset jaune. Page 1 offset vert et rouge, pages 2–3 vert. Plié
Aspect d'une impression en trois couleurs grâce à l'utilisation d'un carton teinté

77   Eurotel Villars, Villars-sur-Ollon, Schweiz
Frühstückskarte. Gestaltung und Druck Gerber-Druckerei, Steffisburg
138 × 238 mm, offen 276 × 238 mm, 4seitig. Offsetkarton gelb. Offset, Seite 1 grün und rot, Seiten 2–3 grün. Gefalzt
Dreifarbige Wirkung durch Verwendung eines getönten Kartons

77   Eurotel Villars, Villars-sur-Ollon, Switzerland
Menu-card for breakfast. Designed and printed by Gerber Druckerei, Steffisburg
138 × 238 mm, open 276 × 238 mm, 4 pages. Offset printing on page 1: green and red, pages 2–3: in green. Folded
A three-coloured effect has been achieved with the use of a coloured paper.

77

Guten Morgen

Frühstück:
Kaffee, Tee oder Schokolade
mit verschiedenen Brötchen, Konfitüre, Butter
auf Verlangen: Toast, Hausbrot, Honig   7.—

Frischer Orangen- oder Grapefruitsaft	20 cl.	3.50
Tomatensaft, nature oder gewürzt	12 cl.	3.—
2 x halbe Grapefruit		3.50
Gemischtes Kompott		4.50
Früchte nach Auswahl	Stk.	1.80
Birchermüesli mit frischen Früchten		6.50
Haferflockenbrei (mit Milch oder Rahm)		5.—
Cornflakes (mit Milch oder Rahm)		4.50
Joghurt nature		2.—
Käse nach Auswahl	ab	4.50
Ein gekochtes Ei		1.80
Zwei Eier im Glas		4.—
Zwei pochierte Eier auf Toast		5.—
Zwei Spiegeleier oder Rührreier		5.—
mit Schinken, Speck oder Chipolatawürstchen		7.—
Omelette nature		6.—
Omelette mit Schinken oder Käse		7.50
Chipolatawürstchen gebraten		7.—
Speck oder Schinken grilliert		8.50
Bündnerfleisch oder Rohschinken		9.50
Schinken oder kaltes Roastbeef		9.50
Aufschnitt-Teller		9.50

SERVICE INBEGRIFFEN

78b

Bonjour

Petit déjeuner:
Café, thé ou chocolat
avec petits pains divers, confiture, beurre
sur demande: toast, pain noir, miel   7.—

Jus d'orange ou de pamplemousse frais	20 cl.	3.50
Jus de tomate, nature ou assaisonné	12 cl.	3.—
2 x un demi pamplemousse		3.50
Compote assortie		4.50
Fruits frais au choix	pièce	1.80
Coupe Dr. Bircher aux fruits frais		6.50
Porridge chaud (avec lait ou crème)		5.—
Cornflakes (avec lait ou crème)		4.50
Yogourt nature		2.—
Grand choix de fromage	dès	4.50
Un œuf à la coque		1.80
Deux œufs en verre		4.—
Deux œufs pochés sur toast		5.—
Deux œufs au plat ou brouillés		5.—
avec jambon, lard ou chipolatas		7.—
Omelette nature		6.—
Omelette au jambon ou au fromage		7.50
Chipolatas rôties		7.—
Lard ou jambon grillé		8.50
Viande séchée des Grisons ou jambon cru		9.50
Jambon ou roastbeef froid		9.50
Assiette de viande froide assortie		9.50

SERVICE COMPRIS

Good morning

Continental breakfast:
Coffee, tea or chocolate
with various rolls, marmalade, jam, butter
by request: toast, brown bread, honey   7.—

Fresh orange or grapefruit juice	20 cl.	3.50
Tomato juice	12 cl.	3.—
2 x a half grapefruit		3.50
Assorted stewed fruit		4.50
Assorted fresh fruit	piece	1.80
Swiss cold porridge with fresh fruit		6.50
Hot porridge (with milk or cream)		5.—
Cornflakes (with milk or cream)		4.50
Yogurt		2.—
Assorted cheese	from	4.50
One boiled egg		1.80
Two eggs in a glass		4.—
Two poached eggs on toast		5.—
Two fried or scrambled eggs		5.—
with ham, bacon or small veal sausages		7.—
Plain omelette		6.—
Omelette with ham or cheese		7.50
Roasted small veal sausages		7.—
Roasted ham or bacon		8.50
Air dried meat or raw ham from the Grisons		9.50
Cold ham or roastbeef		9.50
Assorted cold meat		9.50

SERVICE INCLUDED

300/2/76

78a–b Hotel Glärnischhof, Zurich, Suisse
Carte des petits déjeuners. Création Harro Lang, Zurich; impression: R. Hürlimann, Zurich
102 × 210 mm, ouvert 302 × 210 mm, 6 pages. Chromo double face. Page 1 offset 4 couleurs, pages 2–4 typo noir. Laminé deux faces, rainé deux fois, plis roulés
Présentation des mets trilingue allemand-français-anglais. Ici, c'est le petit déjeuner «continental» qui est mis en valeur – certainement pour inciter les nombreux clients britanniques à y goûter.

78a–b Hotel Glärnischhof, Zürich, Schweiz
Frühstückskarte. Gestaltung Harro Lang, Zürich, Druck R. Hürlimann, Zürich
102 × 210 mm, offen 302 × 210 mm, 6seitig. Chromokarton zweiseitig. Seite 1 Offset 4farbig, Seiten 2–4 Buchdruck schwarz. Beidseitig laminiert, 2mal gerillt, Wickelfalz
Speisenangebot 3sprachig Deutsch, Französisch, Englisch. Die Betonung liegt hier – wohl in Anbetracht der zahlreichen englischen Gäste – auf der Hervorhebung des «kontinentalen» Frühstücks.

78a–b Hotel Glärnischhof, Zurich, Switzerland
Menu-card for breakfast. Designed by Harro Lang, Zurich. Printed by R. Hürlimann, Zurich
102 × 210 mm, open 302 × 210 mm, 6 pages. Two-sided cast-coated card. Page 1: 4-colour offset printing, pages 2–4: letterpress printing in black. Laminated, on both sides, twice scored, reverse accordion fold
Menus in German, French and English. The emphasis lies on the 'Continental' breakfast, obviously with the numerous English guests in mind.

78a

79a–b Twigs, The Capitol Hilton, Washington D.C., USA
Carte des petits déjeuners. Création: Menu Promotion Ideas Inc., Clifton, New Jersey
Couverture: 139×292 mm, ouvert 278×292 mm, 4 pages. Papier structuré à la cuve. Pages 1 et 4 offset vert et brun. Rainé, plié
Intérieur: 133×286 mm, ouvert 266×286 mm, 4 pages. Papier structuré à la cuve. Reproduction texte manuscrit, impression vert et brun. Plié, collé dans la couverture
Dans les pages intérieures, le rameau (twig) se répète, mais légèrement modifié. La couleur et la calligraphie de l'intérieur créent l'unité avec la couverture.

79a–b Twigs, The Capitol Hilton, Washington, D.C., USA
Frühstückskarte. Gestaltung Menu Promotion Ideas Inc., Clifton, New Jersey
Umschlag: 139×292 mm, offen 278×292 mm, 4seitig. Büttenstrukturkarton. Seiten 1 und 4 Offset grün und braun. Gerillt, gefalzt
Innenteil: 133×286 mm, offen 266×286 mm, 4seitig. Büttenstrukturpapier. Handgeschriebene Vorlage reproduziert, Druck grün und braun. Gefalzt und im Rücken am Umschlag angeklebt
Übernahme des Zweigs (= Twig) in abgewandelter Form im Innenteil. Farbe und Kalligraphie des Innenteils schaffen die Verbindung zum Umschlag.

79a–b Twigs, The Capitol Hilton, Washington D.C., USA
Menu-card for breakfast. Designed by Menu Promotion Ideas Inc., Clifton, New Jersey
Cover: 139×292 mm, open 278×292 mm, 4 pages. Card with texture of hand-made paper. Pages 1 and 4: offset printing in green and brown. Scored, folded
Contents: 133×286 mm, open 266×286 mm, 4 pages. Paper with texture of hand-made paper. Hand-written text reproduced, print in green and brown. Folded, glued to the cover in the spine
Adoption of the 'twig' in modified form on the inside pages. Colour and calligraphy achieve the link with the cover.

79a

79b

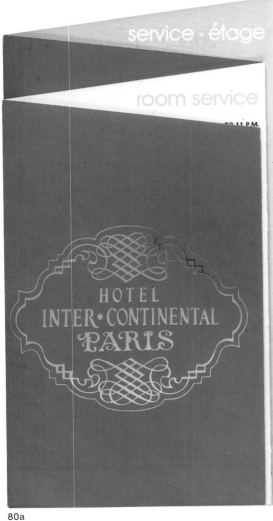

service · étage

room service

...O 11 P.M.

HOTEL
INTER·CONTINENTAL
PARIS

80a

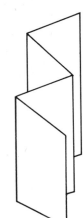

80a–b Hôtel Inter-Continental, Paris
Carte du service-étage. Création et impression: Akila-Pasquet, Pantin
125 × 245 mm, ouvert 486 × 180/245 mm, 8 pages. Chromo double face. Offset rouge et ocre, texte typo noir.

Page 1 dorure à la feuille. Rainé trois fois, plis en zigzag
Présentation des mets bilingue français-anglais. La façon «répertoire» est obtenue par la coupe en diagonale et le pliage en zigzag.

80a–b Hôtel Inter-Continental, Paris, Frankreich
Zimmerkarte. Gestaltung und Druck Akila-Pasquet, Pantin
125 × 245 mm, offen 486 × 180/245 mm, 8seitig. Chromokarton zweiseitig. Offset rot und ocker, Text

Buchdruck schwarz. Seite 1 Goldfolienprägung, 3mal gerillt, Zickzackfalz
Speisenangebot 2sprachig Französisch, Englisch. Durch den Diagonalschnitt und den Zickzackfalz entsteht der Eindruck eines Griffregisters.

80a–b Hôtel Inter-Continental, Paris, France
Room service-card. Designed and printed by Akila-Pasquet, Pantin
125 × 245 mm, open 486 × 180/245 mm, 8 pages. Two-sided cast-coated card. Offset printing in red and

ochre; text: letterpress printing in black. Gold embossing on page 1. Three times scored, accordion fold
Menus in French and English. By means of the diagonal cut and the accordion fold, a type of thumb index is realized.

service · étage

room service

SERVICE DE MIDI A 23 HEURES
Carte du Room - Service

Hors d'Oeuvres et Potages
Cocktail de Pamplemousse	16,00
Cœur de Palmier à l'Huile douce	20,00
Jambon de San Daniele	35,00
Saumon fumé avec toasts	60,00
Médaillon de foie gras	80,00
Pot de caviar Beluga (30 g)	90,00
Consommé double en tasse	16,00
Potage du Jour	15,00

Poissons
Sole meunière ou grillée	56,00
Turbot poché sauce Hollandaise	60,00

Entrées et Grillades
Volaille sautée aux morilles	60,00
Filet minute Maître d'Hôtel	56,00
Côtelettes d'agneau haricots verts	52,00
Côte de veau Bonne Maman	54,00
Hamsteak hawaïenne	36,00

Buffet froid et Sandwiches
Club sandwich	26,00
Sandwich baguette :	
Roast Beef, jambon, poulet	24,00
Assiette anglaise, salade saison	40,00
Omelettes fines herbes, champignons	28,00
Hamburger	28,00
Cheeseburger	30,00
Portion de fromage (au choix)	14,00

Desserts
Pâtisseries françaises assorties (2 pièces)	18,00
Choix de glaces et sorbets	16,00
Mignon vanille ou chocolat	16,00

Boissons
Jus d'orange frais, pamplemousse, tomate	13,00
Pot de thé avec lait ou citron	9,00
Café américain, expresso ou décaféiné	9,00

A l'heure du cocktail
Plateau de canapés (9 pièces)	92,00
(saumon fumé, foie gras, caviar)	
Plateau de petits fours secs (300 g)	66,00
Plateau de petits fours frais (300 g)	70,00
Variété de petit fritots chauds (8 pièces)	50,00
(scampis, poulet, fromage, sole)	

MENU RÉDUIT APRÈS 23 H. - CONSULTEZ LE MAITRE D'HÔTEL
SERVICE 15% NON COMPRIS

SERVED FROM 12 NOON TO 11 P.M.
Carte du Room - Service

Appetizers and Soups
Grapefruit cocktail	16,00
Hearts of Palm vinaigrette	20,00
Cured San Daniele Ham	35,00
Smoked Salmon with toast	60,00
Medaillon of foie gras	80,00
Beluga Caviar (30 g)	90,00
Double consommé	16,00
Soup of the day	15,00

Fish
Grilled or Pan fried sole	56,00
Poached turbot with Hollandaise sauce	60,00

Entrees
Sauteed chicken with morrels	60,00
Broiled minute filet steak	56,00
Grilled lamb chops with green beans	52,00
Sauteed veal cutlet with lardoons	54,00
Grilled hamsteak with pineapple	36,00

Cold buffet and Sandwiches
Club sandwich	26,00
Sandwich on french bread :	
Roast beef, ham, chicken	24,00
Assorted cold meat platter with salad	40,00
Mushroom, ham or fine herb omelette	28,00
Hamburger on a bun	28,00
Cheeseburger	30,00
Cheese (Portion)	14,00

Desserts
Assorted french pastries (2)	18,00
Choice of ice creams and sherbets	16,00
Vanilla or chocolate cream	16,00

Beverages
Grapefruit, tomato or fresh orange juice	13,00
Pot of tea with milk or lemon	9,00
American coffee, expresso or decaffeinated	9,00

At Cocktail time
Tray of canapés (9 pieces)	92,00
(smoked salmon, foie gras, caviar)	
Tray of dry petits fours (300 g)	66,00
Tray of fresh petits fours (300 g)	70,00
Selection of small hot fritters (8 pieces)	50,00
(scampis, chicken, cheese, sole)	

LIMITED MENU AFTER 11 PM - PLEASE CHECK WITH HEADWAITER
15% SERVICE CHARGE WILL BE ADDED TO YOUR CHECK.

Cartes des Vins
Wine List

	Bout.	½ Bout.
Bordeaux blanc		
Château Liot (Barsac) 73	52,00	—
Château J. Gervais (Graves) 74	45,00	24,00
Bordeaux rouges		
Côtes de Bourg 74	32,00	18,00
réserve Inter-Continental		
Château Tanesse 74	48,00	26,00
Mouton Cadet Rothschild 70	58,00	30,00
Clos des Menuts 73	64,00	34,00
(St Emilion)		
Château la Tour Carnet 73	60,00	—
(Haut Médoc)		
Château Branaire Ducru 74	100,00	50,00
(St Julien)		
Bourgognes blancs		
Meursault Blagny (Latour)	110,00	60,00
Puligny Montrachet		
« Clos du Cailleret » (DROUHIN)	120,00	70,00
Bourgognes rouges		
Mercurey (Maufoux)	80,00	45,00
Beaune 1er Cru (Drouhin)	105,00	55,00
Volnay (Maufoux)	105,00	55,00
Aloxe Corton (Latour)	115,00	65,00
Vins Divers		
Château de Selle 74	75,00	35,00
Domaine d'Ott		
Gewurztraminer 74	60,00	32,00
« Les Sorcières »	70,00	35,00
Châteauneuf du Pape		
Champagnes		
Laurent Perrier Brut S.A./N.V.	100,00	—
Moët et Chandon Imp. brut/N.V.	120,00	65,00
Mumm Cordon Rouge 71	150,00	80,00
Dom Perignon 70	280,00	—

CONSULTEZ NOTRE GRANDE CARTE DES VINS
ASK FOR OUR COMPLETE WINE LIST

Bar

(BOUTEILLE ENTIERE - FULL BOTTL

Apéritifs
Dubonnet, Noilly Prat, Martini, Cinzano	80,00
Campari	90,00
Tio Pepe, Dry Sack	85,00
Porto Sandeman Ruby	90,00

Whiskies
Bell's, White Label	120,00
Canadian Club, Seagrams V.O.	130,00
Johnny Walker Red Label, Ballantines	140,00
Jack Daniel's Black Label	220,00
Chivas Regal, Old Parr	
Johnny Walker Black Label	230,00

Rhum
Bacardi	120,00

Gins
Booth's	110,00
Beefeater, Gordon's	120,00

Vodkas
Eristow	115,00
Moskovskaya	115,00

Cognacs et liqueurs Apéritifs
Boulestin	110,00
Cointreau, Grand Marnier	120,00
Courvoisier VSOP, Rémy Martin VSOP	160,00
Armagnac	180,00
Martell Cordon Bleu	290,00
Framboise, Mirabelle	215,00

Chaque commande de bouteille entière est accompagnée de glace, de quatre bouteilles de sodas aux choix, pommes chips et amandes et noisettes salées.

Each bottle order is served with ice, a choice of 4 mixers as well as potato chips and salted nuts.

SERVICE 15% NON COMPRIS
15% SERVICE CHARGE WILL BE ADDED TO YOUR CHECK.

80b

81a

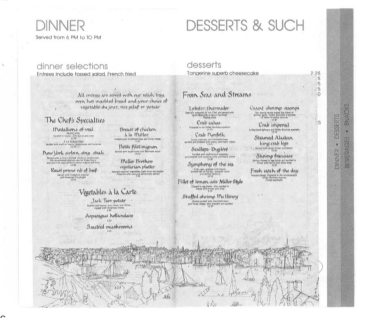

BREAKFAST
Served from 7:00 AM to 11 AM
Sat. and Sun. to Noon

The Continental
Chilled juice
**Danish pastry, muffin,
or toasted English muffin**
Butter and preserves
Coffee, tea, Sanka, milk
2.50

The All American
Choice of juice
Two eggs, any style
Hash browned potatoes
Bacon, sausage or ham
Buttered toast with preserves
Coffee, tea or milk
5.25

Country Special
Choice of juice
Six eggs, any style
Hash browned potatoes
Bacon, sausage or ham
Coffee, tea or milk
6.50

great starts
Choice of chilled juices
Orange, grapefruit, tomato and
prune juice   Sm. 1.15   Lg. 1.40
Half grapefruit   1.35
Chilled quarter melon (in season)   1.65
Fresh strawberries (in season)   1.50
Sliced bananas   1.25

cereals
Assorted cold cereals 1.50   Hot oatmeal   1.65
With fresh fruit   1.95   With cream   1.75

pastries
Toasted English muffin
with butter and preserves   1.15
Toasted bagel with butter and preserves 1.25
Toast with butter and preserves   .95
Assorted hot Danish pastry   1.35

eggs - omelettes
Served with buttered toast and preserves.
With hash browned potatoes add .75
One egg (any style)   1.50
With bacon, sausage or ham   2.75
Two eggs (any style)   2.00
With bacon, sausage or ham   3.25
Plain fluffy omelette   2.95
With bacon, sausage or ham   4.25
American or Swiss cheese omelette   3.50
Fluffy ham and cheese omelette   3.75
Western omelette   3.75

steak n' eggs
A perfectly broiled breakfast steak,
plus two eggs any style, with
hash browned potatoes and toast   6.75

the new yorker
Toasted bagel with cream cheese,
butter and marmalade
Coffee, tea or milk   2.75

french toast
With syrup and butter   2.75
With bacon, sausage or ham   add 1.25
Canadian bacon slices   add 1.50

beverages
Coffee   Tea   Sanka   Milk   75

Minimum order 1.75
Room service charge .75 per person
Gratuities not included

© 1980 DESIGN UNLIMITED, Hempstead, N.Y.

BREAKFAST · LUNCH · DINNER · DESSERTS · BEVERAGES · SNACKS

81b

DINNER
Served from 6 PM to 10 PM

DESSERTS & SUCH

dinner selections
Entrees include tossed salad, French fried

desserts
Tangerine superb cheesecake   2.25

DINNER · DESSERTS · BEVERAGES · SNACKS

81c

81a–c The Baltimore Hilton Hotel,
Baltimore, Maryland, USA
Carte du service-étage. Création: Design Unlimited/Culinary Concepts,
Hempstead, New York
Couverture: 127×217 mm, ouvert
254×217 mm, 4 pages. Chromo une
face argent. Sérigraphie blanc et bleu,
pages 2–3 offset bleu clair et bleu
foncé
Intérieur: 125×217 mm, ouvert
250×217 mm, 8 pages. Papier offset.
Offset bleu clair et bleu foncé. Plié et
agrafé deux fois dans le pli avec la
couverture
Les pages sont pliées de façon asy-
métrique, en forme de répertoire. Une
carte de menu au format réduit
(100×170 mm) des restaurants Miller
Brothers est agrafée au centre.

81a–c The Baltimore Hilton Hotel,
Baltimore, Maryland, USA
Zimmerkarte. Gestaltung Design Un-
limited/Culinary Concepts, Hempstead, New York
Umschlag: 127×217 mm, offen
254×217 mm, 4seitig. Chromokarton
einseitig silber. Siebdruck weiß und
blau, Seiten 2–3 Offset hell- und dunkelblau
Innenteil: 125×217 mm, offen
250×217 mm, 8seitig. Offsetpapier.
Offset hell- und dunkelblau. Gefalzt
und mit dem Umschlag 2mal drahtgeheftet
Die Seiten sind asymmetrisch gefalzt,
so daß ein Griffregister entsteht. In der
Mitte ist eine verkleinerte Menukarte
des Restaurants Miller Brothers im Format 100×170 mm miteingeheftet.

81a–c The Baltimore Hilton Hotel,
Baltimore, Maryland, USA
Room service-card. Designed by
Design Unlimited/Culinary Concepts,
Hempstead, New York
Cover: 127×217 mm, open
254×217 mm, 4 pages. One-sided
cast-coated card in silver. Silk-screen
printing in white and blue, pages 2–3:
offset printing in pale blue and dark
blue
Contents: 125×217 mm, open
250×217 mm, 8 pages. Offset paper.
Offset printing in pale blue and dark
blue. Folded, 2-wire stitched to the
cover
The pages are folded off-centre, thus
creating a thumb index. A reduced
menu-card from the Miller Brothers'
restaurant, size 100×170 mm, is attached in the centre.

Room Service Menu

82

82   Hotel Lanka Oberoi, Colombo, Sri Lanka
Carte du service-étage. Création Dale Keller & Associates Ltd., Hong Kong
Couverture: 293×126 mm, ouvert 293×252 mm, 4 pages. Chromo mat. Pages 1 et 4 offset noir et orange. Page 3 impression typo orange. Laqué, plié, estampé

Intérieur: 293×126 mm, ouvert 293×252 mm, 10 pages. Papier offset. Impression typo orange et noir. Plié, estampé en répertoire, pages 9 et 10 collées dans le pli sur page 8, agrafé deux fois dans le pli avec la couverture Carte au format horizontal dont l'intérieur est uniquement typographique.

82   Hotel Lanka Oberoi, Colombo, Sri Lanka
Zimmerkarte. Gestaltung Dale Keller & Associates Ltd., Hongkong
Umschlag: 293×126 mm, offen 293×252 mm, 4seitig. Matter Chromokarton. Seiten 1 und 4 Offset schwarz und orange. Seite 3 Buchdruck orange. Lackiert, gefalzt, formgestanzt

Innenteil: 293×126 mm, offen 293×252 mm, 10seitig. Offsetpapier. Buchdruck orange und schwarz. Gefalzt, formgestanzt mit Griffregister, Seiten 9 und 10 auf Seite 8 angefälzelt, mit dem Umschlag 2mal drahtgeheftet Horizontale Karte mit rein typographischer Lösung im Innenteil

82   Hotel Lanka Oberoi, Colombo, Sri Lanka
Room service-card. Designed by Dale Keller & Associates Ltd., Hong Kong
Cover: 293×126 mm, open 293×252 mm, 4 pages. Cast-coated card with matt finish. Pages 1 and 4: offset printing in black and orange. Page 3: letterpress printing in orange. Varnished, folded, die-cut

Contents: 293×126 mm, open 293×252 mm, 10 pages. Offset paper. Letterpress printing in orange and black. Folded, die-cut with thumb index, pages 9 and 10 joined on to page 8, 2-wire stitched to the cover Horizontal card with purely typographical solution on the inside pages.

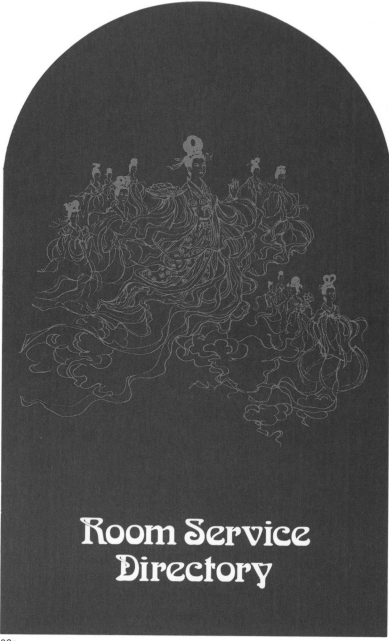

Room Service
Directory

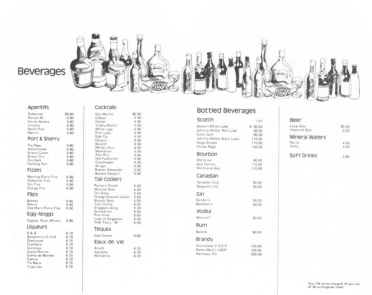

Beverages

83b

83a

83a–b   The Mandarin, Singapour
Carte du service-étage. Création: Overseas Union Advertising
Couverture: 176 × 300 mm, ouvert 352 × 300 mm, 4 pages. Chromo mat double face. Pages 1, 3 et 4 offset brun-rouge. Page 1 dorure à la feuille. Laminé, rainé, plié, estampé
Intérieur: 176 × 300 mm, ouvert 352 × 300 mm, 8 pages. Papier offset gaufré. Offset brun-rouge. Plié et agrafé deux fois dans le pli avec la couverture
A l'intérieur ni le style de l'illustration ni le caractère de l'écriture ne sont repris. Mais la couleur d'impression et la forme d'estampage sont d'importants éléments d'harmonisation.

83a–b   The Mandarin, Singapur
Zimmerkarte. Gestaltung Overseas Union Advertising
Umschlag: 176 × 300 mm, offen 352 × 300 mm, 4seitig. Matter Chromokarton zweiseitig. Seiten 1, 3 und 4 Offset rotbraun. Seite 1 Goldfolienprägung. Laminiert, gerillt, gefalzt, formgestanzt
Innenteil: 176 × 300 mm, offen 352 × 300 mm, 8seitig. Offsetpapier geprägt. Offset rotbraun. Gefalzt und mit dem Umschlag 2mal drahtgeheftet, formgestanzt
Weder der Stil der Illustration noch die Schrift sind im Innenteil übernommen; Druckfarbe und Stanzform bilden aber starke verbindende Elemente.

83a–b   The Mandarin, Singapore
Room service-card. Designed by Overseas Union Advertising
Cover: 176 × 300 mm, open 352 × 300 mm, 4 pages. Two-sided cast-coated card with matt finish. Pages 1, 3 and 4: offset printing in russet. Page 1: gold embossing. Laminated, scored, folded, die-cut
Contents: 176 × 300 mm, open 352 × 300 mm, 8 pages. Embossed offset paper. Offset printing in russet. Folded, 2-wire stitched to the cover and die-cut
Neither style of illustration nor lettering have been adopted on the inside pages; colour of printing and the cutting-die, however, form unifying elements.

84a–b Camellia Corner, Hotel Okura, Tokyo, Japon
Carte de menu
Couverture: 220×310 mm, ouvert 440×310 mm, 4 pages. Carton de boîte pliante. Sérigraphie. Dorure à la feuille, laminage grain. Rainé, plié
Intérieur: 220×310 mm, ouvert 650×310 mm, 6 pages. Papier structuré à la cuve. Offset vert olive. Rainé deux fois, plis roulés, agrafé deux fois dans le pli avec la couverture. 4 paires de pinces en plastique pour insérer le menu du jour
Présentation des mets bilingue japonais-anglais. Sur la première page intérieure, reprise du motif de couverture en impression une couleur. Les pinces en plastique sont pratiques mais laissent de profondes marques au revers du papier lorsqu'il est tendre.

84a–b Camellia Corner, Hotel Okura, Tokio, Japan
Speisekarte
Umschlag: 220×310 mm, offen 440×310 mm, 4seitig. Faltschachtelkarton. Siebdruck. Goldfolienprägung, Prägelaminierung. Gerillt, gefalzt
Innenteil: 220×310 mm, offen 650×310 mm, 6seitig. Papier mit Büttenstruktur. Offset olivegrün. 2mal gerillt, Wickelfalz, mit dem Umschlag 2mal drahtgeheftet. 4 Paar Kunststoffklemmen zum Einschieben der Tagesmenus
Speisenangebot 2sprachig Japanisch, Englisch. Übernahme des Umschlagmotivs als einfarbige Reproduktion auf der ersten Innenseite. Die Kunststoffklemmen sind praktisch, hinterlassen aber bei weichen Papieren tiefe Eindrücke auf der Gegenseite.

84a–b Camellia Corner, Hotel Okura, Tokyo, Japan
Menu-card
Cover: 200×310 mm, open 440×310 mm, 4 pages. Folding-box card. Silk-screen printing. Gold embossing, laminated with embossing. Scored, folded
Contents: 220×310 mm, open 650×310 mm, 6 pages. Paper with texture of hand-made paper. Offset printing in olive-green. Twice scored, reverse accordion fold, 2-wire stitched to the cover. 4 pairs of plastic paper-clips to insert the 'Menu of the Day' cards
Menus in Japanese and English. On the first inside page: adoption of the cover motif reproduced in monochrome. The plastic paper-clips are practical, but leave deep marks on the reverse of the soft paper.

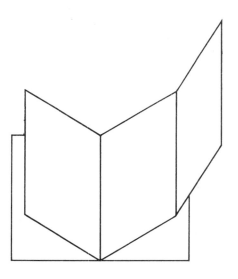

84a

84b

85b

85a–b Café in the Park, Century Park Sheraton, Manille, Philippines
Carte de menu. Création: Eric David
175 × 382 mm, ouvert 530 × 382 mm, 6 pages. Carton de boîte pliante. Impression typo. Pages 1 et 5 8 couleurs, pages 2–4 3 couleurs. Laminé deux faces, rainé, plis roulés
Reprise du motif de couverture en négatif sur les pages intérieures. De brèves descriptions des différents mets facilitent le choix.

85a–b Café in the Park, Century Park Sheraton, Manila, Philippinen
Speisekarte. Gestaltung Eric David
175 × 382 mm, offen 530 × 382 mm, 6seitig. Faltschachtelkarton. Buchdruck Seiten 1 und 5 8farbig, Seiten 2–4 3farbig. Beidseitig laminiert, gerillt, Wickelfalz
Übernahme des Umschlagmotivs negativ auf den Innenseiten. Kurze Beschreibungen der einzelnen Gerichte helfen bei der Auswahl.

85a–b Café in the Park, Century Park Sheraton, Manila, The Philippines
Menu-card. Designed by Eric David
175 × 382 mm, open 530 × 382 mm, 6 pages. Foldingbox card. Letterpress printing on page 1 and 5: in 8 colours, on pages 2–4: in 3 colours. Laminated on both sides, scored, rerverse accordion fold
Adoption of the negative cover motif on the inside pages. Short description of the individual dishes assist one's choice.

85a

86 Café Tuileries, Hôtel Inter-Continental, Paris
Cartes des petits déjeuners. Création et impression: Akila-Pasquet, Pantin
160 × 220 mm, ouvert 320 × 220 mm, 4 pages. Carton offset couleur. Offset brun, rouge et jaune. Laminé deux faces, plié
Présentation des mets bilingue français-anglais. Petite carte conçue avec goût sans effet de décoration particulier.

86 Café Tuileries, Hotel Inter-Continental, Paris, Frankreich
Frühstückskarte. Gestaltung und Druck Akila-Pasquet, Pantin
160 × 220 mm, offen 320 × 220 mm, 4seitig. Offsetkarton farbig. Offset braun, rot, gelb. Beidseitig laminiert, gefalzt
Speisenangebot 2sprachig Französisch, Englisch. Kleine, geschmackvoll konzipierte Karte ohne besondere Gestaltungselemente

86 Café Tuileries, Hotel Inter-Continental, Paris, France
Menu-card for breakfast. Designed and printed by Akila-Pasquet, Pantin
160 × 220 mm, open 320 × 220 mm, 4 pages. Coloured offset card. Offset printing in brown, red and yellow. Laminated on both sides, folded
Menus in French and English. Small, tastefully conceived card without special design elements.

86

87 Sivalai, Siam Inter-Continental, Bangkok, Thaïlande
Carte de menu. Création: Wittle Gouvain & Associate, Bangkok
215×320 mm, ouvert 430×320 mm, 4 pages. Chromo double face. Pages 1 et 4 sérigraphie bleu, pages 2–3 offset bleu, vert, rouge et or. Laminé deux faces
Comme le démontre le grand choix de plats étrangers, cette carte est entièrement basée sur une clientèle touristique internationale.

87 Sivalai, Siam Inter-Continental, Bangkok, Thailand
Speisekarte. Gestaltung Wittle Gouvain & Associate, Bangkok
215×320 mm, offen 430×320 mm, 4seitig. Chromokarton zweiseitig. Seiten 1 und 4 Siebdruck blau, Seiten 2–3 Offset blau, grün, rot, gold. Zweiseitig laminiert
Diese Speisekarte ist ganz auf ein internationales Reisepublikum angelegt, wie die vielen für Thailand eigentlich fremden Gerichte deutlich machen.

87 Sivalai, Siam Inter-Continental, Bangkok, Thailand
Menu-card. Designed by Wittle Gouvain & Associate, Bangkok
215×320 mm, open 430×320 mm, 4 pages. Two-sided cast-coated card. Pages 1 and 4: silk-screen printing in blue, pages 2–3: offset printing in blue, green, red and gold. Laminated on both sides
This menu-card is aimed at the international traveller, a fact which is emphasized by the selection of dishes which, strictly speaking, are foreign to Thailand.

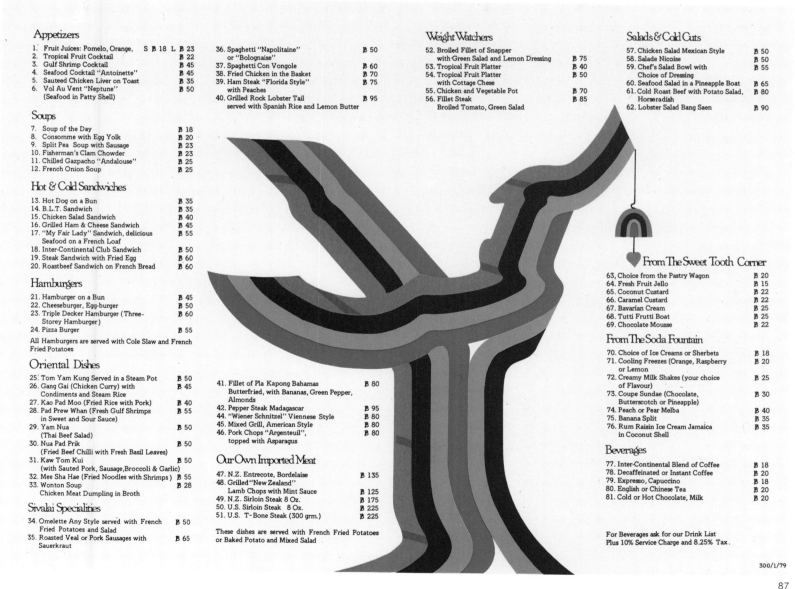

Appetizers

1. Fruit Juices: Pomelo, Orange, S ฿ 18 L ฿ 23
2. Tropical Fruit Cocktail ฿ 22
3. Gulf Shrimp Cocktail ฿ 45
4. Seafood Cocktail "Antoinette" ฿ 45
5. Sauteed Chicken Liver on Toast ฿ 35
6. Vol Au Vent "Neptune" ฿ 50
   (Seafood in Patty Shell)

Soups

7. Soup of the Day ฿ 18
8. Consomme with Egg Yolk ฿ 20
9. Split Pea Soup with Sausage ฿ 23
10. Fisherman's Clam Chowder ฿ 23
11. Chilled Gazpacho "Andalouse" ฿ 25
12. French Onion Soup ฿ 25

Hot & Cold Sandwiches

13. Hot Dog on a Bun ฿ 35
14. B.L.T. Sandwich ฿ 35
15. Chicken Salad Sandwich ฿ 40
16. Grilled Ham & Cheese Sandwich ฿ 45
17. "My Fair Lady" Sandwich, delicious ฿ 55
    Seafood on a French Loaf
18. Inter-Continental Club Sandwich ฿ 50
19. Steak Sandwich with Fried Egg ฿ 60
20. Roastbeef Sandwich on French Bread ฿ 60

Hamburgers

21. Hamburger on a Bun ฿ 45
22. Cheeseburger, Egg-burger ฿ 50
23. Triple Decker Hamburger (Three- ฿ 60
    Storey Hamburger)
24. Pizza Burger ฿ 55

All Hamburgers are served with Cole Slaw and French Fried Potatoes

Oriental Dishes

25. Tom Yam Kung Served in a Steam Pot ฿ 50
26. Gang Gai (Chicken Curry) with ฿ 45
    Condiments and Steam Rice
27. Kao Pad Moo (Fried Rice with Pork) ฿ 40
28. Pad Prew Whan (Fresh Gulf Shrimps ฿ 55
    in Sweet and Sour Sauce)
29. Yam Nua ฿ 50
    (Thai Beef Salad)
30. Nua Pad Prik ฿ 50
    (Fried Beef Chilli with Fresh Basil Leaves)
31. Kaw Tom Kui ฿ 50
    (with Sauted Pork, Sausage, Broccoli & Garlic)
32. Mee Sha Hae (Fried Noodles with Shrimps) ฿ 55
33. Wonton Soup ฿ 28
    Chicken Meat Dumpling in Broth

Sivalai Specialities

34. Omelette Any Style served with French ฿ 50
    Fried Potatoes and Salad
35. Roasted Veal or Pork Sausages with ฿ 65
    Sauerkraut

36. Spaghetti "Napolitaine" ฿ 50
    or "Bolognaise"
37. Spaghetti Con Vongole ฿ 60
38. Fried Chicken in the Basket ฿ 70
39. Ham Steak "Florida Style" ฿ 75
    with Peaches
40. Grilled Rock Lobster Tail ฿ 95
    served with Spanish Rice and Lemon Butter

41. Fillet of Pla Kapong Bahamas ฿ 80
    Butterfried, with Bananas, Green Pepper,
    Almonds
42. Pepper Steak Madagascar ฿ 95
44. "Wiener Schnitzel" Viennese Style ฿ 80
45. Mixed Grill, American Style ฿ 80
46. Pork Chops "Argenteuil", ฿ 80
    topped with Asparagus

Our Own Imported Meat

47. N.Z. Entrecote, Bordelaise ฿ 135
48. Grilled "New Zealand" ฿ 125
    Lamb Chops with Mint Sauce
49. N.Z. Sirloin Steak 8 Oz. ฿ 175
50. U.S. Sirloin Steak 8 Oz. ฿ 225
51. U.S. T-Bone Steak (300 grm.) ฿ 225

These dishes are served with French Fried Potatoes or Baked Potato and Mixed Salad

Weight Watchers

52. Broiled Fillet of Snapper ฿ 75
    with Green Salad and Lemon Dressing
53. Tropical Fruit Platter ฿ 40
54. Tropical Fruit Platter ฿ 50
    with Cottage Chese
55. Chicken and Vegetable Pot ฿ 70
56. Fillet Steak ฿ 85
    Broiled Tomato, Green Salad

Salads & Cold Cuts

57. Chicken Salad Mexican Style ฿ 50
58. Salade Nicoise ฿ 50
59. Chef's Salad Bowl with ฿ 55
    Choice of Dressing
60. Seafood Salad in a Pineapple Boat ฿ 65
61. Cold Roast Beef with Potato Salad, ฿ 80
    Horseradish
62. Lobster Salad Bang Saen ฿ 90

From The Sweet Tooth Corner

63. Choice from the Pastry Wagon ฿ 20
64. Fresh Fruit Jello ฿ 15
65. Coconut Custard ฿ 22
66. Caramel Custard ฿ 22
67. Bavarian Cream ฿ 25
68. Tutti Frutti Boat ฿ 25
69. Chocolate Mousse ฿ 22

From The Soda Fountain

70. Choice of Ice Creams or Sherbets ฿ 18
71. Cooling Freezes (Orange, Raspberry ฿ 20
    or Lemon
72. Creamy Milk Shakes (your choice ฿ 25
    of Flavour)
73. Coupe Sundae (Chocolate, ฿ 30
    Butterscotch or Pineapple)
74. Peach or Pear Melba ฿ 40
75. Banana Split ฿ 35
76. Rum Raisin Ice Cream Jamaica ฿ 35
    in Coconut Shell

Beverages

77. Inter-Continental Blend of Coffee ฿ 18
78. Decaffeinated or Instant Coffee ฿ 20
79. Expresso, Capuccino ฿ 18
80. English or Chinese Tea ฿ 20
81. Cold or Hot Chocolate, Milk ฿ 20

For Beverages ask for our Drink List
Plus 10% Service Charge and 8.25% Tax.

300/1/79

87

88 La Pâtisserie, Kuwait Hilton, Koweït
Carte de table du Coffee-Shop (coin cafés). Création:
Impact Advertising Company, Chypre
180×165 mm, ouvert 180×430 mm, 4 pages plus
2 rabats. Chromo une face. Pages 1 et 4 offset 4
couleurs. Rainé trois fois, estampé
Les deux rabats se plient et se fixent, formant ainsi une
carte de table bien stable. Le texte est bilingue anglais-arabe.

88 La Pâtisserie, Kuwait Hilton, Kuwait
Aufsteller als Hinweis für den Coffee-Shop. Gestaltung
Impact Advertising Company, Zypern
180×165 mm, offen 180×430 mm, 4seitig und 2 Klappen. Chromokarton einseitig. Seiten 1 und 4 Offset
4farbig. 3mal gerillt, gestanzt
Durch Falten und Zusammenstecken der beiden Klappen entsteht ein solider Aufsteller. Text 2sprachig
Englisch, Arabisch

88 La Pâtisserie, Kuwait Hilton, Kuwait
Sign refers to the Coffee-Shop. Designed by Impact
Advertising Company, Cyprus
180×165 mm, open 180×430 mm, 4 pages plus 2
flaps. One-sided cast-coated card. Pages 1 and 4:
4-colour offset printing. Three times scored, die-cut
When folded and assembled, the menu-card becomes
rigid and stands upright on its own. Menus in English
and Arabic.

88

89a

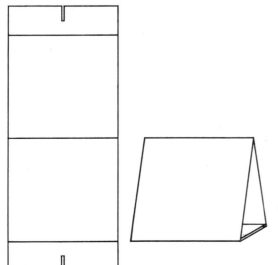

BEVERAGES			المشـروبـات
CAFE VIENNESE MELANGE with chantilly	400	٤٠٠	قهـوة نمـاوية مـع كريم شـانتي
FILTER COFFEE WITH CREAM	350	٣٥٠	قهـوة متطرة مـع الكريما
EXPRESSO	400	٤٠٠	قهـوة إكسبرسو
TEA WITH MILK or LEMON	350	٣٥٠	شـاي مع الحليـب أو الليمون
POT OF HOT CHOCOLATE	400	٤٠٠	شـوكولاتـه سـاخنة
TURKISH COFFEE	350	٣٥٠	قهـوة تركية
CAPPUCCINO	400	٤٠٠	كـبوتشـينو
SOFT DRINKS			**المـرطبـات**
MINERAL WATER	600	٦٠٠	مياه معدنية
PEPSI-COLA or 7UP	300	٣٠٠	بيبسي كولا أو سـفن أب
FRUIT JUICE LARGE	500	٥٠٠	عصير فواكه ، جمـد كبير

89b

89a–b   La Pâtisserie, Kuwait Hilton, Koweït
89a–b   La Pâtisserie, Kuwait Hilton, Koweït
Carte des consommations. Création et impression:
Impact Advertising Company, Chypre
Couverture: 165×205 mm, ouvert 230×205 mm,
4 pages. Chromo une face. Pages 1 et 4 offset 4 couleurs et or, pages 2–3 offset jaune, rouge et brun. Plié
Intérieur: 165×205 mm, ouvert 230×205 mm,
8 pages. Papier couché mat. Offset jaune, rouge et
brun. Plié et cousu à la couverture
Présentation des mets bilingue anglais-arabe. En
fonction du sens de la lecture, la carte se divise en
deux parties; la première partie est en anglais, la
seconde en arabe.

89a–b   La Pâtisserie, Kuwait Hilton, Kuwait
Getränkekarte. Gestaltung und Druck Impact Advertising Company, Zypern
Umschlag: 165×205 mm, offen 230×205 mm, 4seitig.
Chromokarton einseitig. Seiten 1 und 4 Offset 4farbig
und gold, Seiten 2–3 gelb, rot, braun. Gefalzt
Innenteil: 165×205 mm, offen 230×205 mm, 8seitig.
Mattes Kunstdruckpapier. Offset gelb, rot, braun. Gefalzt und mit dem Umschlag fadengeheftet
Speisenangebot 2sprachig Englisch, Arabisch. Entsprechend den Leserichtungen zerfällt die Karte in
zwei Teile, der erste Teil ist englisch, der zweite arabisch.

89a–b   La Pâtisserie, Kuwait Hilton, Kuwait
Menu-card. Designed by Impact Advertising Company, Cyprus
Cover: 165×205 mm, open 230×205 mm, 4 pages.
One-sided cast-coated card. Pages 1 and 4: 4-colour
offset printing plus gold, pages 2–3: printing in yellow,
red and brown. Folded
Contents: 165×205 mm, open 230×205 mm, 8 pages.
Art paper with matt finish. Offset printing in yellow, red
and brown. Folded, thread-sewn to the cover
Menus in English and Arabic. As the direction of reading is taken into consideration, the card falls into two
parts: the first in English and the second in Arabic.

90   L'Apéro, Les Quatre Saisons, Montréal, Canada
Carte de menu. Création et impression: Houston Press
Co. Ltd., Lachine, Québec
97×203 mm, 2 pages. Papier à la cuve. Page 1 offset
brun et noir
Le papier soigneusement choisi et l'impression
soignée font toute l'élégance de cette petite carte.

90   L'Apéro, Les Quatre Saisons, Montreal, Kanada
Speisekarte. Gestaltung und Druck Houston Press Co.
Ltd., Lachine, Quebec
97×203 mm, 2seitig. Büttenpapier. Seite 1 Offset
braun und schwarz
Ein besonders ausgesuchtes Papier und die sorgfäl-
tige Typographie geben dieser kleinen Karte eine elegante Note.

90   L'Apéro, Les Quatre Saisons, Montréal, Canada
Menu-card. Designed and printed by Houston Press
Co. Ltd., Lachine, Quebec
97×203 mm, 2 pages. Hand-made paper. Page 1: offset printing in brown and black
Attractive paper and careful typography give the card
its elegant touch.

90

L'APÉRO

Repas légers servis de midi à 15 hrs.
Light luncheon from noon to 3 p.m.

POTAGE DU JOUR
Soup of the day

ou/or

VICHYSSOISE FRAPPÉE
Chilled Vichyssoise

* * *

QUICHE LORRAINE   4.75

CANAPÉS AU CHOIX (3 PIÈCES)
Choice of Canapés (3 pieces)   4.50

ASSIETTE DE CREVETTES
DE MATANE
Matane Shrimp Salad   6.25

PLAT DU JOUR GARNI
Special of the Day Garnished   5.50

* * *

CAFÉ
Coffee

* * *

PÂTISSERIES ET GÂTEAUX
DU CHARIOT
Pastries and Cakes from
the Wagon   1.75

200/9/79

91a

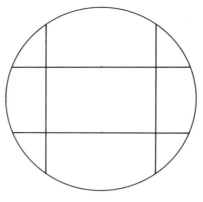

91a–b Paparazzi, New York, N.Y., USA
Carte des crêpes. Création: Design
Unlimited/Culinary Concepts, Hempstead, New York
205×120 mm, ⌀ 354 mm, 2 pages. Carton offset légèrement jaunâtre. Offset
jaune, rouge et brun. Estampé, rainé,
plis croisés

91a–b Paparazzi, New York, N.Y.,
USA
Crêpe-Karte. Gestaltung Design Un-
limited/Culinary Concepts, Hempstead, New York
205×120 mm, ⌀ 354 mm, 2seitig. Offsetkarton leicht gelblich. Offset gelb,
rot, braun. Formgestanzt, gerillt, Kreuz-
bruchfalz

91a–b Paparazzi, New York, N.Y., USA
Crêpe card. Designed by Design Un-
limited/Culinary Concepts, Hempstead, New York
205×120 mm, ⌀ 354 mm, 2 pages. Offset card with yellowish tinge. Offset
printing in yellow, red and brown. Die-
cut, scored, right-angle fold

91b

92a–b Tangerine, The Baltimore Hilton, Baltimore, Maryland, USA
Carte de lunch. Création Design Unlimited/Culinary Concepts, Hempstead, New York
215 × 352 mm, ouvert 430 × 352 mm, 4 pages. Carton offset. Offset bleu, rouge et orange. Soudé sous thermo rétractable.
Il existe également une carte pour le dîner. Différenciation et harmonie sont obtenues grâce à un autre format et à une autre disposition des mêmes éléments graphiques. En page 1, sous l'inscription, le symbole extrême-oriental pour «Tangerine», la mandarine.

92b

92a–b Tangerine, The Baltimore Hilton, Baltimore, Maryland, USA
Lunch-Karte. Gestaltung Design Unlimited/Culinary Concepts, Hempstead, New York
215 × 352 mm, offen 430 × 352 mm, 4seitig. Offsetkarton. Offset blau, rot, orange. Eingeschweißt
Es existiert auch eine Dinner-Karte. Differenzierung und Zusammenhang werden durch ein anderes Format und andere Anordnung der gleichen grafischen Elemente erreicht. Das fernöstliche Symbol für Tangerine = Mandarine erscheint unter dem Schriftzug auf Seite 1.

92a–b Tangerine, The Baltimore Hilton, Baltimore, Maryland, USA
Menu-card for lunch. Designed by Design Unlimited/ Culinary Concepts, Hempstead, New York
215 × 352 mm, open 430 × 352 mm, 4 pages. Offset card. Offset printing in blue, red and orange. Shrink-wrapped
There is also a menu-card for dinner. Distinctiveness and association are arrived at by means of both different size and layout of the same graphic elements. The Far Eastern symbol for tangerine (= mandarine) appears beneath the lettering on page 1.

92a

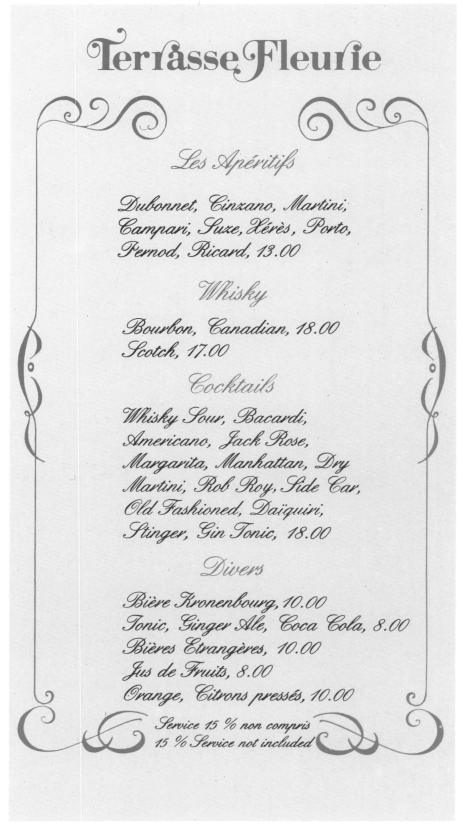

Terrasse Fleurie

Les Apéritifs

Dubonnet, Cinzano, Martini,
Campari, Suze, Xérès, Porto,
Pernod, Ricard, 13.00

Whisky

Bourbon, Canadian, 18.00
Scotch, 17.00

Cocktails

Whisky Sour, Bacardi,
Americano, Jack Rose,
Margarita, Manhattan, Dry
Martini, Rob Roy, Side Car,
Old Fashioned, Daïquiri,
Stinger, Gin Tonic, 18.00

Divers

Bière Kronenbourg, 10.00
Tonic, Ginger Ale, Coca Cola, 8.00
Bières Etrangères, 10.00
Jus de Fruits, 8.00
Orange, Citrons pressés, 10.00

Service 15 % non compris
15 % Service not included

93

93   Terrasse Fleurie, Hôtel Inter-Continental, Paris
Carte des desserts et des consommations. Création et impression: Akila-Pasquet. Pantin
120×230 mm, 2 pages. Chromo double face. Typo 2 couleurs. Laminé deux faces
Exemple de carte élégante et personnelle créée avec un minimum de frais. Cette solution présuppose chez le créateur un art consommé de la typographie et du trait.

93   Terrasse Fleurie, Hôtel Inter-Continental, Paris, Frankreich
Dessert- und Getränkekarte. Gestaltung und Druck Akila-Pasquet, Pantin
120×230 mm, 2seitig Chromokarton zweiseitig. Buchdruck 2farbig. Beidseitig laminiert
Ein Musterbeispiel dafür, wie mit wenig Aufwand eine elegante und persönliche Karte geschaffen werden kann. Diese Lösung verlangt vom Gestalter große Sicherheit in der Behandlung von Schrift und Typografie.

93   Terrasse Fleurie, Hôtel Inter-Continental, Paris, France
Dessert card and wine list. Designed and printed by Akila-Pasquet, Pantin
120×230 mm, 2 pages. Two-sided cast-coated card. Two-coloured letterpress printing. Laminated on both sides
A perfect example of the production of a very elegant and personal card without incurring great expenditure. This solution requires great skill by the designer in the treatment of lettering and typography.

94a–b   Coffee Shop, Kuwait-Sheraton Hotel, Koweït ▷
Carte de menu. Création: Susan Fitze, Zurich
210×397 mm, ouvert 627×397 mm, 6 pages. Newschromo double face. Offset 4 couleurs et couleur spéciale, texte en brun. Laminé, rainé 2 fois, plis roulés
Présentation des mets bilingue anglais-arabe. Cette carte est parfaitement lisible malgré la riche et débordante illustration. Les espaces libres contribuent à une typographie claire et rationnelle.

94a–b   Coffee Shop, Kuwait-Sheraton Hotel, Kuwait
Speisekarte. Gestaltung Susan Fitze, Zürich
210×397 mm, offen 627×397 mm, 6seitig. Newschromo zweiseitig. Offset 4farbig und Sonderfarbe, Texteindruck braun. Laminiert, 2mal gerillt, Wickelfalz
Speisenfolge 2sprachig Englisch, Arabisch. Trotz der Überfülle an Illustration ist die Karte gut durchorganisiert. Die ausgesparten Flächen reichen für eine straffe und klare Typografie.

94a–b   Coffee Shop, Kuwait-Sheraton Hotel, Kuwait
Menu-card. Designed by Susan Fitze, Zurich
210×397 mm, open 627×397 mm, 6 pages. Two-sided super-calendered paper. Four-colour offset printing plus additional colour, text overprinted in brown. Laminated, twice scored, reverse accordion fold
Menus in English and Arabic. Despite its abundance of illustrations, this card has been realized in a flawless manner. The remaining blank spaces permit a rigid and clear typography.

APPETIZERS المقبلات

COLD باردة

001	Fresh Grapefruit Cocktail	0.600
002	Marinated Greenland Salmon «Gravad Laks»	1.500
003	Hummos	0.600
004	Mutabal	0.600
005	Home made liver Pate	0.750
006	Shrimp Cocktail	1.250
007	Fresh Vegetables a la grecque	0.750

HOT ساخنة

011	Seafood Pancake	1.250
012	Chicken and Mushroom Puff Pastry	1.250
013	Quiche Lorraine	1.000
014	Meat and Cheese Sambussek	0.750
015	Creamed Fresh Mushroom on toast	1.000

SOUPS الشوربات

021	Soup of the day	0.600
022	Onion Soup	0.600
023	Arabic Lentil Soup	0.600
024	Filippino Molo Soup	0.600
	Shrimps, Noodles, Chicken, onion and celery	
025	Leberknödel Soup	0.600
	Austrian Soup with liver dumpling	

SEA FOOD مأكولات بحرية

041	Grilled Hamour	2.000
042	Grilled Shrimps	2.250
043	Fried Shrimps	2.250
044	Filet of Zubeidi Belle Meuniere	2.250
045	Shrimp Curry with condiments	2.250

All the above dishes are served with French Fried Potatoes or Buttered Rice

FRENCH SANDWICH BOARD سندويشات على الطريقة الفرنسية

All Sandwiches are prepared on Home made French Bread, served with French Fried Potatoes, Cole slaw and Fresh Onions

031	Roast Beef	1.250
032	Delicatessen Beef	1.250
033	Chicken	1.250
034	Tuna Fish	1.250
035	Salami	1.250
036	Mortadella	1.250
037	Cheese	1.250

LIGHTMEALS وجبات خفيفة

HOT ساخن

051	Green Noodles with Mushroom and meat sauce	1.500
052	Omelette of your choice	1.300
053	Beef Burger with cole slaw and French Fries	1.400
054	Cheese or Egg Burger with cole slaw and French Fries	1.500

COLD باردة

055	Rice Salad Romaine Style	1.250
	Rice, Anchovies, olives, Polish Beef, seasoned with herbs, oil and vinegar	
056	Gourmet Salad	1.250
	Chicken, green pepper, celery, tomato, cucumber, chicory, green beans and swiss cheese, seasoned with oil and vinegar dressing	
057	Chicken Salad	1.500
	Chunks of white chicken, sliced apples mixed with spicy mayonnaise dressing, garnished with egg, tomato and asparagus spears	
058	Cold Meat Platter	1.500
	Roast beef, chicken, delicatessen beef and cheese garnished with fresh salads	
059	Small-Mixed Salad	0.400
	seasonal vegetables with french dressing	

BEEF البقر

061	Hungarian Beef Goulash	2.000
	Chunks of U.S. Beef cooked in a rich meat sauce with paprika	
062	Beef Tenderloin Continental	3.000
	Prime American beef tenderloin served with grilled mushrooms, tomato, and French Fried Potatoes	
063	Sirloin Steak Tyrolienne	3.250
	Cut from prime american beef, served with onion, parsley, tomato and garlic sauce	

VEAL العجل

066	Escalope Viennoise	2.750
067	Veal Kebab with onions and mushrooms	3.000

LAMB الغنم

071	The traditional Irish Stew	2.250
072	Lamb Curry Madras Style	2.250

CHICKEN الدجاج

076	Chicken Mexicaine	2.000
077	Chicken Kebab	2.250

ORIENTAL DISHES أطباق شرقية

081	Lamb Shish Kebab	2.750
	Grilled American Lamb meat, served with raw onions, green pepper, tomato and arabic rice	
082	Kufta Halabia	2.000
	Grilled Spicy Ground Meat, served with arabic rice, raw onions and a bowl of yoghurt	
083	Sayadiya Samak	2.000
	Chunks of fresh fish cooked with onion, rice and pine nuts	

94b

94a

THE SAND BAR

SINGAPORE SNACKS

Chinese Spring Rolls		$2.50
Kajang Kebabs (½ doz) $3.80	(1 doz)	$7.20
Ketupat		$0.70
Malabar Samossas		$3.50
Chin Kai with Kropuk		$6.50

SANDWICHES

Mandarin Special Club	$5.80
Chicken	$5.00
The Apple Topper	$5.50
Egg Sandwich with Spring Onions	$4.00

SANDBAR SPECIALS

The St. Louis Hamburger	$5.40
The Swiss Cheeseburger	$5.80
Steak Sandwich with Fried Onion Rings	$9.00
The Rembrandt: Holland's Favourite	$4.60
Miniature Bratwurst with Potato Salad	$5.00
Grilled Prawns with Lemon	$7.50
Strammer Max	$5.60

FOR WEIGHT-WATCHERS

Melon and Pineapple Cocktail	$2.50
Tropical Fruit Plate with Lime Sherbet	$4.80
Seafood Cocktail in a Coconut	$5.00
Salad Platter	$5.50

THE ICE-BOX

Ice Cream of your choice	$2.20
Banana Split	$3.50
Lemon or Orange Sherbet	$2.20
Coupe Denmark	$3.50
Suntan Coupe	$4.00

BEVERAGES

Pot of Coffee	$1.80
Pot of Tea	$1.50
Iced Lemon Tea	$1.50
Pasteurised Milk Pack	$2.00

MILKSHAKES AND FLOATS

Chocolate	$3.60
Strawberry	$3.60
Hazelnut	$3.60
Coconut	$3.60
The Original O'Leary Iced Irish Coffee	$4.60
Citrus Float	$3.60

Service charge — 10%
Government Tax — 3%
5/78/100

95

---

95 The Sand Bar, The Mandarin, Singapour
Carte de menu. Création: Overseas Union Advertising
∅ 278 mm, 2 pages. Papier couché, offset 3 couleurs. Laminé, contre-collé sur carton gris, estampé
Cette carte est indéchirable et imperméable; au dos, inversion des couleurs: surface pleine en orange, bord et centre en jaune.

95 The Sand Bar, The Mandarin, Singapur
Speisekarte. Gestaltung Overseas Union Advertising
∅ 278 mm, 2seitig. Kunstdruckpapier, Offset 3farbig. Laminiert, auf Graukarton kaschiert, formgestanzt
Die unzerreißbare und wasserfeste Karte bringt auf ihrer Rückseite Umkehrung der Farben: Vollfläche orange, Rand und Zentrum gelb.

95 The Sand Bar, The Mandarin, Singapore
Menu-card. Designed by Overseas Union Advertising
∅ 278 mm, 2 pages. Art paper. Three-colour offset printing. Laminated, mounted on to grey card, die-cut
The indestructible and water-tight card shows a reversal of colours on the back cover: all in orange, except border and centre in yellow.

96a–b Chatterbox, The Mandarin, ▷ Singapour
Carte des petits déjeuners. Création: Overseas Union Advertising
135×304 mm, ouvert 400×304 mm, 6 pages. Chromo pour boîte pliante 7/10. Offset vert, olive, brun et orange, au dos jaune, brun et noir. Laminé deux faces, rainé, plis roulés
L'épaisseur du carton et les marges étroites exigent une légère modification des motifs dans le sens de la largeur; à défaut, un déséquilibre se créerait lors du pliage.

96a–b Chatterbox, The Mandarin, Singapur
Frühstückskarte. Gestaltung Overseas Union Advertising
135×304 mm, offen 400×304 mm, 6seitig. Faltschachtelchromo 7/10. Offset grün, olive, braun, orange, Rückseite gelb, braun, schwarz. Beidseitig laminiert, gerillt, Wickelfalz.
Bei dieser Kartonstärke und solch schmalen Rändern müssen die Motive in der Breite leicht abgeändert werden, da sich sonst beim Falten Standdifferenzen ergeben.

96a–b Chatterbox, The Mandarin. Singapore
Menu-card for breakfast. Designed by Overseas Union Advertising
135×304 mm, open 400×304 mm, 6 pages. Cast-coated folding-box card: 7/10. Offset printing in green, olive, brown and orange, back cover in yellow, brown and black. Laminated on both sides, scored, reverse accordion fold
As this card is particularly strong and has such narrow borders, the motifs require slight alteration in width for otherwise difficulties may arise in making the card stand upright when folded.

97 Chatterbox, The Coffee Shop, The Mandarin, Singapour
Carte de menu. Création: Overseas Union Advertising
213×375 mm, ouvert 433×375 mm, 4 pages. Chromo pour boîte pliante. Offset vert, brun et orange, intérieur jaune, brun et noir. Laminé deux faces, rainé, plié
Belle homogénéité avec la carte des petits déjeuners, par la reprise du motif de la couverture. La différence tient dans le format et le pliage.

97 Chatterbox, The Coffee Shop, The Mandarin, Singapur
Speisekarte. Gestaltung Overseas Union Advertising
213×375 mm, offen 433×375 mm, 4seitig. Faltschachtelchromo. Offset grün, olive, braun, orange, Innenseiten gelb, braun, schwarz. Beidseitig laminiert, gerillt, gefalzt
Schöne Druckgestaltung, wobei der Rapport des Umschlags der Frühstückskarte aufgenommen wird. Der Unterschied liegt im Format und in der Falzung.

97 Chatterbox, The Coffee Shop, The Mandarin, Singapore
Menu-card. Designed by Overseas Union Advertising
213×375 mm, open 433×375 mm, 4 pages. Cast-coated folding-box card. Offset printing in green, olive, brown and orange, inside pages in yellow, brown and black. Laminated on both sides, scored, folded
Fine printing which keeps to the design of the breakfast menu. The difference lies in the format and the fold.

97

96a

96b

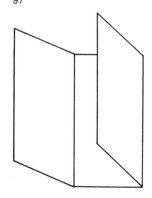

98a

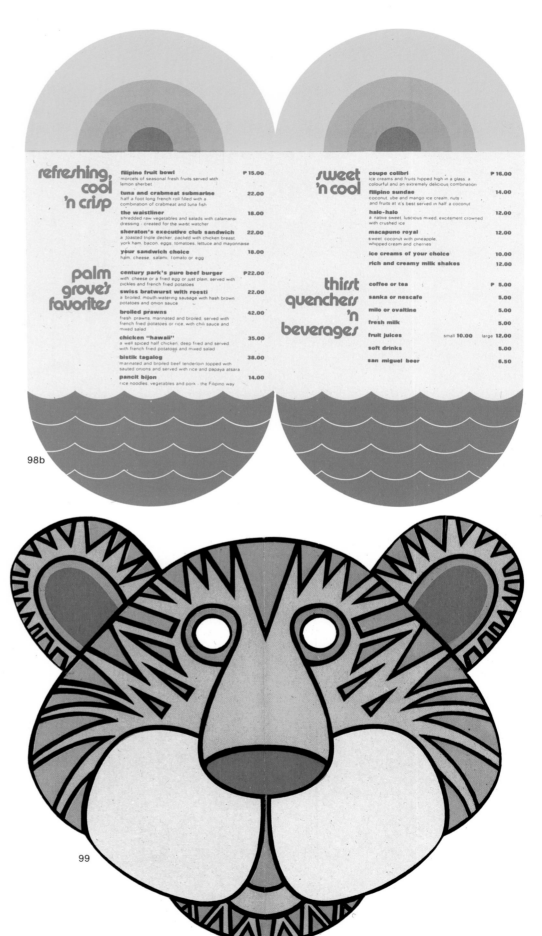

refreshing, cool 'n crisp

filipino fruit bowl		P 15.00
morcels of seasonal fresh fruits served with lemon sherbet		
tuna and crabmeat submarine		22.00
half a foot long french roll filled with a combination of crabmeat and tuna fish		
the waistliner		18.00
shredded raw vegetables and salads with calamansi dressing - created for the waist watcher		
sheraton's executive club sandwich		22.00
a toasted triple decker, packed with chicken breast, york ham, bacon, eggs, tomatoes, lettuce and mayonnaise		
your sandwich choice		18.00
ham, cheese, salami, tomato or egg		

palm grove's favorites

century park's pure beef burger		P 22.00
with cheese or a fried egg or just plain, served with pickles and french fried potatoes		
swiss bratwurst with roesti		22.00
a broiled, mouth-watering sausage with hash brown potatoes and onion sauce		
broiled prawns		42.00
fresh prawns, marinated and broiled, served with french fried potatoes or rice, with chili sauce and mixed salad		
chicken "hawaii"		35.00
a well spiced half chicken, deep fried and served with french fried potatoes and mixed salad		
bistik tagalog		38.00
marinated and broiled beef tenderloin topped with sauted onions and served with rice and papaya atsara		
pancit bijon		14.00
rice noodles, vegetables and pork - the Filipino way		

sweet 'n cool

coupe colibri		P 16.00
ice creams and fruits tipped high in a glass, a colourful and an extremely delicious combination		
filipino sundae		14.00
coconut, ube and mango ice cream, nuts and fruits at it's best served in half a coconut		
halo-halo		12.00
a native sweet, luscious mixed, excitement crowned with crushed ice		
macapuno royal		12.00
sweet coconut with pineapple, whipped cream and cherries		
ice creams of your choice		10.00
rich and creamy milk shakes		12.00

thirst quenchers 'n beverages

coffee or tea		P 5.00
sanka or nescafe		5.00
milo or ovaltine		5.00
fresh milk		5.00
fruit juices	small 10.00	large 12.00
soft drinks		5.00
san miguel beer		6.50

98b

98a–b Palm Grove, Century Park Sheraton, Manille, Philippines
Carte de menu. Création: Eric David
154×305 mm, ouvert 308×305 mm, 4 pages. News-chromo double face. Offset bleu, jaune, rouge et orange. Laminé deux faces, rainé, plié, estampé
Cette petite carte est conçue pour les mets servis au bord de la piscine; ses couleurs sont en accord avec l'eau et le soleil.

98a–b Palm Grove, Century Park Sheraton, Manila, Philippinen
Speisekarte. Gestaltung Eric David
154×305 mm, offen 308×305 mm, 4seitig. News-chromo zweiseitig. Offset blau, gelb, rot, orange. Beidseitig laminiert, gerillt, gefalzt, formgestanzt
Diese für kleine, am Rand des Swimmingpools zu servierende Gerichte vorgesehene Karte stimmt mit ihren Farben (Sonne, Wasser) auf die Umgebung ein.

98a–b Palm Grove, Century Park Sheraton, Manila, The Philippines
Menu-card. Designed by Eric David
154×305 mm, open 308×305 mm, 4 pages. Super-calendered paper. Offset printing in blue, yellow, red and orange. Laminated on both sides, scored, folded, die-cut
This menu-card for snacks to be served by the swimming-pool blends well in its colours with those of the surroundings (sun, water).

99

100 Hyatt Regency, Singapour
Carte de menu imprimée sur ballon de plage
∅ gonflé 410 mm. Plastique. Sérigraphie, bandes blanches et rouges assemblées à chaud
Description des petits déjeuners, des boissons et des grillades quotidiennes. Cette carte de menu est conçue comme jeu et souvenir publicitaire durable.

100 Hyatt Regency, Singapur
Speisekarte als Wasserball
∅ aufgeblasen 410 mm. Kunststoff. Siebdruck. Weiße und rote Bahnen geschweißt
Beschreibung der Frühstücksgerichte und Erfrischungen, Hinweis auf das tägliche Barbecue-Luncheon. Spielgerät und Souvenir mit Langzeitwerbung

100 Hyatt Regency, Singapore
Menu-card in the shape of a water-ball.
∅ when inflated 410 mm. Rubber. Silk screen, white and red stripes welded together
Description of breakfast menus, guide and comments on the daily barbecue luncheon. Toy and memento with long-term advertising effect.

100

REFRESHMENTS & SNACKS
TROPICAL FRUIT COMBINATION   S$6.00
Selection of tropical fruits, topped with cottage cheese and fresh mint leaves

THE FISHERMAN'S PRAWNS COCKTAIL   S$8.00
Served in coconut with tangy hot sauce

THE ONE FOOTER   S$7.50
Hyatt's hot dog with mustard, relishes and cole slaw salad

HYATT POOL OR CHEESE BURGER   S$7.50
Freshly ground beef served with smothered onions, peppers, mustard, pickles and cole slaw salad

CLUB SANDWICH   S$7.00
A triple-decker combination of cole slaw, tomato, eggs, grilled bacon, turkey and pickles

FARMER'S FRIED CHICKEN IN THE BASKET   S$9.00
An old Kentucky recipe served with corn on cob, french fries and crispy greens

POOL BREAKFAST
from 9 am onwards   S$8.50
Choice of Fresh Fruit Juice
Scrambled Eggs on Toast with Chipolatas
Grilled Ham and Bacon Rashers
Selections of fresh Rolls or Pastries with butter, jam and marmalade
Coffee or Tea

DAILY BARBECUE LUNCHEON
Weather permitting from 11.30am to 3.00pm
FOR TODAY'S SPECIALITIES
Please refer to the menu board

◁ 99 Hotel Lanka Oberoi, Colombo, Sri Lanka
Carte de menu pour enfants. Création Gavin Asarappa, Dehiwela
320 × 275 mm, 2 pages. Papier recyclé. Offset rouge, jaune et noir, dos en noir et rouge. Estampé. Elastique de suspension
Modèle de carte pour enfants bien conçue. Après avoir choisi son menu, l'enfant peut mettre le masque de tigre.

99 Hotel Lanka Oberoi, Colombo, Sri Lanka
Kinderkarte. Gestaltung Gavin Asarappa, Dehiwela
320 × 275 mm, 2seitig. Recycling-Papier. Offset rot, gelb, schwarz, Rückseite schwarz, rot. Formgestanzt. Gummiband zum Anhängen
Gutes Beispiel einer interessanten Kinderkarte. Nach dem Wählen des Menus kann die Tigermaske aufgesetzt werden.

99 Hotel Lanka Oberoi, Colombo, Sri Lanka
Menu-card for children. Designed by Gavin Asarappa, Dehiwela
320 × 275 mm, 2 pages. Recycled paper. Offset printing in red, yellow and black, back cover in black and red. Die-cut. Can be hung up by a rubber band
A good example of an interesting menu-card for children. After choosing the menu, the tiger mask may be put on.

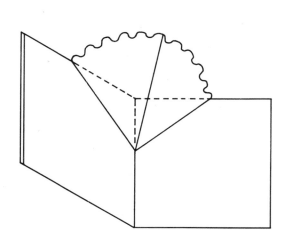

Spritzige Erfrischung
mit einem Sprutz
Mövenpick-Esprit!

So prickelfruchtiggluschtig frischerfrischendzischig...

101a

Erfrischungsdrinks mit...

...im Mövenpick

Lemonsomonsieur –
Lemonsomadame 2.–
Ein Zwei-Dezi-Guterli
zitronignaturliches
Lemonsoda für jedermann.

Schprutzzz Nr. 1:
Winzer-Walzer 4.80
Erfrischender Tanz rund
ums Lemonsoda und
Weisswein.

Schprutzzz Nr. 2:
Pimm's Summertime
7.50
Most like it frisch – mit
einem Lemonsoda-
Pimm's-Gemisch.

Schprutzzz Nr. 3:
Dr Frischzisch 4.–
Zisch en Frische – bisch
frisch und... frei von
Alkohol, doch voll von
Ananas-, Orangen-,
Zitronen- und
Grapefruitsaft.

Schprutzzz Nr. 4:
Le feu de l'amitié
12.50
Gisch Di wie de bisch!
Zu zweit zischt sich's
frischer bei Kerzenlicht,
Rum und Queens Bitter
Orange.

Schprutzzz Nr. 5:
Coqorange 5.50
Ein toller Schprutzzz Eier-
cognac in spritziges
Queens Bitter Orange
gemischt.

Schprutzzz Nr. 6:
Sandokan 10.50
Zisch-misch-frisch-
fernostliche Frische in
einem geheimnisvollen
Becher eingefangen.
Immer nur lächeln...
den Becher darfst Du
behalten.

Schprutzzz Nr. 7:
Piña Colada 7.80
Eine schneefrische
Mischung von Rum,
Kokosnussen und Ananas.

Schprutzzz Nr. 8:
Café Alexander 7.50
Frischer Nach-Tisch –
Eiskaltes Frischissimo mit
Kakao, Kaffee und Cognac.

101b

101a–b Mövenpick, Zurich, Suisse
Carte des consommations. Création:
Bodenmatt-Team
240×240 mm, ouvert 480×373 mm,
4 pages. Carton offset. Offset 4
couleurs. Laqué, rainé, estampé,
contre-collé
Carte axée sur la publicité, tant par sa
conception graphique que par le texte,
un mélange d'allemand et de dialecte.

101a–b Mövenpick, Zürich, Schweiz
Getränkekarte. Gestaltung Bodenmatt-
Team
240×240 mm, offen 480×373 mm,
4seitig. Offsetkarton. Offset 4farbig.
Lackiert, gerillt, formgestanzt, kaschiert
Nicht nur von der Gestaltung her auf
Werbung getrimmt, sondern auch entsprechend in einer Mischung von Dia-
lekt und Hochdeutsch getextet

101a–b Mövenpick, Zurich, Switzer-
land
Wine list. Designed by Bodenmatt-
Team
Cover: 240×240 mm, open
480×373 mm, 4 pages. Offset card.
Four-colour offset printing. Varnished,
scored, die-cut, mounted
Design geared to advertising effect as
is the text which is in both dialect and
High German.

102a–b Mövenpick, Zurich, Suisse ▷
Carte des glaces et des desserts. Création: Service de publicité Mövenpick
153×292 mm, ouvert 608×292 mm,
8 pages. Chromo double face. Offset 4
couleurs. Laminé, rainé trois fois, plis
parallèles
D'appétissantes illustrations présentent toute la gamme des spécialités.

102a–b Mövenpick, Zürich, Schweiz
Eis- und Dessertkarte. Gestaltung
Werbeabteilung Mövenpick
153×292 mm, offen 608×292 mm,
8seitig. Chromokarton zweiseitig.
Offset 4farbig. Laminiert, 3mal gerillt,
parallel gefalzt
Appetitanregende Aufnahmen zeigen
sämtliche angebotenen Eisspeziali-
täten.

102a–b Mövenpick, Zurich, Switzerland
Ice-cream and dessert card. Designed
by the advertising department of Mövenpick
153×292 mm, open 608×292 mm, 8
pages. Two-sided cast-coated card.
Four-colour offset printing. Laminated,
three times scored, folded parallel
Attractive photographs depict the en-
tire selection of ice-cream specialities.

Mövenpick Ice-Cream

Sie aus dem Sortiment der bekanntesten Rahm-Glacen, Sorbets und Joghurt-Glacen unter folgenden Aromen selber wählen:

Caramelita mit Rahmcaramelwürfeln

Chocolat Chips mit Schokosplittern

Maple Walnuts mit caramelisierten Baumnüssen

Pistache mit Pistaziensplittern

Sorbet Fraise

Sorbet Citron

Brombeer Joghurt

Preis per Kugel Fr. 1.70
mit Rahm + Fr. –.80

Ihren Glace-Traum zu Hause:
...nd bei uns auch in der praktischen 1-Liter-...e. Dank 3-stündigem Kälteschutz jederzeit transportbereit.

MÖVENPICK

Vanille-Doppelrahm-Glace mit Fruchtcouli
Eine Kugel Vanille-Doppelrahm-Glace mit Konfekt und einem Fruchtcouli nach Wahl:
- Ananas
- Johannisbeer
- Mango
- Brombeer
Fr. 2.50

Mini-Coupe
Für den kleinen Glace-Gluscht nach dem Essen oder zwischendurch.

4 Mini-Kugeln: Brombeer Joghurt, Sorbets Framboise, Citron und Fraise mit Mango-Fruchtcouli und Konfekt
Fr. 3.80

Degustieren geht über studieren

Mövenpick-Eispalette
Mövenpick bringt erstmals in der »Glacegeschichte« die Eispalette. Damit Sie die beliebtesten 9 Mövenpick-Glacesorten mit ihren echten Aromen zum Anbeissen gegenüberstellen und degustieren können.

Je eine Degustationskugel*
Apple Blossom, Sorbet Fraise, Caramelita, Sorbet Citron, Brombeer Joghurt, Maple Walnuts, Chocolat Chips, Sorbet Framboise, Pistache.

Dazu Konfekt und Brombeer-Fruchtcouli
* Entspricht einem Drittel einer normalen Mövenpick-Glace-Kugel.
Fr. 7.80

102a

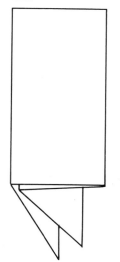

Coupe Senga Sengana
Apple Blossom-, Pistache- und Erdbeer-Glace auf Meringueschalen mit marinierten Erdbeeren, Rahm, Konfekt und Mango-Fruchtcouli Fr. 7.50

Coupe Amarena
Drei Kugeln Vanille-Doppelrahm-Glace auf Meringueschalen mit dunklen, marinierten Amarenen-Kirschen, Rahm und Amaretti Fr. 7.20

Coupe Frou-Frou
Citron-, Maple Walnuts- und Apple Blossom-Glace auf Konfekt mit frischem Fruchtsalat, Johannisbeer-Fruchtcouli, Rahm und Makrönli Fr. 7.80

Coupe Tête-à-Tête
Sechs Traumglacen auf Meringueschalen mit frischem Fruchtsalat, Schokoladensauce, Ananas-Fruchtcouli, Rahm und Konfekt

Für 2 und mehr Personen Fr. 13.50

Eiscafé Mocca Croquant
Mocca-Croquant-Glacé mit Kaffee und Rahm, garniert mit Haselnuss-Croquant und Konfekt Fr. 4.80

Coupe Caramelita
Zwei Kugeln Caramelita- und eine Kugel Maple Walnuts-Glace auf Meringueschalen mit Caramelsirup, Haselnuss-Croquant, Rahm und Amaretti Fr. 6.80

Coppa Mora
Brombeer Joghurt-, Pistache- und Maple Walnuts-Glace auf Konfekt mit marinierten Brombeeren, Brombeer-Fruchtcouli, Rahm und Nusskonfekt Fr. 7.50

Coupe Swiss Chocolat-Doodle
Zwei Kugeln Chocolat- und eine Kugel Vanille-Glace auf Meringueschalen mit Schokoladen-Sauce, Schokoladenspänen, Rahm und Amaretti Fr. 6.50

Irish Coff
Fr. 6.—
Er sieht so fröhlich aus un... schmeckt so wundervoll.

Desserts
Birchermüesli nature
Birchermüesli mit Rahm
Crème Caramel
  mit Rahm
Frischer Fruchtsalat
  mit Rahm
  mit Kirsch
Meringue mit Rahm
Meringue glacée

Käse
Unser Servicepersonal ber... gerne über unser Käseang...
Portion
Brotauswahl und Butter inbegriffen.

102b

103a–b, 104a–b   The Capital Hilton, Washington D.C., USA
Carte de menu pour enfants. Création: Menu Promotion Ideas Inc., Clifton, New Jersey
348×264 mm, 2 pages. Papier pigmenté une face, satiné. Recto offset 4 couleurs, verso offset noir. Estampé
Le nez se déplie, les yeux sont perforés et peuvent être enlevés. Le masque s'accroche derrière les oreilles. Les menus des deux cartes sont identiques, mais les noms sont assortis au sujet du masque, selon qu'il est pour fille ou pour garçon.

103a–b, 104a–b   The Capital Hilton, Washington, D.C., USA
Kinderkarte. Gestaltung Menu Promotion Ideas Inc., Clifton, New Jersey
348×264 mm, 2seitig. Einseitig pigmentiertes Papier, satiniert. Vorderseite Offset 4farbig, Rückseite Offset schwarz. Formgestanzt
Die Nase kann vorgeklappt werden, die Augen sind vorgestanzt und können herausgenommen werden. Die Maske wird hinter den Ohren eingehängt. Die Speisenangebote sind auf beiden Karten identisch, die Namen jedoch den Masken angepaßt, einmal für Jungen, einmal für Mädchen.

103a–b, 104a–b   The Capital Hilton, Washington, D.C., USA
Menu-card for children. Designed by Menu Promotions Ideas Inc., Clifton, New Jersey
348×264 mm, 2 pages. One-sided pigmented paper with satin finish. Front cover: 4-colour offset printing; back cover: offset printing in black. Die-cut
The nose may be pulled forward, the eyes are also perforated and may be removed. The mask is tied behind the ears. The menus are identical on both cards; the names, however, are adapted to the mask; one for boys, one for girls.

103a

104a

The Capital Hilton
16TH AND K STREETS, N.W.
WASHINGTON, D.C.

THE PIRATE BURGER
Grilled Hamburger on Bun
Fried Potatoes
Ice Cream or Sherbet
Milk or Soda

4.75

THE SEAFARER
Fried Shrimp
with Cocktail Sauce
Fried Potatoes
Cole Slaw
Milk or Soda

4.95

THE TREASURE CHEST
Grilled Cheese with Bacon
Sandwich
Cole Slaw
Potato Chips
Milk or Soda

3.75

LONG JOHN SILVERS
Peanut Butter and Jelly
Sandwich
Potato Chips
Milk or Soda

2.75

THE CAPTAIN HOOK
A Stack of Pancakes
with Maple Flavored
Syrup
Crisp Bacon
Milk or Soda

4.25

FISHERMAN'S CATCH
Tuna Salad on Toast
Potato Chips and Pickle
Milk or Soda

3.95

103b

The Capital Hilton
16TH AND K STREETS, N.W.
WASHINGTON, D.C.

THE PANDA BURGER
Grilled Hamburger on Bun
Fried Potatoes
Ice Cream or Sherbet
Milk or Soda

4.75

FLIPPER'S FAVORITE
Fried Shrimp
with Cocktail Sauce
Fried Potatoes
Cole Slaw
Milk or Soda

4.95

THE NATIONAL VELVET
Grilled Cheese with Bacon
Sandwich
Cole Slaw
Potato Chips
Milk or Soda

3.75

BAMBI'S CHOICE
Peanut Butter and Jelly
Sandwich
Potato Chips
Milk or Soda

2.75

BENGI'S BEST
A Stack of Pancakes
with Maple Flavored
Syrup
Crisp Bacon
Milk or Soda

4.25

FLICKA'S TREAT
Tuna Salad on Toast
Potato Chips and Pickle
Milk or Soda

3.95

104b

CHILDREN'S MENU

105

105   The Manila Mandarin, Manille, Philippines
Carte de menu pour enfants. Création: Studio de publicité interne
252 × 236 mm, 2 pages. Papier couché contre-collé sur carton gris ¹²/₁₀. Recto offset 4 couleurs, verso bleu. Laminé
La partie bleue de l'illustration est répétée en fond au verso, le texte est repiqué en bleu foncé. Quant à l'illustration même, l'accent a été mis sur l'épi de maïs, si apprécié des enfants. Il leur sera servi sous toutes les formes.

105   The Manila Mandarin, Manila, Philippinen
Kinderkarte. Gestaltung im hauseigenen Werbestudio
252 × 236 mm, 2seitig. Kunstdruckpapier auf Graukarton ¹²/₁₀ kaschiert. Vorderseite Offset 4farbig, Rückseite blau. Laminiert
Die Blauplatte der Abbildung der Vorderseite wird als Hintergrund für die Rückseite verwendet, Text als Eindruck dunkelblau. Die Titelseite zielt besonders auf die bei Kindern so beliebten Maiskolben ab, die in allen möglichen Variationen serviert werden.

105   The Manila Mandarin, Manila, The Philippines
Menu-card for children. Designed by the establishment's own advertising studio
252 × 236 mm, 2 pages. Art paper mounted on to grey card: ¹²/₁₀. Front cover: 4-colour offset printing; back cover: offset printing in blue. Laminated
The blue printing plate of the illustration on the front is used for the background on the rear; the text is overprinted in dark blue. The title-page emphasizes corn-on-the-cob, always popular with children, which is served in every possible variation.

Cartes spéciales

Spezialkarten

Special menus

Certains événements fournissent l'occasion de créer une carte de circonstance; il est évident que le graphiste s'inspirera des raisons mêmes de l'événement. Ainsi la carte d'une semaine gastronomique se rapportera à la décoration choisie par le restaurant. Les participants à un congrès ou un jubilé seront agréablement surpris par une carte de forme rappelant l'activité de l'association ou de l'entreprise organisatrice. Lors de rencontres à caractère privé, une carte originale à emporter et utiliser en d'autres circonstances est vivement appréciée: des pochettes de tissu, par exemple, dont les fabricants offrent de vastes collections aux motifs variés et assurent également l'impression.

Hier sind ein paar Beispiele von Spezialkarten zu besonderen Anlässen zusammengefaßt. Bei der Gestaltung solcher Karten muß der Grafiker auf den besonderen Charakter des Anlasses eingehen.
Karten für gastronomische Wochen zum Beispiel sollten immer Bestandteil der gesamten Dekoration des Restaurants sein. Bei Kongressen und Betriebsjubiläen kann der Zusammenhang mit dem Ereignis durch eine spezielle Formgebung hergestellt werden.
Beliebt sind bei geschlossenen Gesellschaften Karten, die nach Hause mitgenommen und weiter benützt werden können. Taschentuchfabrikanten bieten ganze Kollektionen von Motiven an und besorgen auch den Eindruck des Textes.

Here are a few examples of special menus for particular occasions. The designer should take account of the circumstances in each case. Menus for *semaines gastronomiques,* for example, should always be an integral part of the restaurant's basic decorative style. A special form may be adopted for congresses and anniversaries (e.g. a firm's jubilee). Members of private associations and clubs often like to take the menu home and use it again. Handkerchief manufacturers offer whole ranges of motifs and will print the text as well.

106   Brasserie, Hotel Inter-Continental, Cologne, RFA
Carte de menu spéciale pour la période de la chasse
250 × 370 mm, 2 pages. Carton offset couleur. Offset brun
Une ancienne représentation d'un chasseur et de son chien souligne le but de cette carte.

106   Brasserie, Hotel Inter-Continental, Köln, Bundesrepublik Deutschland
Spezialkarte für Wildwochen
250 × 370 mm, 2seitig. Offsetkarton bunt. Offset braun
Eine alte Darstellung eines Jägers und seines Hundes unterstreicht den Anlaß dieser Karte.

106   Brasserie, Hotel Inter-Continental, Cologne, West Germany
Special menu-card for the game season
250 × 370 mm, 2 pages. Coloured offset card. Offset printing in brown
An old illustration of a hunter and his dog emphasizes the occasion of this card.

Wildwochen

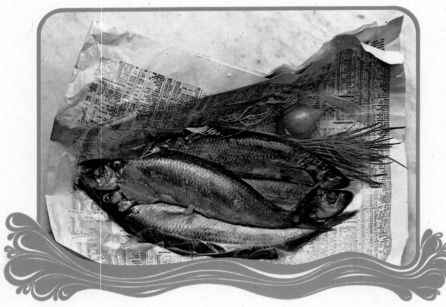

Matjeszeit

107

107 Romantik Hotel Schwan, Östrich-Winkel, RFA
Carte spéciale pour le hareng.
210 × 230 mm, ouvert 420 × 230 mm, 4 pages. Papier couché. Page 1 offset 4 couleurs, pages 2–4 offset noir. Plié
En page 2, texte sur le hareng, sa pêche et sa préparation. En page 4, texte publicitaire sur les hôtels Romantik.

107 Romantik Hotel Schwan, Östrich-Winkel, Bundesrepublik Deutschland
Spezialkarte für «Matjeszeit»
210 × 230 mm, offen 420 × 230 mm, 4seitig. Kunstdruckpapier. Seite 1 Offset 4farbig, Seiten 2–4 Offset schwarz. Gefalzt
Auf Seite 2 befindet sich Text über den Hering, den Fang und die Zubereitung, auf Seite 4 Werbetext für die Romantik Hotels.

107 Romantik Hotel Schwan, Östrich-Winkel, West Germany
Special menu-card for the herring season
210 × 230 mm, open 420 × 230 mm, 4 pages. Art paper. Page 1: 4-colour offset printing; pages 2–4: offset printing in black. Folded
On page 2: text about the herring in general, as well as the catching of the fish and its preparation. On page 4: advertising text for Romantik Hotels.

108 Hotel St. Gotthard, Zurich, Suisse
Carte spéciale pour amateurs d'huîtres. Création: CEM Management AG, Zurich
⌀ 300 mm, 2 pages. Papier offset couleur. Page 1 offset 4 couleurs, verso vierge. Estampé

108 Hotel St. Gotthard, Zürich, Schweiz
Spezialkarte «Austrologie-Kongreß». Gestaltung CEM Management AG, Zürich
⌀ 300 mm, 2seitig. Offsetpapier bunt. Offset 4farbig auf Seite 1, Rückseite unbedruckt. Formgestanzt

108 Hotel St. Gotthard, Zurich, Switzerland
Special menu card for an 'oyster congress'. Designed by CEM Management AG, Zurich
⌀ 300 mm, 2 pages. Coloured offset paper. Four-colour offset printing on page 1, back cover left unprinted. Die-cut

108

109 Arbalète, Hotel Monopol,
Lucerne, Suisse
Carte spéciale pour homards du vivier.
Création Jörg Wey, Lucerne
265×340 mm, 2 pages. Chromo une
face. Page 1 offset 4 couleurs, page 2
offset noir
Présentation des plats trilingue allemand-français-anglais. Au dos, texte
trilingue sur le homard, son origine, sa
préparation et la manière correcte de le
manger. L'illustration de la page 1 y est
reproduite en noir et blanc, les différentes parties du homard étant nu-
mérotées pour le mode d'emploi.

109 Arbalète, Hotel Monopol, Luzern,
Schweiz
Spezialkarte für frischen Hummer. Gestaltung Jörg Wey, Luzern
265×340 mm, 2seitig. Chromokarton
einseitig. Seite 1 Offset 4farbig, Seite 2
Offset schwarz
Angebot 3sprachig Deutsch, Französisch, Englisch. Auf der Rückseite
3sprachiger Text über den Hummer,
seine Herkunft, seine Zubereitung und
die korrekte Art, ihn zu essen. Die Abbildung der Vorderseite ist, mit Ziffern
versehen, als Gebrauchsanleitung auf
der Rückseite in Schwarz reproduziert.

109 Arbalète, Hotel Monopol,
Lucerne, Switzerland
Special menu-card for fresh lobster.
Designed by Jörg Wey, Lucerne
265×340 mm, 2 pages. One-sided
cast-coated card. Page 1: 4-colour offset printing; page 2: offset printing in
black
Menus in German, French and English.
On the back: text in three languages on
the lobster in general, its origin, preparation and the correct manner of eating
it. The illustration on the front page is
annotated with numbers similar to an
instruction leaflet and is reproduced in
black on the back.

✳✳✳✳✳✳✳✳✳✳✳ Frischer Hummer ✳✳✳✳✳✳✳✳✳✳✳

HOMARD DE NOTRE VIVIER
Fresh lobster «as you like it»

Arbalète
RESTAURANT FRANÇAIS

KALTE UND WARME VORSPEISEN
HORS-D'OEUVRE FROIDS ET CHAUD
WARM AND COLD SIDE DISHES

Hummer mit Orangen an Mango-Chutney und Curry-Mayonnaise
COCKTAIL DE HOMARD NEPTUNE   Fr. 24.—
Lobster cocktail with oranges, mango chutney and curry-mayonnaise

Halber Hummer mit Gemüsesalat, Spargel, Ei und Caviar
DEMI HOMARD A LA PARISIENNE   Fr. 26.—
Half a lobster with vegetable salad, asparagus, egg and caviar

Pfannkuchen mit feiner Füllung aus Hummer und Champignons
CREPES FARCIES ARMORICAINE   Fr. 15.—
Pancakes stuffed with lobster and mushrooms

SUPPEN
POTAGES
SOUPS

Klare Hummersuppe
BOUILLON DE HOMARD CLAIR   Fr. 8.—
Clear lobster soup

Hummersuppe
BISQUE DE HOMARD   Fr. 8.—
Cream of lobster soup

HAUPTGERICHTE
PLAT DE RÉSISTANCE
MAIN DISHES

Gekochter, ganzer Hummer im Sud
HOMARD ENTIER A LA NAGE AUX AROMATES   Fr. 50.—
Whole poached lobster

Hummer an Hummersauce mit Champignons
HOMARD THERMIDOR   Fr. 32.—
Lobster in lobster sauce and mushrooms

Halber Hummer an Senfrahmsauce mit Crevetten
LA DEMOISELLE DE CHERBOURG   Fr. 32.—
Half a lobster in a mustard cream sauce with shrimps

Halber Hummer an Cognac-Sauce mit Tomaten
HOMARD A L'AMERICAINE   Fr. 34.—
Lobster on brandy sauce with tomatoes

Zubereitungszeit minimum 30 Minuten
Préparation des mets environ 30 minutes
Time for preparation at least 30 minutes

✳✳✳✳✳✳✳✳✳✳✳✳✳✳✳✳✳✳✳✳✳✳✳✳✳✳✳✳✳

109

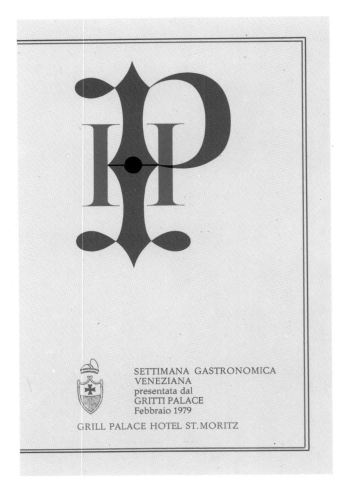

111 Hotel Inter-Continental, Cologne, RFA
Carte des spécialiteś de la semaine hongroise
245×352 mm, ouvert 490×352 mm, 4 pages. Carton couché. Impression typo 8 couleurs. Rainé, plié

Présentation des mets bilingue alle-mand-anglais. Les personnages styli-sés de la couverture et la conception de l'intérieur, simple et facile à consul-ter, rendent cette carte claire et agré-able.

111 Hotel Inter-Continental, Köln, Bundesrepublik Deutschland
Spezialitätenkarte für Ungarische Woche
245×352 mm, offen 490×352 mm, 4seitig. Kunstdruckkarton. Buchdruck 8farbig. Gerillt, gefalzt

Speisenangebot 2sprachig Deutsch, Englisch. Modern stilisierte Personen auf der Umschlagseite und einfach, aber klar gestalteter Innenteil ergeben eine klare und angenehm erschei-nende Karte.

111 Hotel Inter-Continental, Cologne, West Germany
Menu-card for specialities on the occa-sion of a Hungarian Week
245×352 mm, open 490×352 mm, 4 pages. Art card. Eight-colour letter-press printing. Scored, folded

Menus in German and English. The modern, stylized presentation of people on the front cover and the simple, yet clearly compiled inside pages make this a well-organized and pleasing card.

110 Grill, Palace Hotel, St-Moritz, Suisse
Carte des spécialités de la semaine vénitienne. Créa-tion: Direction de l'hôtel, Walter Gammeter, St-Moritz
185×280 mm, ouvert 370×280 mm, 4 pages. Chromo double face. Impression typo vert et rouge. Rainé, plié
L'impression en rouge et vert de la carte de la «Setti-mana Gastronomica Veneziana» fait immédiatement penser aux couleurs nationales italiennes.

110 Grill, Palace Hotel, St. Moritz, Schweiz
Spezialitätenkarte für Venezianische Woche. Gestal-tung Direktion des Hotels, Walter Gammeter, St. Moritz
185×280 mm, offen 370×280 mm, 4seitig. Chromo-karton zweiseitig. Buchdruck grün und rot. Gerillt, ge-falzt
Die Karte für eine «Settimana Gastronomica Vene-ziana» ruft durch die Verwendung der italienischen Nationalfarben sofort die Assoziation mit dem Land hervor.

110 Grill, Palace Hotel, St. Moritz, Switzerland
Menu-card for specialities on the occasion of a Vene-tian Week. Designed by the management of the hotel, Walter Gammeter, St. Moritz
185×280 mm, open 370×280 mm, 4 pages. Two-sided cast-coated card. Letterpress printing in green and red. Scored, folded
The use of Italy's national colours for the card, created for a 'Settimana Gastronomica Veneziana', immedi-ately evokes the association with the country.

112 Hotel Wittelsbacher Hof, Oberstdorf, RFA
Carte spéciale à l'occasion du 75ᵉ anniversaire de
l'établissement. Création: Ilse Ortlieb. Impression: Karl
Hofmann, Oberstdorf
Couverture: 210 × 297 mm, ouvert 420 × 297 mm,
4 pages. Papier couché. Pages 1 et 4 offset bleu et or,
pages 2 et 3, 4 couleurs et gris. Plié
Intérieur: 207 × 293 mm, ouvert 414 × 293 mm,
4 pages. Papier chiné à la cuve. Offset noir. Plié, relié à
la couverture par un ruban blanc et bleu, aux couleurs
bavaroises
Cette carte-anniversaire présente des mets tirés du
livre de cuisine de grand-mère: excellente idée qui
crée une atmosphère du temps passé.

112 Hotel Wittelsbacher Hof, Oberstdorf, Bundes-
republik Deutschland
Spezialkarte anläßlich des 75jährigen Bestehens des
Hauses. Gestaltung Ilse Ortlieb, Druck Karl Hofmann,
Oberstdorf
Umschlag: 210 × 297 mm, offen 420 × 297 mm, 4seitig.
Kunstdruckpapier. Seiten 1 und 4 Offset blau und gold,
Seiten 2–3 4farbig und grau. Gefalzt
Innenteil: 207 × 293 mm, offen 414 × 293 mm, 4seitig.
Bütten meliert. Offset schwarz. Gefalzt und durch
Band in den bayerischen Landesfarben Weiß-Blau mit
dem Umschlag verbunden
In dieser Jubiläumskarte sind Gerichte aus Großmut-
ters Kochbuch aufgenommen, ein besonders histori-
sierend wirkender Einfall.

112 Hotel Wittelsbacher Hof, Oberstdorf, West Ger-
many
Special menu-card for the 75th anniversary celebra-
tion of the establishment
Designed by Ilse Ortlieb, printed by Karl Hofmann,
Oberstdorf
Cover: 210 × 297 mm, open 420 × 297 mm, 4 pages. Art
paper. Pages 1 and 4: offset printing in blue and gold,
pages 2 and 3: 4-colour offset printing plus grey.
Folded
Contents: 207 × 293 mm, open 414 × 293 mm, 4 pages.
Marbled hand-made paper. Offset printing in black.
Folded and attached to the cover with a ribbon in the
national colours of Bavaria
This 'jubilee' card offers menus from 'Grandmother's
Cookery Book', an original idea combined with a touch
of history.

1905 — 1980

75 JAHRE

HOTEL WITTELSBACHER HOF

OBERSTDORF

112

En toutes choses l'hôte doit faire la joie
de son hôte *(et réciproquement)*

Convier Quelqu'un

disait, comme on sait, Brillat-Savarin, c'est se charger de
son

Bonheur

pendant tout le temps qu'il est sous votre toit.

Nous en avons fait évidemment notre devise.

Qu'elle soit donc la vôtre également, quand c'est à la
Tour d'Argent que vous entendez les traiter.

Ne faites pour cela confiance qu'à vous-même.

Nous serons les musiciens et les solistes. Mais le chef
d'orchestre

C'eſt vous

Ante portas iam laetitiae initium 9
Que les festivités commencent
dès votre arrivée

Voici enfin venu le jour que vous avez désiré.

Sitôt franchies les grilles de la Tour, un peu avant
même, j'aimerais que pour vous la fête commence. Que
d'abord, vous oubliiez tout des tracas quotidiens : les
embarras d'une cité impraticable, la morosité bétonnière,
la Seine même hélas... mais vous en verrez bientôt danser
les étincelles dans les plafonds miroitants de la salle d'en
haut.

Vous quittez vos soucis et vos prisons d'acier en
confiant au chasseur votre voiture. Vous êtes *attendu*.
L'implacable vingtième siècle s'abolit dans le temps
retrouvé, et vous pouvez désormais suivre le précepte
de l'*Alexandre* de Racine (qui s'appliquait à toute autre
chose, j'en conviens, mais qu'importe!)

Garde dans ce déſordre une Aſſiette tranquille

113

---

113 La Tour d'Argent, Paris
Création: Y. de Farcy. Impression:
Lannay, Paris
Couverture: 115×170 mm, ouvert
230×170 mm, 4 pages. Chromo argent
une face. Page 1 gaufrage
Intérieur: 113×170 mm, 16 pages. Papiers vergé à la cuve. Offset noir, rouge,
argent et vert. Plié et encarté dans la
couverture

**113 La Tour d'Argent, Paris, Frank-
reich**
Gestaltung Y. de Farcy, Druck Lannay,
Paris
Umschlag: 115×170 mm, offen
230×170 mm, 4seitig. Silberchromo-
karton einseitig. Blindprägung auf
Seite 1
Innenteil: 113×170 mm, 16seitig. Büttenpapier vergé. Offset schwarz, rot,
silber, grün. Gefalzt und in den Umschlag eingesteckt

113 La Tour d'Argent, Paris, France
Designed by Y. de Farcy, printed by
Lannay, Paris
Cover: 115×170 mm, open
230×170 mm, 4 pages. One-sided
cast-coated silver paper. Blind embossing on page 1
Contents: 113×170 mm, 16 pages. Laid
hand-made paper. Offset printing in
black, red, silver, green. Folded and inserted

---

114 Hotel St. Gotthard, Zurich, Suisse
Création: CEM Management AG, Zurich
Couverture: 132×250 mm, ouvert 264×250 mm,
4 pages. Carton offset. Page 1 offset brun. Rainé, plié
Intérieur: 130×242 mm, 8 pages. Papier offset couleur. Offset brun. Plié et relié à la couverture par un
cordon brun
Carte de menu en forme de petit livre de recettes. Les
pages sont extraites du livre «Aechti Schwyzer Chuchi», de Marianne Kaltenbach (édité par Hallwag Verlag, Berne et Stuttgart); simple adjonction des prix.

114 Hotel St. Gotthard, Zürich, Schweiz
Gestaltung CEM Management AG, Zürich
Umschlag: 132×250 mm, offen 264×250 mm, 4seitig.
Offsetkarton. Seite 1 Offset braun. Gerillt, gefalzt
Innenteil: 130×242 mm, 8seitig. Offsetpapier bunt.
Offset braun. Gefalzt und durch braune Kordel mit dem
Umschlag verbunden
Speisekarte in Form eines Rezeptbüchleins. Die Sei-
ten sind unter Beifügung der Preise dem Buch «Ächti
Schwizer Chuchi» von Marianne Kaltenbach (erschie-
nen im Hallwag Verlag Bern und Stuttgart) entnommen.

114 Hotel St. Gotthard, Zurich, Switzerland
Designed by CEM Management AG, Zurich
Cover: 132×250 mm, open 264×250 mm, 4 pages.
Offset card. Page 1: offset printing in brown. Scored,
folded
Contents: 130×242 mm, 8 pages. Coloured offset
paper. Offset printing in brown. Folded and attached to
the cover with a brown cord
Menu-card in the form of a recipe book. The pages are
taken from the book 'Aechti Schwizer-Chuchi' by
Marianne Kaltenbach (published by Hallwag Verlag,
Berne and Stuttgart)

Busecca 5.80
(Tessiner Kuttelsuppe)

Für 4 Personen

1 Zwiebel
2 Knoblauchzehen
2 Essl. Olivenöl
50 g Speckwürfelchen
5 Kartoffeln
3 Rüebli
½ Sellerieknolle
3 Tomaten
2 Lauchstengel
400 g vorgekochte, in
Streifen geschnittene
Kutteln
1 Teel. Salz, 1 Prise
Pfeffer
Je 1 Prise Safran,
Majoran, Basilikum,
Rosmarin
2 Essl. Tomatenpüree
1 l Fleischbrühe
Geriebener Sbrinz

Zwiebeln und Knoblauch fein hacken, zusammen
mit Speckwürfelchen im heissen Öl hellgelb rö-
sten. Kartoffeln, Rüebli, Sellerie und Tomaten in
Würfel, den Lauch in feine Rädchen schneiden.
Alles zusammen mit den Kutteln beigeben und
kurz dämpfen. Mit den Gewürzen überstreuen,
Tomatenpüree beifügen, alles vermischen, mit
Fleischbrühe aufgiessen. 30 Minuten kochen. Ge-
riebenen Sbrinz dazu servieren.

Schunggebegräbnis mit Apfelmus 7.50
(Hörnli mit Schinken)

Für 4 Personen

250 g gekochte Hörnli,
Nudeln oder Makkaroni
1 Essl. Butter
150 g Schinken
3 Eier
2 Essl. Käse
2½ dl Milch oder
Rahm
Salz, Pfeffer,
Muskatnuss

Die Butter in einer Bratpfanne erhitzen. Die
Teigwaren mit dem gehackten Schinken hinein-
geben und alles gut mischen. Eier, Käse und
Milch oder Rahm verquirlen. Mit Salz, Pfeffer
und Muskatnuss würzen. Diese Mischung über
die Teigwaren giessen. Mehrmals wenden. dann
alles zu einer Art Kuchen zusammenpressen. Zu-
decken und auf kleinem Feuer braten, bis eine
goldbraune Kruste entsteht. Auf eine Platte stür-
zen und mit Salat servieren.

Spaghetti nach Asconeser Art 9.50

Für 4 Personen

4 schöne Tomaten
100 g Champignons
400 g Spaghetti
Salz, schwarzer,
grobgemahlener Pfeffer
400 g Kalb- oder
Geflügelfleisch,
geschnetzelt
2 Essl. Butter
1 Zwiebel, fein gehackt
1 Knoblauchzehe
1 Prise Oregano
100 g Rohschinken
2 Essl. gehackte
Petersilie
100 g Sbrinz

Die Tomaten kurz in kochendes Wasser tauchen.
Die Haut abziehen und das Fruchtfleisch würfeln.
Die Champignons scheibeln und sofort mit den
Tomaten mischen.
Die Spaghetti in viel kochendes Salzwasser geben.
Mit einer Holzkelle etwas eintauchen und darauf
achten, dass sie nicht zusammenkleben. Ungefähr
10 Minuten kochen. Die Spaghetti sollen «al
dente» bleiben.
Inzwischen das Fleisch in der Butter 3–4 Minuten
braten. Aus der Pfanne nehmen. Zuerst die Zwiebeln im Bratenfond leicht dünsten, dann Tomaten, Champignons und durchgepressten Knoblauch beifügen. Mit Salz, Pfeffer und Oregano
würzen. Kurz vor dem Anrichten den in Streifen
geschnittenen Rohschinken beifügen und 10 Minuten mitdämpfen. Die Sauce über die gut abge-
tropften Spaghetti giessen. Mit Petersilie be-
streuen. Den Sbrinz am Tisch frisch gerieben dar-
übergeben.

115 The Colony House, Charleston, Caroline du Sud, USA
Création: Design Unlimited/Culinary Concepts, Hempstead, New York
152×228 mm, 16 pages. Papier à la cuve couleur. Offset brun et noir, agrafé deux fois dans le pli
De vieilles gravures, des cartes et un texte sur l'histoire de Charleston confèrent à cette carte l'allure d'une brochure vivante et intéressante.

115 The Colony House, Charleston, South Carolina, USA
Gestaltung Design Unlimited/Culinary Concepts, Hempstead, New York
152×228 mm, 16seitig. Büttenpapier bunt. Offset braun und schwarz, 2mal drahtgeheftet
Alte Stiche, Karten und ein Text über die Geschichte von Charleston ergänzen diese Speisekarte zu einer lebendigen, interessanten Broschüre

115 The Colony House, Charleston, S.C., USA
Designed by Design Unlimited/Culinary Concepts, Hempstead, New York
152×228 mm, 16 pages. Coloured hand-made paper. Offset printing in brown and black, 2-wire stitched
Old prints, maps and a text on the history of Charleston complement this menu-card, rendering it a lively, interesting brochure.

the story of
THE COLONY HOUSE
is the story of Charleston

Though the Spanish had trod the shores of Charleston Harbor some 150 years earlier, the history of Charleston (or Charles Town, as it was first known) really begins in 1670, with the establishment of the settlement that was to become the City. The early years were replete with stories of hardships and triumphs, Indian conflicts and Indian friendships, famine and plenty... but trade began, first with the Indians, then with occasional ships from Barbados and England, and even with the Spanish settlements far to the west.

Charlestown's waterfront was the first area to be developed, with wharves extended out into the water, and a seawall.

Through the 1700's, Charleston (by now known as Charlestown) grew and prospered. Years of Indian attacks gave way to the era of the pirate, and even the notorious "Blackbeard" himself had to be dealt with. After one attack, in which Samual Wragg, a member of the Provincial Congress and his four-year-old son were taken by Blackbeard and held for ransom, one Colonel Rhett was commissioned to end the scourge. Within a month, some 49 pirates had been caught, tried and executed.

With relative peace, and the growth of trade, Charleston entered her golden age, becoming one of the most important centers of the arts and commerce in North America.

Continued on page 7

4

It has always been the aim of the Management to offer our guests the opportunity to sample a wide variety of wines at minimum cost, in order to promote familiarity with the many fine choices available. Thus, your attention is invited to

OUR LIST OF
FINE WINES
by the
CARAFE

CONSIDERED BY MANY TO BE THE LARGEST AND FINEST SELECTION IN THE CITY OF CHARLESTON

IN ADDITION...
OUR BOTTLED WINES FEATURE
THE BEST VINTAGES OF THE COLONIES AND THE MOTHER COUNTRY
and are commended to your attention

APPETIZERS

ESCARGOTS BAKED IN MUSHROOM CAPS
With garlic, special spices and a dash of chablis 3.50

POTTED CREEK SHRIMP
Tiny local shrimp, in our special marinade 2.95

SHRIMP COCKTAIL
Large local shrimp with a fine cocktail sauce 3.75

ATLANTIC BLUE CRAB FINGERS
With Dijon mustard mayonnaise 3.25

LUMP CRABMEAT COCKTAIL
Choice nuggets from local blue crab with cocktail sauce 3.95

ONION PIE
Onions, bacon, cheese and egg custard, baked fresh daily in a pie shell 1.75

THINLY SLICED PROSCIUTTO HAM AND RIPE SEASONAL MELON 2.50

SOUPS

CHARLESTON SHE-CRAB SOUP
The Carolina classic, with our chef's special touch 1.95

SHELLFISH CHOWDER
A hearty soup, full of shrimp, scallops and crabmeat 1.95

POT LUCK SOUP *The chef's selection* 1.25

BAKED SWISS ONION SOUP
A generous serving, topped with genuine Swiss gruyere 2.25

THE SALAD CART
You are invited to partake of our ample selection of greens and garnishes, crisps and savories, relishes and salads, and to carve your own crusty chunk of assorted breads. Return for more should the mood prevail.
Salad cart a la carte... 4.95

5

115

VSPPF

VERBAND SCHWEIZERISCHER
PAPIER- UND PAPIERSTOFF-FABRIKANTEN

HOTEL DU GOLF
CRANS - MONTANA
22 JUIN 1979

MENU

SAUMON EN BELLEVUE
GARNI DE FRIVOLITES
SAUCE VERTE

* * *

CONSOMME DOUBLE
AU FUMET DE TOMATES
A L'ANDALOUSE

*

TRAIN DE COTES DU CHAROLAIS ROTI
SAUCE MARCHANDE DE VIN
POMMES CHATEAU
AUBERGINES FARCIES

*

CREPES SOUFFLEES DES PERES CHARTREUX

LE PAPIER SUISSE

VINS

DEZALEY "PERTUIZET" CHAUDET
CHATEAU PAVEIL DE LUZE 1969 HAUT-MEDOC
PINOT NOIR ROMERBLUT, ORSAT

EAU DE VIE DU PAYS
CAFE

116

116   Hôtel du Golf, Crans-Montana,
Suisse
Carte de menu. Impression: J. Périsset,
Sierre
210×310 mm, 2 pages. Carton couché.
Offset argent et rouge. Estampé
Cette carte, destinée à une réception
privée, a la forme d'une channe. Elle
évoque ainsi les régions viticoles du
Valais.

116   Hôtel du Golf, Crans-Montana,
Schweiz
Spezialkarte. Druck J. Périsset, Sierre
210×310 mm, 2seitig. Kunstdruckkarton. Offset silber und rot. Formgestanzt
Diese für eine geschlossene Gesellschaft entworfene Karte ist in Form
einer Weinkanne in Anlehnung an das
Weinbaugebiet des Wallis konzipiert.

116   Hôtel du Golf, Crans-Montana,
Switzerland
Special menu-card. Printed by J. Périsset, Sierre
210×310 mm, 2 pages. Art card. Offset
printing in silver and red. Die-cut
This card, specially designed for a
private party, is conceived in the shape
of a wine-jug, alluding to the wine-
growing Valais district.

117   Hôtel du Golf, Crans-Montana,
Suisse
Carte de menu spéciale. Création:
Amag, Suisse
235×123 mm, ouvert 235×246 mm,
4 pages. Papier structuré à la cuve.
Offset brun. Plié, estampé
Carte créée pour la soirée du personnel
d'une entreprise importatrice d'auto-
mobiles.

117   Hôtel du Golf, Crans-Montana,
Schweiz
Spezialkarte.
Gestaltung Amag, Schweiz
235×123 mm, offen 235×246 mm,
4seitig. Papier mit Büttenstruktur.
Offset braun. Gefalzt, formgestanzt
Für den Familienabend des Personals
einer Autoimportfirma gestaltete Karte

117   Hôtel du Golf, Crans-Montana,
Switzerland
Special menu-card. Designed by
Amag, Switzerland
235×123 mm, open 235×246 mm, 4
pages. Paper with texture of hand-
made paper. Offset printing in brown.
Folded, die-cut
For a family celebration held for em-
ployees of a car-import business.

GOLF

117

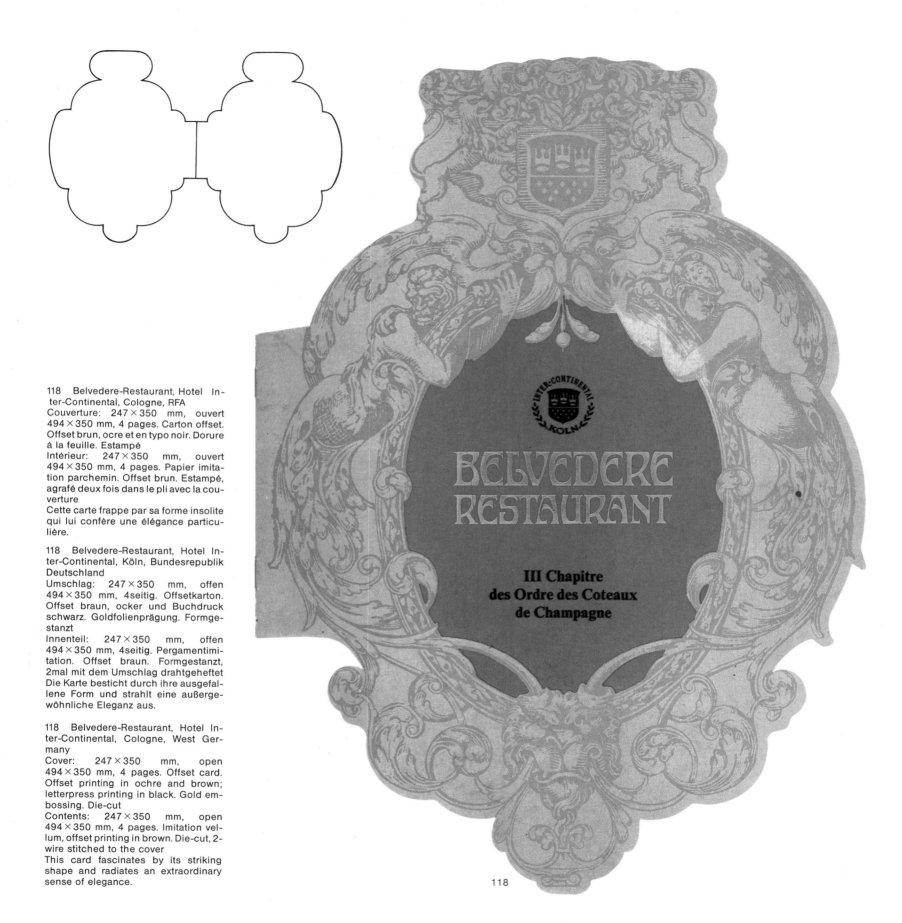

118 Belvedere-Restaurant, Hotel Inter-Continental, Cologne, RFA
Couverture: 247×350 mm, ouvert
494×350 mm, 4 pages. Carton offset.
Offset brun, ocre et en typo noir. Dorure
à la feuille. Estampé
Intérieur: 247×350 mm, ouvert
494×350 mm, 4 pages. Papier imitation parchemin. Offset brun. Estampé,
agrafé deux fois dans le pli avec la couverture
Cette carte frappe par sa forme insolite
qui lui confère une élégance particu-
lière.

118 Belvedere-Restaurant, Hotel Inter-Continental, Köln, Bundesrepublik
Deutschland
Umschlag: 247×350 mm, offen
494×350 mm, 4seitig. Offsetkarton.
Offset braun, ocker und Buchdruck
schwarz. Goldfolienprägung. Formgestanzt
Innenteil: 247×350 mm, offen
494×350 mm, 4seitig. Pergamentimitation. Offset braun. Formgestanzt,
2mal mit dem Umschlag drahtgeheftet
Die Karte besticht durch ihre ausgefal-
lene Form und strahlt eine außergewöhnliche Eleganz aus.

118 Belvedere-Restaurant, Hotel Inter-Continental, Cologne, West Germany
Cover: 247×350 mm, open
494×350 mm, 4 pages. Offset card.
Offset printing in ochre and brown;
letterpress printing in black. Gold embossing. Die-cut
Contents: 247×350 mm, open
494×350 mm, 4 pages. Imitation vellum, offset printing in brown. Die-cut, 2-
wire stitched to the cover
This card fascinates by its striking
shape and radiates an extraordinary
sense of elegance.

INTER-CONTINENTAL
KÖLN

BELVEDERE
RESTAURANT

**III Chapitre
des Ordre des Coteaux
de Champagne**

118

Speiserestaurant Löwen
Rôtisserie Pfeffermühle
Büren an der Aare

Konfirmationsfeier

ANGELA WEIBEL

LE MENU

Le Pâté maison en croûte
La sauce Cumberland
La salade Waldorf

•

Le Mixed-Grill riche Pfeffermühle
Le Roesti-bernois
Le riz aux amandes
La Bouquetière de légumes

•

Le Vacherin glacé aux fraises

•

Le bon café et liqueurs
Les friandises

LES VINS

Epesses le Rocanel 1975
Fleurie 1976

Palmsonntag, 19. März 1978

119

119   Restaurant Löwen, Büren an der Aare, Suisse
Carte de menu spéciale pour une confirmation. Impression: Alba, Appenzell
310 × 310 mm, batiste coton avec impression textile couleur. Texte en sérigraphie noir
Carte établie pour une fête de famille. Le mouchoir peut être emporté comme souvenir. D'autres motifs peuvent être obtenus.

119   Restaurant Löwen, Büren an der Aare, Schweiz
Spezialkarte für Konfirmationsfeier. Druck Alba, Appenzell
310 × 310 mm, Baumwollbattist mit farbigem Textildruck. Text Siebdruck schwarz
Menü für einen festlichen Familienanlaß. Das Taschentuch kann als Andenken mitgenommen werden. Es sind verschiedene Motive erhältlich.

119   Restaurant Löwen, Büren on the Aare, Switzerland
Special menu-card for a confirmation celebration
310 × 310 mm, voile with design printed in colour on to the material. Text: screen printing in black
Menu for a family celebration. The handkerchief may be kept as a memento. Various motifs are available.

120 Palace Hotel, Gstaad, Suisse
Carte de menu spéciale à l'occasione de la soirée de gala du sport suisse. Fabrication et impression: Kreier
300 × 300 mm, batiste coton rouge. Texte en sérigraphie noir
Une réalisation simple, bien étudiée pour une clientèle choisie.

120 Palace Hotel, Gstaad, Schweiz
Spezialkarte für Gala-Abend des Schweizer Sports. Herstellung und Druck Kreier
300 × 300 mm, Baumwollbattist rot. Text Siebdruck schwarz
Einfach gestaltete und gut wirkende Möglichkeit für ein ausgesuchtes Publikum

120 Palace Hotel, Gstaad, Switzerland
Special menu-card for a gala evening of Swiss sport. Designed and printed by Kreier
300 × 300 mm, red voile. Text: screen printing in black
Simple design and pleasing effect for a select public.

120

121

121 Hôtel du Golf, Crans-Montana, Suisse
Carte de menu spéciale pour le Saint-Sylvestre. Fabrication et impression: Fisba-Stoffels, St-Gall
310 × 310 mm, batiste coton rouge. Texte et illustration en sérigraphie noir
Petit cochon porte-bonheur et objets amusants servent de cadre et donnent le ton de la fête.

121 Hôtel du Golf, Crans-Montana, Schweiz
Spezialkarte für Silvester-Menu. Herstellung und Druck Fisba-Stoffels, St. Gallen
310 × 310 mm, Baumwollbattist rot. Text und Illustration in Siebdruck schwarz
Glücksschwein und Festdekoration als Rahmen für die Silvesterfeier

121 Hôtel du Golf, Crans-Montana, Switzerland
Special menu-card for a New Year's Eve celebration. Designed and printed by Fisba-Stoffels, St. Gallen
310 × 310 mm, red voile. Text and illustration: screen printing in black
The little pig as symbol of good luck and festive decorations create a suitable atmosphere for a New Year's Eve celebration.

Cartes de compagnies d'aviation

Luftfahrtgesellschaften

Airlines

Dans la plupart des cas, les compagnies d'aviation s'identifient à leur pays d'origine. Ainsi, les cartes de menus jouent-elles le double rôle de publicité de prestige en faveur de la compagnie et du pays dont elle porte les couleurs. L'objectif de ces cartes n'étant pas de vendre des repas, elles contribuent en revanche efficacement à imposer une image de marque. La reproduction de gravures anciennes, d'œuvres d'art ou d'objets artisanaux, illustre la culture du pays; il est également possible de faire appel à d'autres aspects typiques, tels que paysages, architecture, us et coutumes nationaux. La destination du vol ou des informations sur les liaisons internationales sont aussi parmi les thèmes présentés, fréquemment sous forme de séries de cartes. Les textes publicitaires, multilingues, fournissent d'intéressantes précisions sur les sujets illustrés, créant l'identité compagnie-pays d'origine.

Luftfahrtgesellschaften werden in der Regel mit dem Land, dessen Hoheitszeichen sie tragen, identifiziert. Die Speisekarten sind Teil der Prestigewerbung für die Gesellschaft und damit auch für das Land. Sie müssen hier nicht Mahlzeiten verkaufen, aber sie tragen entscheidend zur Prägung eines Markenbildes bei.
Mit der Abbildung von Werken aus Kunst und Kunsthandwerk oder der Reproduktion alter Stiche kann das kulturelle Prestige eines Landes dokumentiert werden. Weitere Themen sind zum Beispiel Landschaft, Architektur, Brauchtum des betreffenden Landes, aber auch das angeflogene Ziel oder Hinweise auf weltweite Verbindungen. Diese Themen werden oft in Form von Serien gezeigt. Werbetexte, in der Regel mehrsprachig, können interessante Erklärungen zu den Abbildungen enthalten und den gedanklichen Zusammenhang mit der Fluggesellschaft herstellen.

Airline companies are usually identified with the country of origin. Their menus seek to win prestige for the company and thus also for the nation concerned. They do not need to sell the food they list but serve simply to buttress an image.
A nation's prestige may be demonstrated by reproductions of works of art or handicrafts. Other themes include scenic views, important buildings and folk customs of the country concerned, as well as references to the place of destination or to the airline's services in other parts of the world. These themes often form part of a series. Advertising matter, usually in several languages, may explain what is illustrated and direct the passenger's thoughts to the airline.

122a–b Concorde, Air France, Paris
Carte de menu. Création: Service Publicité et Créativité d'Air France, Paris. Impression: Imprimerie Debar, Reims
Couverture: 210 × 297 mm, ouvert 420 × 297 mm, 4 pages. Papier offset. Page 1 offset 4 couleurs, page 2 offset gris. Rainé, plié
Intérieur: 210 × 297 mm, ouvert 420 × 297 mm, 4 pages. Carte des vins 80 × 297 mm, ouvert 160 × 297 mm, 4 pages. Papier couché mat. Impression en gris. Plié. Les deux cartes sont insérées l'une dans l'autre, agrafées deux fois dans le pli et assemblées à la couverture par un cordon blanc
En page 2 de la couverture, description détaillée de l'illustration avec mention des sources; texte bilingue français-anglais. Présentation des mets également bilingue.

122a–b Concorde, Air France, Paris, Frankreich
Speisekarte. Gestaltung Service Publicité et Créativité d'Air France, Paris. Druck Imprimerie Debar, Reims
Umschlag: 210 × 297 mm, offen 420 × 297 mm, 4seitig. Offsetpapier. Seite 1 Offset 4farbig, Seite 2 Offset grau. Gerillt, gefalzt
Innenteil: 210 × 297 mm, offen 420 × 297 mm, 4seitig. Weinkarte 80 × 297 mm, offen 160 × 297 mm, 4seitig. Mattgestrichenes Kunstdruckpapier. Druck grau. Gefalzt. Beide Karten ineinandergesteckt, 2mal drahtgeheftet und durch weiße Kordel mit dem Umschlag verbunden
Auf Seite 2 des Umschlags ausführliche Bildbeschreibung mit Quellenangabe, Text 2sprachig Französisch, Englisch. Speisenangebot ebenfalls in beiden Sprachen

122a–b Concorde, Air France, Paris, France
Menu-card. Designed by Service Publicité et Créativité d'Air France, printed by Imprimerie Debar, Rheims
Cover: 210 × 297 mm, open 420 × 297 mm, 4 pages. Offset paper. Page 1: 4-colour offset printing; page 2: offset printing in grey. Scored, folded
Contents: 210 × 297 mm, open 420 × 297 mm, 4 pages, wine list: 80 × 297 mm, open 160 × 297 mm, 4 pages. Art paper with matt finish. Printing in grey. Folded, cards tucked into each other, 2-wire stitched and attached to the cover with a white cord
On page 2 of the cover: detailed picture captions with references in French and English. Menu also in French and English.

22a

122b

---

124   Air France, Paris
Création: Service Publicité et Créativité d'Air France, Paris. Impression: Imprimerie Maquet
Couverture: 210 × 297 mm, ouvert 420 × 297 mm, 4 pages. Carton couché mat. Page 1 offset 4 couleurs, page 4 offset noir. Rainé, plié, illustrations vernies

En quatrième page de couverture, bref texte bilingue français-anglais sur l'artiste et l'affiche. Il existe également une série de même format consacrée aux «Peintres contemporains de France».

---

124   Air France, Paris, Frankreich
Gestaltung Service Publicité et Créativité d'Air France, Paris. Druck Imprimerie Maquet
Umschlag: 210 × 297   mm, offen 420 × 297 mm, 4seitig. Mattgestrichener Kunstdruckkarton. Offset, Seite 1 4farbig, Seite 4 schwarz. Gerillt, gefalzt, Illustration lackiert

Auf der vierten Umschlagseite kurzer Text über den Künstler und das Plakat. 2sprachig Französisch, Englisch. In der gleichen Form existiert auch eine Reihe «Zeitgenössische Maler in Frankreich».

---

124   Air France, Paris, France
Designed by Service Publicité et Créativité d'Air France, Paris, printed by Imprimerie Maquet
Cover: 210 × 297 mm, open 420 × 297 mm, 4 pages. Art card with matt finish. Page 1: 4-colour offset printing, page 4: offset printing in

black. Scored, folded, illustration varnished
On page 4 of the cover: a short text on the artist and the poster in French and English. Further, there is a series in similar style entitled 'Contemporary Painters in France'.

---

123   Air France, Paris
Création: Service Publicité et Créativité d'Air France, Paris. Impression: Imprimerie Maillet, Saint-Ouen, Photo ABC (Guyomard)
Couverture: 210 × 297   mm, ouvert 420 × 297 mm, 4 pages. Chromo une face. Page 1 offset 4 couleurs, page 2 en gris. Rainé, plié
En page 2 texte publicitaire sur des horloges et des avions, descriptions détaillées des illustrations avec mention des sources. Texte bilingue français-anglais.

123   Air France, Paris, Frankreich
Gestaltung Service Publicité et Créativité d'Air France, Paris. Druck Imprimerie Maillet, Saint-Ouen, Foto ABC (Guyomard)
Umschlag: 210 × 297   mm, offen 420 × 297 mm, 4seitig. Chromokarton einseitig. Seite 1 Offset 4farbig, Seite 2 grau. Gerillt, gefalzt
Auf Seite 2 Werbetext über Uhren und Flugzeuge sowie ausführliche Bildlegende mit Quellenangabe, Text 2sprachig Französisch, Englisch

123   Air France, Paris, France
Designed by Service Publicité et Créativité d'Air France, printed by Imprimerie Maillet, Saint-Ouen, photograph by ABC (Guyomard)
Cover: 210 × 297   mm, open 420 × 297 mm, 4 pages. One-sided cast-coated card. Page 1: 4-colour offset printing; page 2: offset printing in grey. Scored, folded
On page 2: advertising text on clocks and aeroplanes, as well as detailed captions with references in French and English.

123

124

132

MENU

125

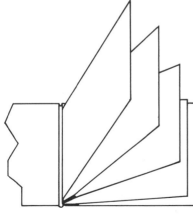

125 Sabena, Bruxelles, Belgique
Carte de menu. Création: Service de Publicité de Sabena
Couverture: 295 × 230 mm, ouvert 490 × 230 mm, 4 pages. Chromo une face. Page 1 offset 4 couleurs, page 4 offset noir. Rainé, plié
Intérieur: 220 × 290 mm, ouvert 440 × 290 mm, 4 pages. Papier couché mat. Impression typo noir. Plié et collé au dos avec la couverture
Légende de l'illustration en quatre langues: français-flamand-anglais-allemand. Présentation des mets en français. En page 1, portrait d'Hélène Fourment de P. P. Rubens.

125 Sabena, Brüssel, Belgien
Speisekarte. Gestaltung Service de Publicité de Sabena
Umschlag: 295 × 230 mm, offen 490 × 230 mm, 4seitig. Chromokarton einseitig. Offset, Seite 1 4farbig, Seite 4 schwarz. Gerillt, gefalzt
Innenteil: 220 × 290 mm, offen 440 × 290 mm, 4seitig. Mattgestrichenes Kunstdruckpapier. Buchdruck schwarz. Gefalzt und im Rücken mit dem Umschlag zusammengeklebt
Bildlegende 4sprachig Französisch, Flämisch, Englisch, Deutsch, Speisenangebot Französisch. Die Seite 1 zeigt das Porträt der Hélène Fourment von P. P. Rubens.

125 Sabena, Brussels, Belgium
Menu-card. Designed by Service de Publicité de Sabena
Cover: 295 × 230 mm, open 490 × 230 mm, 4 pages. One-sided cast-coated card. Page 1: 4-colour offset printing, page 4: offset printing in black. Scored, folded
Contents: 220 × 290 mm, open 440 × 290 mm, 4 pages. Art paper with matt finish. Letterpress printing in black. Folded and glued to the cover on the spine
Picture captions in French, Flemish, English and German. Menu in French. Page 1 reproduces the portrait of Hélène Fourment by P. P. Rubens.

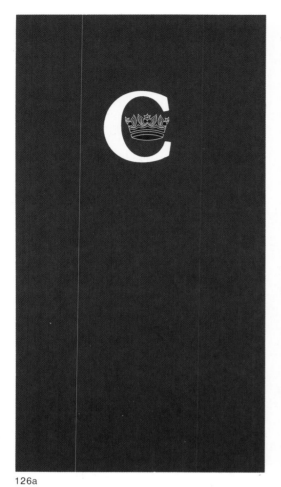

126a

127a

William Shakespeare

In the 16th century town of Stratford-on-Avon, around 1570, a small boy of about six or seven was going 'unwillingly to school'. The working day would have been painfully long, the curriculum almost exclusively Latin Grammar. His name was William Shakespeare.

Elizabeth I had been on the throne for about six years when Shakespeare was born, of good middle-class stock, the son of a respected tradesman.

Not much is known of Shakespeare's early life. He went to the local grammar school – plenty of evidence in his plays subsequently suggests that he knew the classics. Documents do exist to show that he married Anne Hathaway, the daughter of a substantial yeoman family from nearby Shottery, in 1582. The story goes that Shakespeare left Stratford soon afterwards to avoid prosecution for poaching deer, and went to London, a four-day walk, probably in 1587, probably to realise an ambition to become an actor. He was soon to become connected with companies of players and the stage and, in 1589, he was involved with the Blackfriars Theatre. From 1594 he was one of the Chamberlain's Men, charged with providing Court entertainment, and many of his plays were written for them. The original publication of 'A Midsummer's Night Dream' bears the inscription 'As it hath beene sundry times publikely acted, by the Right Honourable, the Lord Chamberlaine his servants.' His name appears on the cast list of Ben Johnson's 'Every Man in his Humour' in 1597, and before the end of the century he was one of the proprietors of the Globe Theatre on Bankside. He was not only an actor and playwright, but a successful business man, and his work was known and respected by his contemporaries.

Between 1590 and 1612 Shakespeare contributed a glorious profusion of masterworks to English literature and the world. Profound and moving tragedies. Light, delicate romances. Historical dramas with a remarkable understanding of events. Delicious comedies that were wise and witty, occasionally foolish, always amusing. The First Folio, the first collected edition of his plays, contained thirty-five.

Visits to Stratford alternated with his busy working life in London and, in 1597, he bought New Place, one of the largest houses in the town, where he was to spend his retirement among family and friends. He died, aged 52, on 23 April, 1616, and was buried in the Parish Church on the Avon riverside. These words are incised on his tomb:

Good frend for Jesus sake forbeare
To digg the dust enclosed heare;
Blese be ye man yt spares these stones
And curst be he yt moves my bones.

A
Midsommer nights
dreame.

As it hath beene sundry times publikely acted, by the Right Honourable, the Lord Chamberlaine his servants.

Written by William Shakespeare.

Printed by Iames Roberts, 1600.

127b

126b

126a–b   Concorde, British Airways, Londres, GB
Création: Richard Negus PPSIAD/FSTD
Couverture: 151×190 mm, ouvert 302×190 mm, 4 pages. Chromo double face. Pages 1 et 4 offset bleu foncé. Dorure à la feuille. Laminé, rainé, plié
Utilisation intéressante du sigle «C» avec couronne du graphisme Concorde. Adaptation en or du logo «British Airways».

126a–b   Concorde, British Airways, London, Großbritannien
Gestaltung Richard Negus PPSIAD/FSTD
Umschlag: 151×190 mm, offen 302×190 mm, 4seitig. Chromokarton zweiseitig. Seiten 1 und 4 Offset dunkelblau. Goldfolienprägung. Laminiert, gerillt, gefalzt
Interessant die signetartige Verwendung des «C» mit Krone aus dem Concorde-Schriftzug. Anpassung des «British Airways»-Schriftzugs in Gold

126a–b   Concorde, British Airways, London, Great Britain
Designed by Richard Negus PPSIAD/FSTD
Cover: 151×190 mm, open 302×190 mm, 4 pages. Two-sided cast-coated card. Pages 1 and 4: offset printing in dark blue. Gold embossing. Laminated, scored, folded
An elegant solution. Of particular interest is the emblematic use of the 'C' with crown taken from Concorde's characteristic lettering. Adaptation of the British Airways logo in gold.

127a–b, 128a–c   British Airways, Londres, GB
Impression: W. R. Royle & Son Ltd.
Couverture: 151×190 mm, ouvert 302×190 mm, 4 pages. Carton couché mat. Page 1 offset 4 couleurs, combinaison fond et cadre. Page 2 offset noir. Rainé, plié, laminé
Légendes des illustrations et graphisme en page 4. En page 2, texte sur l'auteur et son œuvre.

127a–b, 128a–c   British Airways, London, Großbritannien
Druckerei W. R. Royle & Son Ltd.
Umschlag: 151×190 mm, offen 302×190 mm, 4seitig. Mattgestrichener Kunstdruckkarton. Seite 1 Offset 4farbig und Kombination Hintergrund/Rahmen, Seite 2 Offset schwarz. Gerillt, gefalzt, laminiert
Bildlegenden und Schriftzug auf Seite 4. Seite 2 Text über den Dichter und sein Werk

127a–b, 128a–c   British Airways, London, Great Britain
Printed by W. R. Royle & Son Ltd.
Cover: 151×190 mm, open 302×190 mm, 4 pages. Art paper with matt finish. Four-colour offset printing on page 1, background and border are silk-screen combinations; page 2: offset printing in black. Scored, folded, laminated
Picture captions and logo on page 4. On page 2: a text on the poet and his work.

Menu

British airways

1	4
2	3

1 The family house at Chawton.
2 Relics at Chawton.
3 Lansdown Crescent, Bath.
4 A contemporary portrait.

Jane Austen

Jane Austen was born in 1775, the last child but one of the Rector of Steventon in Hampshire. As a young girl she was said to be an attractive, charming girl with a sweet disposition and was largely educated by her father, a classical scholar with a well-stocked library. It was a large and happy family (Jane had six brothers and a sister, Cassandra), typical of the middle-class English society of the late 18th century.

In such an untroubled environment, Jane grew up and lived her whole life among the families of land owners and professional men with strictly conventional attitudes to politics, religion, morals and manners. It was this society that provided the characters and situations for her writing. Despite a lack of wordly experience, she described the life she knew and understood with insight, wit, accuracy and a remarkable ear for contemporary dialogue.

It was at Steventon, when she was still very young, that she first drafted 'Pride and Prejudice', 'Sense and Sensibility' and 'Northanger Abbey'; she revised them later at Chawton, near Alton, where the Austens lived after spending some years in Bath. 'Pride and Prejudice', probably the most celebrated of all her novels, was begun as early as 1796, but did not appear until 1813. 1,500 copies were printed, at 18 shillings each. The later books – 'Emma', 'Mansfield Park' and, last, 'Persuasion' – were all written at Chawton.

Jane Austen achieved little public recognition, not only during her short lifetime, but for most of the nineteenth century. She was, however, highly regarded by her literary contemporaries; Lord Macaulay declared that 'she approaches Shakespeare nearer than any of our writers in drawing character'; in 1815, 'Emma' was dedicated, with his permission, to the Prince Regent. She never married although she once made a mysterious reference to 'an attachment'.

At the beginning of 1817, living in a cottage at Winchester with her sister, and despite ill-health, she began a new novel, eventually titled 'Sanditon'. It remained unfinished; on 18 July she died in Cassandra's arms, at the age of 41, and was buried in the Cathedral.

Royal Class

129

130

129 Royal Class, KLM Royal Dutch Airlines, Amstelveen, Pays-Bas
Création: Service de publicité KLM, Amstelveen. Photo: KLM Aerocarto, La Haye
174 × 300 mm, ouvert 430 × 300 mm, 4 pages et rabat de 83 mm de largeur. Chromo une face. Page 1 offset 4 couleurs, les autres pages en typo noir. Plis roulés
Présentation des mets bilingue français-anglais; toutefois le texte français est recouvert par le rabat de la carte des consommations. Autres textes ainsi que la carte des vins en anglais.

129 Royal Class, KLM Royal Dutch Airlines, Amstelveen, Niederlande
Gestaltung Werbeabteilung KLM, Amstelveen, Foto KLM Aerocarto, Den Haag
174 × 300 mm, offen 430 × 300 mm, 4seitig und 83 mm breite Klappe. Chromokarton einseitig. Seite 1 Offset 4farbig, übrige Seiten Buchdruck schwarz. Wickelfalz
Speisenangebot 2sprachig Französisch, Englisch, wobei der französische Text von der Klappe der Getränkekarte verdeckt wird. Übrige Texte und Weinkarte Englisch

129 Royal Class, KLM Royal Dutch Airlines, Amstelveen, The Netherlands
Designed by the advertising department of KLM, Amstelveen, photograph by KLM Aerocarto, The Hague
174 × 300 mm, open 430 × 300 mm, 4 pages plus flap of 83 mm width. One-sided cast-coated card. Page 1: 4-colour offset printing, remaining pages: letterpress printing in black. Reverse accordion fold
Menu in French and English, the French text covered by the wine list's flap. Remaining texts and wine list in English

130 Business Class, KLM Royal Dutch Airlines, Amstelveen, Pays-Bas
Carte de menu. Création: Service de publicité KLM, Amstelveen. Photo: KLM Aerocarto, La Haye
187 × 241 mm, ouvert 308 × 241 mm, 4 pages. Carton couché. Page 1 offset 4 couleurs, texte en typo noir. Rainé, plié

130 Business Class, KLM Royal Dutch Airlines, Amstelveen, Niederlande
Speisekarte. Gestaltung Werbeabteilung KLM, Amstelveen, Foto KLM Aerocarto, Den Haag
187 × 241 mm, offen 308 × 241 mm, 4seitig. Kunstdruckkarton. Seite 1 Offset 4farbig, Text Buchdruck schwarz. Gerillt, gefalzt

130 Business Class, KLM Royal Dutch Airlines, Amstelveen, The Netherlands
Menu-card. Designed by the advertising department of KLM, Amstelveen, photograph by KLM Aerocarto, The Hague
187 × 241 mm, open 308 × 241 mm, 4 pages. Art paper. Page 1: 4-colour offset printing. Letterpress printing in black. Scored, folded

131 UTA, Paris
Carte de menu. Création: Créations
Fournier, Paris, d'après un document
tiré du livre «Faïences Françaises»
207×210 mm, ouvert 414×210 mm,
4 pages. Newschromo une face. Page 1
offset 4 couleurs, texte des pages 3 et 4
en typo gris. Plié, estampé, en page 1
gaufrage
Le gaufrage accentue le relief de l'illustration. La France est représentée ici,
d'une manière originale, par l'association des arts décoratifs et de l'art culinaire.

131 UTA, Paris, Frankreich
Speisekarte. Gestaltung Créations
Fournier, Paris, nach einem Dokument
aus dem Buch «Faïences Françaises»
207×210 mm, offen 414×210 mm,
4seitig. Newschromo einseitig. Seite 1
Offset 4farbig, Text Seiten 3 und 4
Buchdruck grau. Gefalzt, formgestanzt,
Seite 1 geprägt (Relief)
Die Prägung verleiht der Abbildung
noch mehr Tiefe. Die Verbindung mei-
sterhaftes Kunsthandwerk und Eßkul-
tur steht für Frankreich. Diese Assoziation wird hier auf originelle Weise hergestellt.

131 UTA, Paris, France
Menu-card. Designed by Créations
Fournier, Paris, based on a document
from the book *Faïences Françaises*
207×210 mm, open 414×210 mm, 4
pages. One-sided super-calendered
paper. Page 1: 4-colour offset printing,
text on pages 3 and 4: letterpress printing in grey. Folded, die-cut, page 1:
embossed (relief)
The embossing gives yet more depth to
the illustration. The association of
masterly craftsmanship with *haute cuisine* epitomizes France, and this link is
presented in a highly original manner.

131

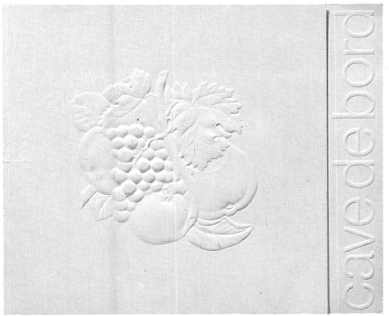

132

132 UTA, Paris
Carte des consommations. Création: Créations Fournier, Paris
210×175 mm, ouvert 388×175 mm, 4 pages. Carton
offset. Gaufrage en pages 1 et 3, pages 2 et 3 offset
gris
Seules la magistrale maîtrise du procédé et l'utilisation
d'un papier de première qualité permettent des gau-
frages d'une telle profondeur.

132 UTA, Paris, Frankreich
Getränkekarte. Gestaltung Créations Fournier, Paris
210×175 mm, offen 388×175 mm, 4seitig. Offsetkarton. Seiten 1 und 3 Blindprägung, Seiten 2–3 Offset
grau
Nur die meisterliche Beherrschung des Verfahrens
und die Verwendung eines erstklassigen Papiers erlauben Prägungen von solcher Tiefe.

132 UTA, Paris, France
Wine list. Designed by Créations Fournier, Paris
210×175 mm, open 388×175 mm, 4 pages. Offset
card. Pages 1 and 3: blind embossing, pages 2–3:
offset printing in grey
Only skilful mastery of technique and use of first-class
paper permit embossing to such a degree of depth.

133

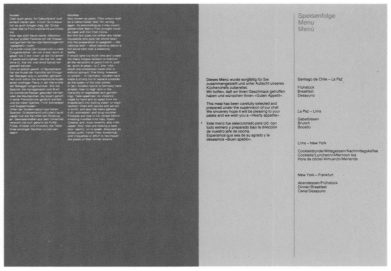

134a

133, 134a–c Lufthansa, Cologne, RFA
Carte de menu. Conception, graphisme et direction artistique: Klaus Wille, Cologne. Typographie intérieur: Rolf Querengässer, Cologne. Photo: Siegfried Himmer, Cologne
Couverture: 210 × 297 mm, ouvert 420 × 297 mm, 4 pages. Carton offset.

Pages 1 et 4 offset 4 couleurs, graphisme en couleur spéciale, pages 2 et 3 offset brun, texte en négatif. Rainé, plié, verni
Intérieur: 210 × 297 mm, 8 pages. Papier structuré à la cuve. Offset brun et rouge. Plié et agrafé deux fois dans le pli avec la couverture

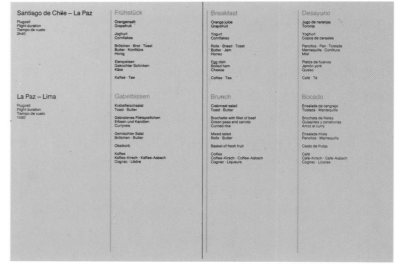

134b

133, 134a–c Lufthansa, Köln, Bundesrepublik Deutschland
Speisekarte. Konzeption, Design und Art Director Klaus Wille, Köln. Typografie Innenteil Rolf Querengässer, Köln, Foto Siegfried Himmer, Köln
Umschlag: 210 × 297 mm, offen 420 × 297 mm, 4seitig. Offsetkarton.

Seiten 1 und 4 Offset 4farbig, Schriftzug Sonderfarbe, Seiten 2–3 Offset braun, Text negativ. Gerillt, gefalzt, lackiert
Innenteil: 210 × 297 mm, 8seitig. Papier mit Büttenstruktur. Offset braun und rot. Gefalzt und mit dem Umschlag 2mal drahtgeheftet

133, 134a–c Lufthansa, Cologne, West Germany
Menu-card. Idea, design and art director: Klaus Wille, Cologne; typography of inside pages by Rolf Querengässer, Cologne; photograph taken by Siegfried Himmer, Cologne

Cover: 210 × 297 mm, open 420 × 297 mm, 4 pages. Offset card. Pages 1 and 4: 4-colour offset printing plus additional colour for lettering, pages 2–3: offset printing in brown, negative text. Scored, folded, varnished

135 Lufthansa, Cologne, RFA
Carte des vins. Conception, graphisme et direction artistique: Klaus Wille, Cologne. Photo: Hans Hansen, Hambourg

210 × 297 mm, ouvert 420 × 297 mm, 4 pages. Carton offset. Pages 1 et 4 offset 4 couleurs. Pages 2 et 3 offset vert et noir

135 Lufthansa, Köln, Bundesrepublik Deutschland
Weinkarte. Konzeption, Design und Art Director Klaus Wille, Köln. Foto Hans Hansen, Hamburg

210 × 297 mm, offen 420 × 297 mm, 4seitig. Offsetkarton. Seiten 1 und 4 Offset 4farbig, Seiten 2–3 Offset grün, schwarz

135 Lufthansa, Cologne, West Germany
Wine list. Idea, design and art director: Klaus Wille, Cologne, photograph by Hans Hansen, Hamburg

210 × 297 mm, open 420 × 297 mm, 4 pages. Offset card. Pages 1 and 4: 4-colour offset printing; pages 2–3: offset printing in green and black

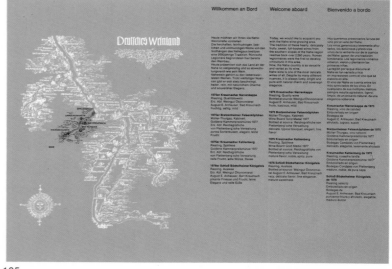

135

Gasthof «Zur Flut»
Saint-Saphorin, Kt. Waadt
(1750)

The Flood Inn
Saint-Saphorin, ct. of Vaud
(1750)

Auberge «A l'Onde»
Saint-Saphorin, ct. de Vaud
(1750)

In längst vergangenen Zeiten, als das Reisen noch mühsam und beschwerlich war, verhiess der Anblick eines Wirtshausschildes oft die höchste Glückseligkeit: Obdach, eine währschafte Mahlzeit, frohe Geselligkeit, ein Nachtlager... In dieser Ur-Form der Werbung fand edle Handwerkskunst, von traditioneller Gastfreundschaft inspiriert, ihren Ausdruck. Heute fliegen wir mit nahezu Schallgeschwindigkeit über Meere und Kontinente. Doch die Gastlichkeit vergangener Zeiten lebt weiter. Das möchte Ihnen die Swissair in einigen Minuten (d.h. in 100, vielleicht 150 Kilometern) beweisen. Guten Appetit!

In days of old, when travelling was at best an irksome and laborious operation, the sight of an inn sign was often a reason for relief and rejoicing. It meant a square meal, jolly company, a bed for the night... This early form of advertising found expression in artistic craftsmanship inspired by traditional hospitality.
Nowadays we fly over seas and continents almost with the speed of sound. Yet the old-time hospitality lives on. Swissair will prove this to you in a few minutes—say in 60 or 100 miles. Bon appétit!

Dans le bon vieux temps, quand les voyages étaient encore pénibles et difficiles, la vue d'une enseigne d'auberge promettait souvent la plus grande des félicités: un asile, un repas plantureux, une joyeuse compagnie, un gîte. Inspiré de l'hospitalité traditionnelle, le noble art artisanal trouva son expression dans cette forme primitive de publicité: l'enseigne. Aujourd'hui, nous survolons les mers et les continents presque à la vitesse du son. Mais l'hospitalité des temps passés demeure. Swissair voudrait vous le prouver dans quelques minutes (c'est-à-dire dans 100 ou 150 kilomètres). Bon appétit!

SWISSAIR

Printed in Switzerland

Menu

136

136   Swissair, Zurich, Suisse
Création: Service de publicité Swissair, Zurich
146×195 mm, ouvert 292×195 mm, 4 pages. Chromo une face. Page 1 offset 4 couleurs et couleur spéciale pour le fond, page 4 offset noir. Rainé, plié, verni
En page 4 bref texte trilingue allemand-anglais-français sur les enseignes d'auberges, l'artisanat et l'hospitalité.

136   Swissair, Zürich, Schweiz
Gestaltung Werbeabteilung Swissair, Zürich
146×195 mm, offen 292×195 mm, 4seitig. Chromokarton einseitig. Seite 1 Offset 4farbig und Sonderfarbe für Hintergrund, Seite 4 Offset schwarz. Gerillt, gefalzt, lackiert
Seite 4 kurzer Text über Wirtshausschilder, Handwerkskunst, Gastlichkeit, 3sprachig Deutsch, Englisch, Französisch

136   Swissair, Zurich, Switzerland
Designed by the advertising department of Swissair, Zurich
146×195 mm, open 292×195 mm, 4 pages. One-sided cast-coated card. Page 1: 4-colour offset printing plus additional colour for background; page 4: offset printing in black. Scored, folded, varnished
Page 4: a short text on pub signs, arts and crafts, hospitality. Menu in German, English and French.

137   Swissair, Zurich, Suisse
Création: Service de publicité Swissair, Zurich. Gouache: Kurt Wirth
185×255 mm, ouvert 370×255 mm, 4 pages. Newschromo une face. Page 1 offset 4 couleurs et couleur spéciale pour le fond. Rainé, plié
La représentation de quelques fermes typiques suisses, de construction massive, s'associe à une impression de confiance et de sécurité.

137 Swissair, Zürich, Schweiz
Gestaltung Werbeabteilung Swissair, Zürich.
Gouache Kurt Wirth
185×255 mm, offen 370×255 mm, 4seitig. Newschromo einseitig. Seite 1 Offset 4farbig und Sonderfarbe für den Hintergrund. Gerillt, gefalzt
Die Bildfolge typischer solider Schweizer Bauernhäuser stimmt ein auf Gediegenheit und Zuverlässigkeit.

137   Swissair, Zurich, Switzerland
Designed by the advertising department of Swissair, Zurich, gouache by Kurt Wirth
185×255 mm, open 370×255 mm, 4 pages. One-sided super-calendered paper. Page 1: 4-colour offset printing plus additional colour for background. Scored, folded
The picture sequence of typical solid Swiss farmhouses lends a touch of genuineness and reliability.

137

138 Swissair, Zurich, Suisse
Création: Service de publicité Swissair, Zurich. Gouache: Kurt Wirth
185 × 255 mm, ouvert
370 × 255 mm, 4 pages. News-chromo une face. Page 1 offset 4 couleurs et couleur spéciale pour le fond. Rainé, plié
Texte trilingue anglais-allemand-français sur l'origine des plantes, ainsi que leur utilisation en cuisine.

138 Swissair, Zürich, Schweiz
Gestaltung
Werbeabteilung Swissair, Zürich. Gouache Kurt Wirth
185 × 255 mm, offen
370 × 255 mm, 4seitig. News-chromo einseitig. Seite 1 Offset 4farbig und Sonderfarbe für den Hintergrund. Gerillt, gefalzt
Text 3sprachig Englisch, Deutsch, Französisch. Geschildert werden Geschichte und Herkunft der Pflanzen sowie deren Verwendung in der Küche.

138 Swissair, Zurich, Switzerland
Designed by the advertising department of Swissair, Zurich, gouache by Kurt Wirth
185 × 255 mm, open
370 × 255 mm, 4 pages. One-sided super-calendered paper. Page 1: 4-colour offset printing plus additional colour for background. Scored, folded
Text in English, German and French. Depicted are the history and provenance of plants, as well as their use in cooking.

138

139

139 EL AL, Israël
Création: W. Turnowsky & Son Ltd. Photo: Ben Lamon
220 × 232 mm, ouvert 440 × 232 mm, 4 pages. Chromo
une face. Page 1 offset 4 couleurs. Rainé, plié
En page 4, légende d'illustration détaillée bilingue
anglais-français avec mention des sources. Les
photos de cette série présentent des récipients anti-
ques trouvés en Israël, représentés parmi des fruits du
pays.

139 EL AL, Israel
Gestaltung W. Turnowsky & Son Ltd., Foto Ben Lamon
220 × 232 mm, offen 440 × 232 mm, 4seitig. Chromokarton einseitig. Seite 1 Offset 4farbig. Gerillt, gefalzt
Seite 4 ausführliche Bildlegende mit Quellenangaben
2sprachig Englisch, Französisch. Die Fotos der Serie
zeigen in Israel gefundene antike Gefäße in Verbindung mit landeseigenen Früchten.

139 EL AL, Israel
Designed by W. Turnowsky & Son Ltd., photograph by
Ben Lamon
220 × 232 mm, open 440 × 232 mm, 4 pages. One-
sided cast-coated card. Page 1: 4-colour offset printing. Scored, folded
On page 4: detailed picture captions with references
in English and French. The photographs of the series
depict antique vessels found in Israel associated with
native fruits.

140b

140c

140a

140a–c Air Canada, Montréal, Canada
Carte de menu. Création: Air Canada, Montréal. Impression: Plow & Waters, Montréal. Photo: William Notmann (1826–1891)
Couverture: 191×305 mm, ouvert 382×305 mm, 4 pages. Carton structuré à la cuve. Offset duplex brun, texte en négatif. Rainé, plié
Intérieur: 184×279 mm, ouvert 368×279 mm, 4 pages. Papier structuré à la cuve. Pages 2 et 3 offset brun. Plié et agrafé deux fois dans le pli avec la couverture
En pages 2 et 3 de couverture, brève biographie du photographe, ainsi que légende détaillée bilingue anglais-français. Une bonne conception et un beau papier donnent de la classe à cette carte de réalisation peu coûteuse.

140a–c Air Canada, Montreal, Kanada
Speisekarte. Gestaltung Air Canada, Montreal, Druck Plow & Waters, Montreal. Foto William Notmann (1826–1891)
Umschlag: 191×305 mm, offen 382×305 mm, 4seitig. Karton mit Büttenstruktur. Offset Duplex braun, Text negativ. Gerillt, gefalzt
Innenteil: 184×279 mm, offen 368×279 mm, 4seitig. Papier mit Büttenstruktur. Seite 2–3 Offset braun. Gefalzt und mit dem Umschlag 2mal drahtgeheftet
Auf der zweiten und dritten Umschlagseite Kurzbiografie des Fotografen sowie ausführliche Bildlegende 2sprachig Englisch, Französisch. Gute Gestaltung und schönes Papier sichern dieser in der Herstellung nicht aufwendigen Karte ihre Wirkung.

140a–c Air Canada, Montréal, Canada
Menu-card. Designed by Air Canada, Montréal, printed by Plow & Waters, Montréal, photograph by William Notmann (1826–1891)
Cover: 191×305 mm, open 382×305 mm, 4 pages. Card with texture of hand-made paper. Duo-tone offset printing in brown, negative text. Scored, folded
Contents: 184×279 mm, open 368×279 mm, 4 pages. Paper with texture of hand-made paper. Pages 2–3: offset printing in brown. Folded and 2-wire stitched to the cover
On pages 2 and 3 of the cover: a short biography of the photographer, as well as detailed picture captions in English and French. Good design and attractive paper give this card its quality without incurring high production costs.

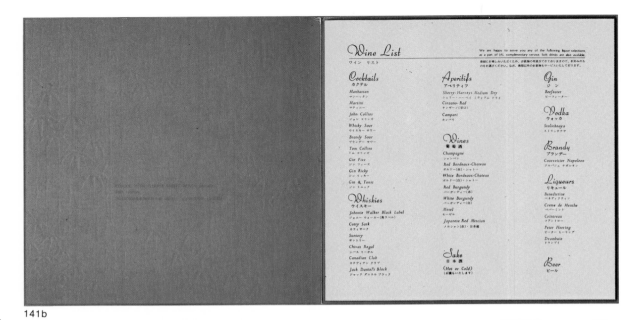

141b

141a–c Japan Airlines, Tokyo, Japon
Carte de menu
Couverture: 250×250 mm, ouvert
500×250 mm, 4 pages. Carton mat.
Page 1 offset 4 couleurs, pages 2 et 3
rouge et noir. Gaufrage. Plié
Intérieur: 244×244 mm, 14 pages. Papier offset légèrement satiné. Offset
gris et vert clair. Pliage par cahiers de 4
pages, collage dans le dos et assemblage à la couverture par un cordon
blanc
Présentation des mets bilingue anglais-japonais. Rappel du motif gaufré
par impression en fond en une seule
couleur.

141a–c Japan Airlines, Tokio, Japan
Speisekarte
Umschlag: 250×250 mm, offen
500×250 mm, 4seitig. Mattkarton.
Seite 1 Offset 4farbig, Seiten 2–3 rot
und schwarz. Blindprägung. Gefalzt
Innenteil: 244×244 mm, 14seitig.
Leicht satiniertes Offsetpapier. Offset
grau und hellgrün. Vierseitenweise gefalzt, im Bund zusammengeklebt und
durch weiße Kordel mit dem Umschlag
verbunden
Speisenangebot 2sprachig Englisch,
Japanisch. Wiederholung des Prägemotivs im Innenteil als einfarbiger Hintergrund

141a–c Japan Airlines, Tokyo, Japan
Menu-card
Cover: 250×250 mm, open
500×250 mm, 4 pages. Card with matt
finish. Page 1: 4-colour offset printing,
pages 2–3: offset printing in red and
black. Blind embossing. Folded
Contents: 244×244 mm, 14 pages. Offset paper with satin finish. Offset printing in grey and pale green. Four-page
fold, glued into gutter and attached to
cover with a white cord
Menu in English and Japanese. Repetition of the blocked motif as single-coloured background on inside pages.

141c

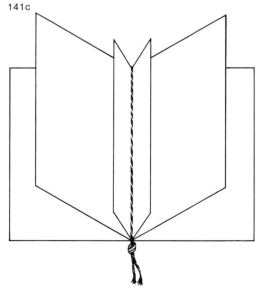

141a

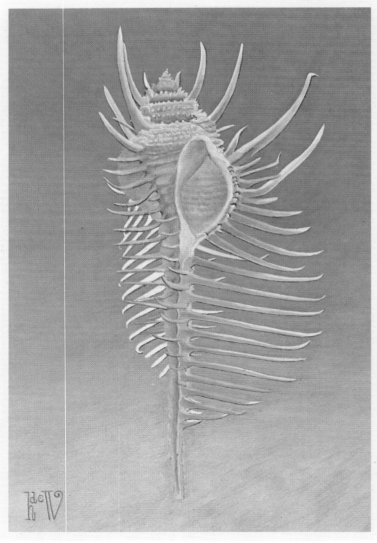

142a

Glory-of-Bengal
Conus Bengalensis
Indian Ocean

Like several hundred other Conus species, the rare Glory-of-Bengal can deliver a toxic sting from harpoon-like teeth carried in its proboscis. Some human deaths have resulted from the sting of some South Sea species.

The beguiling shape and rich coloration of its shell makes this one of the most highly valued family of snails for collectors.

Paper Nautilus
Argonauta Nodusa
Tropical Western Pacific

The Argonauta Nodusa (named for the Argonauts who sailed on the ship Argo to find the Golden Fleece) produce very handsome, fragile, thin, shell-like structures.

They are not true shells. The Paper Nautilus is the egg case of an animal resembling the octopus.

The female constructs the case with special tentacles and the eggs incubate within.

These "shells" can reach ten inches in length and unbroken specimens are highly prized.

Alabaster Murex
Murex Alabaster
Philippines to Taiwan

This very rare and much coveted Murex is decorated with fluted frills of unusual delicacy.

Scarcely known since its discovery on a Philippine beach in the 1830's until Asian fishermen began hauling them up in their nets in the 1960's.

Carrier Shell
Xenophora Pallidula
Tropical Western Pacific

These moderately large (2 to 3 inches) snails begin-with a simple clean shell. Then they cement dead material, such as rocks and shells, to their own shells until they resemble a pile of debris . . . a form of camouflage.

The upper specimen also has a substantial piece of coral which grows naturally on the already attached dead shells.

ON THE COVER:

Venus Comb
Murex Pecten
Tropical Western Pacific

Cherished as a collector's item from very early days for delicacy of its spines and perfection of form.

This striking shell, though not rare, has been sought after in the West as The Comb-of-Venus and in the East as The-Comb-of-Allah.

The spines may also have a "snowshoe" effect supporting the Murex on soft-sediment bottoms.

ABOUT THE ARTIST

HELEN de WERD lives on a quiet piece of desert near Palm Springs, California. A self-taught artist whose formal training was in photography, stage design and dance, Helen has been painting about fifteen years, working primarily with palette knife and oil on canvas for larger pieces, but has developed a technique for finely detailed smaller works of oil on plastic. A fine Arts graduate of Mills College in Oakland, California, she has exhibited at The Maxwell Galleries and The Pantechnicon in California, at Cabell-Massey, Lusara Ltd., and The Houston Galleries in Texas, and at Canyon Gallery in New Mexico. She is represented in a dozen states and two foreign countries.

Ms. de Werd has painted this seashell series exclusively for United Airlines. 12" x 18" full color lithograph prints are available from the Strathmore Company, P.O. Box 391, Geneva, Illinois 60134, shipped postpaid. Please send check or money order in the amount of $6.00 for any one print, or $10.00 for the complete set of five.

/// UNITED AIRLINES

142b

142a–c United Airlines, Chicago, Illinois, USA
Carte de menu. Lithographie: Helen de Werd, Palm Springs
190 × 278 mm, ouvert 380 × 278 mm, 4 pages. Carton offset. Pages 1 et 4 offset 4 couleurs, pages 2 et 3 offset noir. Plié
A l'intérieur, développement du thème «coquillages». En page 4, quatre autres illustrations, avec légendes détaillées. Brève présentation de l'artiste.

142a–c United Airlines, Chicago, Illinois, USA
Speisekarte. Lithographien von Helen de Werd, Palm Springs
190 × 278 mm, offen 380 × 278 mm, 4seitig. Offsetkarton. Seiten 1 und 4 Offset 4farbig, Seiten 2–3 Offset schwarz. Gefalzt
Fortführung des Muschelmotivs im Innenteil. Auf Seite 4 werden die 4 weiteren Abbildungen der Serie gezeigt. Ausführliche Bildlegenden. Kurztext über die Künstlerin. Die Originallithographien können einzeln oder als Serie bestellt werden.

142a–c United Airlines, Chicago, Ill., USA
Menu-card. Lithographs by Helen de Werd, Palm Springs
190 × 278 mm, open 380 × 278 mm, 4 pages. Offset card. Pages 1 and 4: 4-colour offset printing, pages 2–3: offset printing in black. Folded
Continuation of the shell motif on inside pages. The four addtitional illustrations of the series are shown on page 4. Detailed picture captions. A short text on the artist. The original lithographs may be ordered individually or as a series.

From the Cheese Board
Be our guest and select your favorite natural cheese and cracker combination served with grapes. Today's cheeses are sharp cheddar, baby gouda and Danish bleu cheese.

Cocktails
United's Very Dry Beefeater Martini
United's Very Dry Smirnoff Vodka Martini
Manhattan
Screwdriver
Bloody Mary
Whiskey Sour
Dry Sack Sherry
Domestic Beer

Spirits
Old Forester Bourbon
Cutty Sark's 12 Year Old Scotch
Dewar's White Label Scotch
Canadian Club
Jack Daniels Tennessee Whiskey
Beefeater Gin
Smirnoff Vodka
Bacardi Rum

Wines
Mirassou Cabernet Sauvignon
Almaden Pinot Blanc — Vintage 1977
Paul Masson Brut Champagne

Liqueurs
Creme de Menthe
Courvoisier
Benedictine and Brandy
Drambuie
Kahlua
Grand Marnier
Amaretto di Saronno

Soft Beverages
Tomato Juice
Perrier Water
Coca-Cola
Minors Cannot Be Served Alcohol

Salad Offering
A selection of greens and garnishes to start. The Chef has personally selected either a spinach leaf, romaine or bib lettuce salad for your meal today, and offers a choice of dressing.
Javanese
United Airlines Special Bleu Cheese

Your Choice
Roast Strip Sirloin of Beef, au jus
We start with USDA Choice sirloin of beef, rub it with herbs and spices, then roast it with its natural juices. This favorite will be carved at your seat . . . for the perfect accompaniment try our mild horseradish sauce.
Chateau Potatoes
Baby Carrots with Dill

The Chef's Specialty
Breast of Chicken Archidu
This breast of chicken is sauteed to a golden brown, then braised in Sherry wine sauce with mushrooms.
Chateau Potatoes
Baby Carrots with Dill

Our Lighter Air Fare
A piping hot bowl of hearty soup along with our salad is popular with many passengers. It is satisfying, but not quite as filling as our more elaborate entrees. Just ask for today's selection.

Oven Warmed Specialty Breads with Butter

Desserts
Old Fashioned Hot Fudge Sundae Cart

Cappuccino
This recent addition to our inflight fare features piping hot coffee with brandy, chocolate and whipped cream topping.

Beverages
Maxwell House Coffee
Tea
Milk
Sanka

It has been our pleasure to prepare this repast for your enjoyment.

Raoul Delbel, Executive Chef, United Airlines Flight Kitchen at Los Angeles. Member, Epicurean Club.

Please accept our apology if, due to previous passenger selections, your choice is not available.

142c

143 United Airlines, Chicago, Illinois, USA
Carte de menu
Couverture: 190×278 mm, ouvert 380×278 mm, 4 pages. Papier à structure «peau de crocodile». Pages 1 et 4 offset 4 couleurs
Intérieur: 190×278 mm, ouvert 380×278 mm, 4 pages. Papier chiné. Offset noir et brun. Plié et agrafé deux fois dans le pli avec la couverture
Le thème «d'océan à océan», représenté par d'anciennes cartes, symbolise l'activité internationale de la compagnie.

143 United Airlines, Chicago, Illinois, USA
Speisekarte
Umschlag: 190×278 mm, offen 380×278 mm, 4seitig. Papier mit Elefantenhautstruktur. Seiten 1 und 4 Offset 4farbig
Innenteil: 190×278 mm, offen 380×278 mm, 4seitig. Meliertes Papier. Offset schwarz und braun. Gefalzt und mit dem Umschlag 2mal drahtgeheftet
Das Motto «Von Ozean zu Ozean», unterlegt mit Motiven aus alten Karten, weist auf die weltweite Aktivität der Gesellschaft hin.

143 United Airlines, Chicago, Ill., USA
Menu-card
Cover: 190×278 mm, open 380×278 mm, 4 pages. Paper with elephant-hide grained texture. Pages 1 and 4: 4-colour offset printing
Contents: 190×278 mm, open 380×278 mm, 4 pages. Marbled paper. Offset printing in black and brown. Folded, 2-wire stitched to the cover
The motto 'From Ocean to Ocean', underlined with motifs from old maps, alludes to the company's world-wide activities.

143

144a–b Trans World Service, TWA, New York, N.Y., USA
Carte de menu. Création: Directeur artistique Jules Rondepierre, TWA, New York. Illustration de couverture: Barron Storey; agent: Jane Lander Associates, New York. Impression: B.R. Doerfler Co, New York; typographie: Thomas, Richards & Harris, Inc., Wilmington
Couverture: 208×275 mm, ouvert 416×275 mm, 4 pages. Papier gaufré une face. Page 1 et 4 offset 4 couleurs. Rainé, plié
Intérieur: 208×275 mm, ouvert 416×275 mm, 4 pages. Papier chiné à la cuve. Offset brun et bleu. Plié et agrafé deux fois dans le pli avec la couverture

144a–b Trans World Service, TWA, New York, N.Y., USA
Speisekarte. Gestaltung Art Director Jules Rondepierre, TWA, New York. Umschlagbild Barron Storey, Agent Jane Lander Associates, New York. Druck B.R. Doerfler Co. New York, Tyopografie Thomas, Richards & Harris, Inc., Wilmington
Umschlag: 208×275 mm, offen 416×275 mm, 4seitig. Einseitig strukturiertes Papier. Seiten 1 und 4 Offset 4farbig. Gerillt, gefalzt
Innenteil: 208×275 mm, offen 416×275 mm, 4seitig. Papier Bütten meliert. Offset braun und blau. Gefalzt und mit dem Umschlag 2mal drahtgeheftet

144a–b Trans-World Service, TWA, New York, N.Y., USA
Menu-card. Designed by Art Director Jules Rondepierre, TWA, New York; cover illustration by Barron Storey; agent Jane Lander Associates, New York; printed by B.R. Doerfler Co., New York; typography by Thomas, Richards & Harris, Inc., Wilmington, Del.
Cover: 208×275 mm, open 416×275 mm, 4 pages. Paper with embossed texture on one side. Pages 1 and 4: 4-colour offset printing. Scored, folded
Contents: 208×275 mm, open 416×275 mm, 4 pages. Hand-made paper with marbled effect. Offset printing in brown and blue. Folded and 2-wire stitched to the cover

144a

144b

145 TWA, New York, N.Y., USA
Carte de menu. Création: Directeur artistique Jules Rondepierre, TWA, New York. Illustration de couverture: Bob Peak; agent: Harvey Kahn Studio, Milburn, N.J. Impression: B.R. Doerfler Co., New York; typographie: Foodservice Graphics, Inc., New York
Couverture: 208×275 mm, ouvert 416×275 mm, 4 pages. Papier structuré à la cuve. Pages 1 et 4 offset 4 couleurs. Rainé, plié
Intérieur: 208×275 mm, ouvert 416×275 mm, 4 pages. Papier gris clair structuré à la cuve. Offset brun et rouge. Rainé, plié et agrafé deux fois dans le pli avec la couverture

145 TWA, New York, N.Y., USA
Speisekarte. Gestaltung Art Director Jules Rondepierre, TWA, New York. Umschlagbild Bob Peak, Agent Harvey Kahn Studio, Millburn, N.J. Druck B.R. Doerfler Co., New York. Typografie Foodservice Graphics, Inc., New York
Umschlag: 208×275 mm, offen 416×275 mm, 4seitig. Papier mit Büttenstruktur. Seiten 1 und 4 Offset 4farbig. Gerillt, gefalzt
Innenteil: 208×275 mm, offen 416×275 mm, 4seitig. Papier mit hellgrauer Büttenstruktur. Offset braun und rot. Gerillt, gefalzt und mit dem Umschlag 2mal drahtgeheftet

145 TWA, New York, N.Y., USA
Menu-card. Designed by Art Director Jules Rondepierre, TWA, New York; cover illustration by Bob Peak; agent Harvey Kahn Studio, Millburn, New Jersey; printed by B.R. Doerfler Co., New York; typography by Foodservice Graphics Inc., New York
Cover: 208×275 mm, open 416×275 mm, 4 pages. Paper with texture of hand-made paper. Pages 1 and 4: 4-colour offset printing. Scored, folded
Contents: 208×275 mm, open 416×275 mm, 4 pages. Paper with texture of hand-made paper in pale grey. Offset printing in brown and red. Scored, folded and 2-wire stitched to the cover

WASHINGTON

Cartes de compagnies maritimes

Schiffahrtslinien

Shipping lines

Elles remplissent a peu près le même rôle de publicité de prestige que celles des compagnies d'aviation. A bord d'une unité marine, les repas sont souvent l'occasion de «mondanités» et constituent une part importante du programme de croisière ou de traversée. Certaines cartes, élégantes et raffinées, expriment nettement cette tendance. Tous les sujets en rapport direct avec la mer et la navigation conviennent comme thèmes d'illustration: modèles réduits de bateaux, instruments et objets de navigation anciens, par exemple. Les escales sont parfois présentées par l'image, le texte, les informations sur les curiosités, les manifestations culturelles et les possibilités d'achat.

Die Prestigewerbung liegt ganz ähnlich wie bei den Fluggesellschaften. Die Mahlzeiten werden aber hier zu einem gesellschaftlichen Anlaß und bilden einen wesentlichen Bestandteil des Programms der Kreuzfahrten und Überfahrten. Die Eleganz gewisser Menukarten bringt diese festliche Art zu speisen deutlich zum Ausdruck.
Als Sujet eignet sich natürlich alles, was zur See- und zur Schiffahrt gehört: Schiffsmodelle, alte Instrumente und Utensilien. Auch die angelaufenen Häfen können in Bild und Text vorgestellt werden. Nützlich sind Hinweise auf Sehenswürdigkeiten, kulturelle Veranstaltungen oder Einkaufsmöglichkeiten.

A shipping line's means of winning prestige are similar to those employed by an airline. But meals on board ship are social occasions and form an important part of the traveller's programme, whether he or she be crossing the ocean or on a cruise.
Certain menus have an elegance that expresses well the festive nature of such a meal. Anything to do with the sea or ships may serve as a subject: e.g. ship's models, old nautical instruments and paraphernalia. The ports on route may also be represented visually or mentioned in the text, as may tourist attractions, cultural events and shopping hints.

146a–b, 147   Norwegian America Line, Oslo, Norvège
Création: Arnold Rakeng. Photo: Arne Tangen. Impression: Optimal Offset, Oslo
198 × 268 mm, ouvert 396 × 268 mm, 4 pages. Chromo une face. Pages 1 et 4 offset 4 couleurs, texte en négatif. Rainé, plié
En page 4, brève légende d'illustration bilingue anglais-allemand. La série illustre la navigation ancienne par des objets appartenant au Musée de la Navigation norvégien: ustensiles de cambuse, un sextant et un chronomètre de marine.

146a–b, 147   Norwegian America Line, Oslo, Norwegen
Gestaltung Arnold Rakeng, Foto Arne Tangen. Druck Optimal Offset, Oslo
198 × 268 mm, offen 396 × 268 mm, 4seitig. Chromokarton einseitig. Seiten 1 und 4 Offset 4farbig, Text negativ. Gerillt, gefalzt
Kurze Bildlegende auf Seite 4 2sprachig Englisch, Deutsch. Die Serie zeigt alte, zur Schiffahrt gehörende Gegenstände aus dem Norwegischen Schiffahrtsmuseum: Geschirr aus der Kombüse, einen Sextanten und ein Schiffschronometer.

146a–b, 147   Norwegian America Line, Oslo, Norway
Designed by Arnold Rakeng, photograph by Arne Tangen, printed by Optimal Offset, Oslo
198 × 268 mm, open 396 × 268 mm, 4 pages. One-sided cast-coated card. Pages 1 and 4: 4-colour offset printing, negative text. Scored, folded
Short picture captions on page 4 in English and German. The series shows old objects pertaining to shipping exhibited in the Maritime Museum of Norway: tableware from the galley, a sextant and a ship's chronometer.

The rapid evolution that is apparent in the design of ships, is hardly any less noticeable in the victualling. These charming objects reflect a manner of catering which is indeed far from the present day menu.

Wie die Entwicklung von Schiffen und ihrer Einrichtungen fortschreitet, zeigt sich auch in der Kombüse - so hiess die Küche der Segler. Diese hübschen Geräte deuten auf eine Verpflegung hin, die tatsächlich noch weit entfernt ist von ihrem heutigen Menü.

147

Navigare necesse est. However romantic thoughts the stars may provoke, to the sailor the heavenly bodies were first of all an essential aid in finding the way across the seven seas.

Navigare necesse est. So notwendig wie die Seefahrt selbst ist die Kunst, sich auf den sieben Meeren zu orientieren. Welch romantische Träume sonst Sterne auch wecken mögen - für den Seemann dienen sie in erster Linie der Navigation.

146b

148

148 Norwegian America Line,
Oslo, Norvège
Création et photo: Arne Fossen
198 × 268 mm, ouvert 396 × 268
mm, 4 pages. Pages 1 et 4 offset
4 couleurs, texte en négatif.
Rainé, plié
Cette série présente l'art po-
pulaire norvégien: ustensiles de
cuisine, vaisselle, etc., et plus
particulièrement des objets de
vannerie et de tissage.

148 Norwegian America Line,
Oslo, Norwegen
Gestaltung und Foto Arne Fossen
198 × 268 mm, offen 396 ×
268 mm, 4seitig. Seiten 1 und 4
Offset 4farbig, Text negativ. Ge-
rillt, gefalzt
Diese Serie zeigt norwegische
Volkskunst: Küchengeräte, Ge-
schirr usw. vor alten Flecht- und
Weberzeugnissen.

148 Norwegian America Line,
Oslo, Norway
Design and photograph by Arne
Fossen
198 × 268 mm, open
396 × 268 mm, 4 pages. Pages 1
and 4: 4-colour offset printing,
negative text. Scored, folded
This series shows old Norwegian
arts and crafts: kitchen appli-
ances, tableware etc. in front of
old wickerwork and textiles.

May we
recommend

*from the wine locker
a chilled bottle of*

*Niersteiner
Rhine Wine
or
Bourgogne Passetoutgrain 1972
Red Burgundy*

*Please consult
the Wine List for a selection
exactly to your taste*

149

149   Fred. Olsen Lines, Londres, GB
Carte des vins. Création et dessin:
Graham Wrightson Ltd., Londres
171×101 mm, ouvert 171×202 mm,
4 pages. Chromolux une face. Page 1
offset 2 couleurs. Rainé, plié

Carte des vins simple présentant deux
qualités de vin du continent les plus ap-
préciées des Anglais.

149   Fred. Olsen Lines, London, Großbritannien
Weinkarte. Gestaltung und Zeichnung
Graham Wrightson Ltd., London
171×101 mm, offen 171×202 mm, 4sei-

tig. Einseitiger Chromoluxkarton. Seite
1 Offset 2farbig. Gerillt, gefalzt
Eine einfache Weinkarte, die zwei in
England bevorzugte kontinentale
Weine anbietet

149   Fred. Olsen Lines, London, Great
Britain
Wine list. Design and drawing by
Graham Wrightson Ltd., London
171×101 mm, open 171×202 mm, 4
pages. One-sided Astralux card. Page
1: 2-colour offset printing. Scored,
folded
A simple wine list offering two continental wines popular in England.

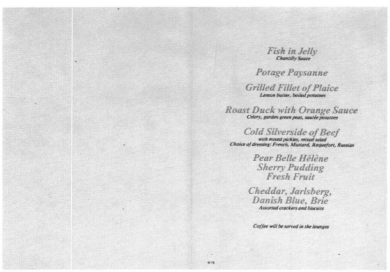

150b

Fish in Jelly
Chantilly Sauce

Potage Paysanne

Grilled Fillet of Plaice
Lemon butter, boiled potatoes

Roast Duck with Orange Sauce
Celery, garden green peas, sauté potatoes

Cold Silverside of Beef
with mixed pickles, mixed salad
Choice of dressing: French, Mustard, Roquefort, Russian

Pear Belle Hélène
Sherry Pudding
Fresh Fruit

Cheddar, Jarlsberg,
Danish Blue, Brie
Assorted crackers and biscuits

Coffee will be served in the lounges

150a–b   Fred. Olsen Lines, Londres, GB
Carte de menu. Création et dessin: Graham Wrightson Ltd., Londres
163×236 mm, ouvert 326×236 mm,

4 pages. Chromo une face. Pages 1 et 3
offset brun et noir. Rainé, plié
Pages intérieures: fond imitation papier
vergé, imprimé en même temps et dans
la même couleur que le texte.

150a–b   Fred. Olsen Lines, London,
Großbritannien
Speisekarte. Gestaltung und Zeichnung Graham Wrightson Ltd., London
163×236 mm, offen 326×236 mm,
4seitig. Einseitiger Chromokarton. Sei-

ten 1 und 3 Offset braun, schwarz. Gerillt, gefalzt
Auf den Innenseiten wird als Hintergrund die Reproduktion eines Vergé-
Papiers verwendet. Einfarbig, zusammen mit dem Text gedruckt

150a–b   Fred. Olsen Lines, London,
Great Britain
Menu-card. Designed and drawing by
Graham Wrightson Ltd., London
163×236 mm, open 326×236 mm, 4
pages. One-sided cast-coated card.

Pages 1 and 3: offset printing in brown
and black. Scored, folded
On inside pages: reproduction of laid
paper for the background. Printed in
monochrome together with the text.

Menu

150a

151, 152 Hapag-Lloyd AG, Brême, RFA
Création: Barbara Geissler
210 × 297 mm, ouvert 420 × 297 mm, 4 pages. Chromo une face. Pages 1 et 4 offset 4 couleurs, fond en combinaison de trames. Rainé, plié, verni
Cachet personnalisé grâce à la combinaison des photos et dessins. L'illustration 152 présente la couverture d'une carte de menu d'adieux.

151, 152 Hapag-Lloyd AG, Bremen, Bundesrepublik Deutschland
Gestaltung Barbara Geißler
210 × 297 mm, offen 420 × 297 mm, 4seitig. Einseitiger Chromokarton. Seiten 1 und 4 Offset 4farbig, Hintergrund Rasterkombination. Gerillt, gefalzt, lackiert
Durch Kombination von Foto und Zeichnung erhält die Karte eine ganz persönliche Note. Abbildung 152 zeigt den Umschlag einer Abschiedsmenukarte.

151–152 Hapag-Lloyd AG, Bremen, West Germany
Designed by Barbara Geissler
210 × 297 mm, open 420 × 297 mm, 4 pages. One-sided cast-coated card. Pages 1 and 4: 4-colour offset printing, background: silk-screen combination. Scored, folded, varnished
A personal touch is achieved with a combination of photograph and drawing. Ill. 152: menu for a farewell celebration.

Hapag-Lloyd AG

151

152

153

152 Hapag-Lloyd AG, Brême, RFA
Carte de menu d'adieux (voir ill. 151).

152 Hapag Lloyd AG, Bremen, Bundesrepublik
Deutschland
Abschiedsmenukarte (vgl. Abb. 151)

152 Hapag-Lloyd AG, Bremen, West Germany
Menu for a farewell celebration: see III. 151

153, 155 Hapag-Lloyd AG, Brême, RFA
Création: Barbara Geissler
210×297 mm, ouvert 420×297 mm, 4 pages. Chromo une face. Pages 1 et 4 offset 4 couleurs. Rainé, plié, verni
Cette nouvelle série illustre les ports d'escale: les Caraïbes, le Grand Nord, etc.

153, 155 Hapag-Lloyd AG, Bremen, Bundesrepublik Deutschland
Gestaltung Barbara Geißler
210×297 mm, offen 420×297 mm, 4seitig. Einseitiger Chromokarton. Seiten 1 und 4 Offset 4farbig. Gerillt, gefalzt, lackiert
Die Sujets der neuen Serie weisen auf angelaufene Häfen hin: Karibik, Hoher Norden usw.

153, 155 Hapag-Lloyd AG, Bremen, West Germany
Designed by Barbara Geissler
210×297 mm, open 420×297 mm, 4 pages. One-sided cast-coated card. pages 1 and 4: 4-colour offset printing. Scored, folded, varnished
The individual subjects of the new series pertain to the ports of destination in the Caribbean, Scandinavia etc.

◁ 154 Hapag-Lloyd AG, Brême, RFA
Carte des petits déjeuners. Création: Barbara Geissler
148×210 mm, ouvert 296×210 mm, 4 pages. Carton offset. Page 1 offset 4 couleurs. Rainé, plié
Diverses variantes sur le thème «petit déjeuner». Les sujets sont du même style que ceux de la grande carte de menu.

154 Hapag-Lloyd AG, Bremen, Bundesrepublik Deutschland
Frühstückskarte. Gestaltung Barbara Geißler
148×210 mm, offen 296×210 mm, 4seitig. Offsetkarton. Seite 1 Offset 4farbig. Gerillt, gefalzt
Verschiedene Varianten zum Thema Frühstück. Die Sujets sind im Hausstil der großen Menukarte gehalten.

154 Hapag-Lloyd AG, Bremen, West Germany
Designed by Barbara Geissler
148×210 mm, open 296×210 mm, 4 pages. Offset card. Page 1: 4-colour offset printing. Scored, folded
Variations on the breakfast theme. The individual subjects retain the characteristic house style of the large menucard.

MS Europa Menuekarte

155

THE GREAT PACIFIC & ORIENT CRUISE

Bali, off the Eastern tip of Indonesia, has long been synonymous with paradise. This magical, serene island with its deserted beaches, tropical forests and lush paddy fields, magnificent temples and shell-pink houses, strikingly attractive people. Do your shopping in picturesque villages housing woodcarvers, silversmiths, painters. And don't miss the traditional Balinese dancers, graceful, agile, humorous — and very photogenic.

QUEEN ELIZABETH 2 BALI

Designed by Christopher R. Foster, Southampton. Photography by Gordon Hammond, Southampton. Printed by Botley Printers Limited, Southampton.

156

156, 157   Cunard Line Ltd., GB
Création: Christopher R. Foster, Southampton. Photo: Gordon Hammond, Southampton. Impression: Botley Printers Ltd., Southampton
210 × 297 mm, ouvert 420 × 297 mm, 4 pages. Carton couché. Page 1 et 4 offset 4 couleurs, texte en négatif. Rainé, plié
Le texte en négatif de la page 4 traite de curiosités touristiques, de possibilités d'achats, etc., aux différentes escales d'une croisière autour du monde.

156, 157   Cunard Line Ltd., Großbritannien
Gestaltung Christopher R. Foster, Southampton, Foto Gordon Hammond, Southampton, Druck Botley Printers Ltd., Southampton
210 × 297 mm, offen 420 × 297 mm, 4seitig. Kunstdruckkarton. Seiten 1 und 4 Offset 4farbig, Text negativ. Gerillt, gefalzt
Die Negativtexte auf Seite 4 bringen Hinweise auf Sehenswürdigkeiten, Einkaufsmöglichkeiten usw. in den angelaufenen Häfen während einer Weltkreuzfahrt.

156–157   Cunard Line Ltd., Great Britain
Designed by Christopher R. Foster, Southampton, photograph by Gordon Hammond, Southampton, printed by Botley Printers Ltd., Southampton
210 × 297 mm, open 420 × 297 mm, 4 pages. Art paper. Pages 1 and 4: 4-colour offset printing, negative texts. Scored, folded
Negative texts on page 4: guide and comments on sights of interest, shopping etc. in the various ports visited on a world cruise.

158   Cunard Line Ltd., GB
Création: Christopher R. Foster, Southampton. Impression: Thamesfleet Printers Limited, Teddington, Middlesex
210 × 297 mm, ouvert 420 × 297 mm, 4 pages. Carton couché. Dorure à la feuille, fond offset noir, texte en négatif. Rainé, plié, verni

158   Cunard Line Ltd., Großbritannien
Gestaltung Christopher R. Foster, Southampton, Druck Thamesfleet Printers Limited, Teddington, Middlesex
210 × 297 mm, offen 420 × 297 mm, 4seitig. Kunstdruckkarton. Goldfolienprägung, Hintergrund Offset schwarz, Text negativ. Gerillt, gefalzt, lackiert

158   Cunard Line Ltd., Great Britain
Designed by Christopher R. Foster, Southampton, printed by Thamesfleet Printers Ltd., Teddington, Middlesex
210 × 297 mm, open 420 × 297 mm, 4 pages. Art card. Gold embossing, background: offset printing in black, negative texts. Scored, folded, varnished

Honolulu is one of the world's greatest resort centres with beautiful forests, mountains, lagoons and waterfalls behind the splendid beaches and bright lights. The famed Waikiki Beach is two miles of palm fringed sand, washed by deliciously warm sea and backed by plush hotels. Sightseeing? Take a sunset cruise on a catamaran, study underwater life over the coral reefs, drive out to the Polynesian Culture Center or Ulu Mau Village, an intriguing replica that shows off native life, arts, culture, songs and dances. Shopping? There are super shopping centers and complexes; Ala Moana, just one, has 50 splendidly landscaped acres laced with pools and gardens, sculptures and fountains, and a dazzling array of international merchandise. You'll want to take home one of those riotous Hawaiian shirts, maybe a 'muu muu', the traditional dress for women, coral jewelry. Nightlife? Anything from hula shows to Broadway names; many of the big hotels feature Polynesian spectaculars, local entertainers.

Designed by Christopher R. Foster, Southampton. Photography by Gordon Hammond, Southampton. Printed by Botley Printers Limited, Southampton.

157

QUEEN ELIZABETH 2 MEXICO

158

159

159   Cunard Line Ltd., GB
Création: Christopher R. Foster, Southampton. Impression: Thamesfleet Printers Limited, Teddington, Middlesex
210 × 297 mm, ouvert 420 × 297 mm, 4 pages. Carton couché. Impression irisé rose et orange. Fond noir, texte en négatif. Rainé, plié verni
Menu de fête pour le jour de l'An. Réalisé avec seulement deux reproductions au trait et deux passages en machine, mais très réussi.

159   Cunard Line Ltd., Großbritannien
Gestaltung Christopher R. Foster, Southampton, Druck Thamesfleet Printers Limited, Teddington, Middlesex
210 × 297 mm, offen 420 × 297 mm, 4seitig. Kunstdruckkarton. Druck irisierend rosa, orange. Hintergrund schwarz, Text negativ. Gerillt, gefalzt, lackiert
Festmenufolge für den Neujahrstag. Effektvolle Lösung mit nur 2 Strichreproduktionen und 2 Druckgängen

159   Cunard Line Ltd., Great Britain
Designed by Christopher R. Foster, Southampton, printed by Thamesfleet Printers Ltd., Teddington, Middlesex
210 × 297 mm, open 420 × 297 mm, 4 pages. Art card. Printing in iridescent pink and orange. Background in black, negative texts. Scored, folded, varnished
Celebration menu on the occasion of the first day of the New Year, 1980. Effective solution with only two line-drawings and two pressruns.

Index – Register – Index

Les chiffres correspondent à la numérotation des illustrations.
Die Zahlen beziehen sich auf die Bildnummern.
The numbers refer to the plate numbers.

Air Canada, Montréal 140
Air France, Paris 123, 124
    Concorde 122
Alain Chapel, Mionnay 9
L'Apéro, Les Quatre Saisons, Montréal 90
Arbalète, Hotel Monopol, Luzern 109
L'Archestrate, Paris 8
Ashby's, Hilton, Washington 48
Asia Chinese Grill Room, Ramada Continental, Tel
    Aviv 64
Hôtel Atlantic, Nice, New Bar 71
Atlantic Hotel Kempinski, Hamburg 24
Atlantis Hotel, Zürich
    Döltschistube 33
    Rôtisserie 59
Badrutt's Palace Hotel, St. Moritz, Grill-Room 62
The Baltimore Hilton, Baltimore 81
    Miller Brothers 49
    Tangerine 92
Hotel Basel, Basel 76
La Bastide de Tourtour, Tourtour 6
The Beanstalk, Rockefeller Center, New York 43
Beef Club, Mövenpick, Bern 35
Belvedere Club, Hotel Inter-Continental, Köln 72
Belvedere Restaurant, Hotel Inter-Continental,
    Köln 118
Bistrothèque, Hôtel Inter-Continental, Paris 69
Brasserie, Hotel Inter-Continental, Köln 17, 106
Le Bristol, Paris 7
British Airways, London 127, 128
    Concorde 126
Bruegel, Oostkerke-Damme 31
Café in the Park, Century Park Sheraton, Manila 85
Cagliostro, München 23
Camellia Corner, Hotel Okura, Tokyo 84
The Capital Hilton, Washington 103
    Twigs 79
Carlton Grill, Hôtel Carlton, Cannes 57
Carousel Bar, The Mandarin, Manila 67
Casino, Grand Hôtel de Divonne, Divonne 3
Century Park Sheraton, Manila
    Café in the Park 85
    Palm Grove 98
Chapel, Alain, Mionnay 9
Château du Domaine St-Martin, Vence 4
Chatterbox, The Mandarin, Singapore 96
    The Coffee Shop 97
Chinese Grill Room, Ramada Continental, Tel Aviv 64
Chinoiserie, Hyatt Regency, Singapore 74
Coffee Shop, Kuwait-Sheraton, Kuwait 94
The Colony House, Charleston 41, 115
Crazy Bar, Hôtel Plaza, Nice 71
Cunard Line Ltd., GB 156, 157, 158, 159
Döltschistube, Atlantis Hotel, Zürich 33
Hotel Eisenhut, Rothenburg ob der Tauber 19, 20
EL AL, Israel 139
El Terral, Las Hadas, Manzanillo 39
Eurotel Villars, Villars-sur-Ollon 77
Feringgi Grill, Rasa Sanyang Hotel, Penang 63
Frankfurt-Sheraton Hotel, Frankfurt am Main
    Maxwell's 28, 66, 75
    Palette 27
Frankfurter Hof, Frankfurt am Main, Restaurant
    Français 22
Franziskaner (Zum), München, Fuchs'nstub'n 26
Les Frères Troisgros, Roanne 5

Fuchs'nstub'n, Zum Franziskaner, München 26
Hotel Glärnischhof, Zürich 78
Golden Cape, Hawaii 47
Hôtel du Golf, Crans-Montana 116, 117, 121
Grand Hôtel de Divonne, Divonne, Casino 3
Greentrees, Ambridge 44
Grill des Ambassadeurs, Hôtel Métropole, Monte-
    Carlo 56
Gualtiero Marchesi, Milano 13
Half Moon Inn, San Diego, Humphrey's 45
Hapag-Lloyd AG, Bremen 151–155
Hilton Hotels
    Baltimore, The Baltimore 81
        Miller Brothers 49
        Tangerine 92
    Kuwait, La Pâtisserie 88, 89
    Washington, Ashby's 48
        The Capital 103
            Twigs 79
Hugenotten (Zum), Hotel Inter-Continental, Berlin 16
Humphrey's, Half Moon Inn, San Diego 45
Hyatt Regency, Singapore 100
    Chinoiserie 74
Inter-Continental Hotels
    Bangkok, Sivalai 87
    Berlin, Zum Hugenotten 16
    Köln 111
        Belvedere Club 72
        Belvedere Restaurant 118
        Brasserie 17, 106
    Paris 80
        Bar 68
        Bistrothèque 69
        Café Tuileries 86
        Rôtisserie Rivoli 55
        Terrasse Fleurie 93
Japan Airlines, Tokyo 141
KLM Royal Dutch Airlines, Amstelveen
    Business Class 130
    Royal Class 129
Kockska Krogen, Savoy Hotel, Malmö 29
Kronenhalle, Zürich 32
Kuwait-Sheraton Hotel, Kuwait
    Coffee Shop 94
    La Pâtisserie 88, 89
Hotel Lanka Oberoi, Colombo 82, 99
Las Hadas, Manzanillo
    El Terral 39
    Legazpi 38
The Last Hurrah!, Parker House, Boston 40
The Left Bank, Treadway Inn, Wilkes-Barre 42
Legazpi, Las Hadas, Manzanillo 38
The Library, The Mandarin, Singapore 70
Hotel Löwen, Sihlbrugg 34
    Bar Dancing 73
Restaurant Löwen, Büren an der Aare 119
Lufthansa, Köln 133, 134, 135
The Mandarin Hotels
    Hong Kong 53
        The Mandarin Grill 65
    Manila 105
        Carousel Bar 67
    Singapore 83
        Chatterbox 96
        Chatterbox, The Coffee Shop 97
        The Library 70
        Pine Court 52
        The Sand Bar 95
        Top of the M 50
The Mandarin Grill, The Mandarin, Hong Kong 65
Marchesi, Gualtiero, Milano 13
Mariott Hotels, Orlando, Samantha's 46
Maxwell's, Frankfurt-Sheraton Hotel, Frankfurt am
Main 28, 66, 75
Hôtel Métropole, Monte-Carlo, Grill des Ambassa-
    deurs 56

Miller Brothers, The Baltimore Hilton Hotel, Baltimore
    49
Hotel Monopol, Luzern, Arbalète 109
Le Moulin de Mougins, Mougins 1, 2
Mövenpick
    Bern, Beef Club 35
    Zürich 101, 102
Münchner Kindl-Stuben, Penta Hotel, München 15
Le Neptune, Grill Room, Hôtel du Rhône, Genève 60
New Bar, Hôtel Atlantic, Nice 71
Norwegian America Line, Oslo 146, 147, 148
Hotel Okura, Tokyo
    Camellia Corner 84
    Yamazato 54
L'Olivo, Park Hotel, Siena 14
Fred. Olsen Lines, London 149, 150
Palace Hotel, Gstaad 120
Palace Hotel, St. Moritz, Grill-Room 62, 110
Palette, Frankfurt-Sheraton Hotel, Frankfurt am
    Main 27
Palm Grove, Century Park Sheraton, Manila 98
Paparazzi, New York 91
Hôtel Park, Nice, Passage 71
Park Hotel, Siena, L'Olivo 14
Park-Restaurant, Kaiserau 18
Parker House, Boston, The Last Hurrah! 40
Passage, Hôtel Park, Nice 71
La Pâtisserie, Kuwait Hilton, Kuwait 88, 89
Penta Hotel, München, Münchner Kindl-Stuben 15
Pine Court, The Mandarin, Singapore 52
Hôtel Plaza, Nice, Crazy Bar 71
Les Quatre Saisons, Montréal, L'Apéro 90
Ramada Continental, Tel Aviv, Chinese Grill Room 64
Rasa Sanyang Hotel, Penang, Feringgi Grill 63
Restaurant Français, Steigenberger Hotel, Frankfurter
    Hof, Frankfurt am Main 22
Hôtel du Rhône, Genève, Grill-Room Le Neptune 60
Rôtisserie Rivoli, Hôtel Inter-Continental, Paris 55
Romantik Hotel Schwan, Östrich-Winkel 107
Sabena, Bruxelles 125
Samantha's, Mariott Hotels, Orlando 46
The Sand Bar, The Mandarin, Singapore 95
Savoy Hotel, Malmö
    Grillen 58
    Kockska Krogen 29
Hotel Schwan, Östrich-Winkel 107
Schweizer Stuben, Wertheim-Bettingen 25
Sheraton Hotels
    Frankfurt am Main, Maxwell's 28, 66, 75
        Palette 27
    Honolulu, Volcano House 51
    Kuwait, Coffee Shop 94
    Manila, Café in the Park 85
        Palm Grove 98
Sivalai, Siam Inter-Continental, Bangkok 87
Hotel St. Gotthard, Zürich 36, 108, 114
Steigenberger Hotels
    Bad Kissingen, Kurhaushotel 21
    Frankfurt am Main, Frankfurter Hof, Restaurant Fran-
    çais 22
Swissair, Zürich 136, 137, 138
Tangerine, The Baltimore Hilton, Baltimore 92
Terrasse Fleurie, Hôtel Inter-Continental, Paris 93
Top of the M, The Mandarin, Singapore 50
La Tour d'Argent, Paris 10, 11, 12, 113
Trans World Airlines, New York 144, 145
Treadway Inn, Wilkes-Barre, The Left Bank 42
Troisgros, Les Frères, Roanne 5
Café Tuileries, Hôtel Inter-Continental, Paris 86
Twigs, The Capital Hilton, Washington 79
United Airlines, Chicago 142, 143
UTA, Paris 131, 132
Volcano House, Sheraton Hotels in the Pacific,
    Honolulu 51
Hotel Wittelsbacher Hof, Oberstdorf 112
Yamazato, Hotel Okura, Tokyo 54

160